Zaire

WORLD BIBLIOGRAPHICAL SERIES

General Editors:
Robert G. Neville (Executive Editor)
John J. Horton

Robert A. Myers   Hans H. Wellisch
Ian Wallace   Ralph Lee Woodward, Jr.

John J. Horton is Deputy Librarian of the University of Bradford and currently Chairman of its Academic Board of Studies in Social Sciences. He has maintained a longstanding interest in the discipline of area studies and its associated bibliographical problems, with special reference to European Studies. In particular he has published in the field of Icelandic and of Yugoslav studies, including the two relevant volumes in the World Bibliographical Series.

Robert A. Myers is Associate Professor of Anthropology in the Division of Social Sciences and Director of Study Abroad Programs at Alfred University, Alfred, New York. He has studied post-colonial island nations of the Caribbean and has spent two years in Nigeria on a Fulbright Lectureship. His interests include international public health, historical anthropology and developing societies. In addition to *Amerindians of the Lesser Antilles: a bibliography* (1981), *A Resource Guide to Dominica, 1493-1986* (1987) and numerous articles, he has compiled the World Bibliographical Series volumes on *Dominica* (1987), *Nigeria* (1989) and *Ghana* (1991).

Ian Wallace is Professor of German at the University of Bath. A graduate of Oxford in French and German, he also studied in Tübingen, Heidelberg and Lausanne before taking teaching posts at universities in the USA, Scotland and England. He specializes in contemporary German affairs, especially literature and culture, on which he has published numerous articles and books. In 1979 he founded the journal *GDR Monitor*, which he continues to edit under its new title *German Monitor*.

Hans H. Wellisch is Professor emeritus at the College of Library and Information Services, University of Maryland. He was President of the American Society of Indexers and was a member of the International Federation for Documentation. He is the author of numerous articles and several books on indexing and abstracting, and has published *The Conversion of Scripts and Indexing and Abstracting: an International Bibliography*, and *Indexing from A to Z*. He also contributes frequently to *Journal of the American Society for Information Science*, *The Indexer* and other professional journals.

Ralph Lee Woodward, Jr. is Professor of History at Tulane University, New Orleans. He is the author of *Central America, a Nation Divided*, 2nd ed. (1985), as well as several monographs and more than seventy scholarly articles on modern Latin America. He has also compiled volumes in the World Bibliographical Series on *Belize* (1980), *El Salvador* (1988), *Guatemala* (Rev. Ed.) (1992) and *Nicaragua* (Rev. Ed.) (1994). Dr. Woodward edited the Central American section of the *Research Guide to Central America and the Caribbean* (1985) and is currently associate editor of Scribner's *Encyclopedia of Latin American History*.

VOLUME 176

Zaire

Dawn Bastian Williams,
Robert W. Lesh
and Andrea L. Stamm

CLIO PRESS
OXFORD, ENGLAND · SANTA BARBARA, CALIFORNIA
DENVER, COLORADO

British Library Cataloguing in Publication Data

Zaire. – (World Bibliographical
series; vol. 176)
I. Williams, D. E. II. Series
016.96751

ISBN 1–85109–218–8

ABC-CLIO Ltd.,
Old Clarendon Ironworks,
35A Great Clarendon Street,
Oxford OX2 6AT, England.

————

ABC-CLIO Inc.,
130 Cremona Drive,
Santa Barbara,
CA 93116 USA.

Designed by Bernard Crossland.
Typeset by Columns Design and Production Services Ltd, Reading, England.
Printed and bound in Great Britain by Bookcraft (Bath) Ltd., Midsomer Norton.

THE WORLD BIBLIOGRAPHICAL SERIES

This series, which is principally designed for the English speaker, will eventually cover every country (and many of the world's principal regions), each in a separate volume comprising annotated entries on works dealing with its history, geography, economy and politics; and with its people, their culture, customs, religion and social organization. Attention will also be paid to current living conditions – housing, education, newspapers, clothing, etc.– that are all too often ignored in standard bibliographies; and to those particular aspects relevant to individual countries. Each volume seeks to achieve, by use of careful selectivity and critical assessment of the literature, an expression of the country and an appreciation of its nature and national aspirations, to guide the reader towards an understanding of its importance. The keynote of the series is to provide, in a uniform format, an interpretation of each country that will express its culture, its place in the world, and the qualities and background that make it unique. The views expressed in individual volumes, however, are not necessarily those of the publisher.

VOLUMES IN THE SERIES

1 *Yugoslavia*, Rev. Ed., John J. Horton
2 *Lebanon*, Rev. Ed., C. H. Bleaney
3 *Lesotho*, Shelagh M. Willet and David Ambrose
4 *Zimbabwe*, Rev. Ed., Deborah Potts
5 *Saudi Arabia*, Rev. Ed., Frank A. Clements
6 *Russia/USSR*, Second Ed., Lesley Pitman
7 *South Africa*, Rev. Ed., Geoffrey V. Davis
8 *Malawi*, Robert B. Boeder
9 *Guatemala*, Rev. Ed., Ralph Lee Woodward, Jr
10 *Pakistan*, David Taylor
11 *Uganda*, Robert L. Collison
12 *Malaysia*, Ian Brown and Rajeswary Ampalavanar
13 *France*, Rev. Ed., Frances Chambers
14 *Panama*, Eleanor DeSelms Langstaff
15 *Hungary*, Thomas Kabdebo
16 *USA*, Sheila R. Herstein and Naomi Robbins
17 *Greece*, Richard Clogg and Mary Jo Clogg
18 *New Zealand*, R. F. Grover
19 *Algeria*, Richard I. Lawless
20 *Sri Lanka*, Vijaya Samaraweera
21 *Belize*, Second Ed., Peggy Wright and Brian E. Coutts
23 *Luxembourg*, Carlo Hury and Jul Christophory
24 *Swaziland*, Rev. Ed., Balam Nyeko
25 *Kenya*, Robert L. Collison
26 *India*, Brijen K. Gupta and Datta S. Kharbas
27 *Turkey*, Merel Güçlü
28 *Cyprus*, P. M. Kitromilides and M. L. Evriviades
29 *Oman*, Rev. Ed., Frank A. Clements
31 *Finland*, J. E. O. Screen
32 *Poland*, Rev. Ed., George Sanford and Adriana Gozdecka-Sanford
33 *Tunisia*, Allan M. Findlay, Anne M. Findlay and Richard I. Lawless
34 *Scotland*, Eric G. Grant
35 *China*, Peter Cheng
36 *Qatar*, P. T. H. Unwin
37 *Iceland*, John J. Horton
38 *Nepal*, John Whelpton
39 *Haiti*, Rev. Ed., Frances Chambers
40 *Sudan*, Rev. Ed., M. W. Daly
41 *Vatican City State*, Michael J. Walsh

Contents

Contents

Contents

Introduction

By the time Zaire finally became an independent country in 1960, it had already experienced a disruptive and turbulent history, chiefly characterized by plunder and exploitation. When in 1885 the territory became the personal property of Belgium's King Leopold II, under the name of the Congo Free State, he personally benefitted from ruthlessly exploiting its vast riches. Reports of forced labour and brutalities inflicted upon the indigenous population, however, led to international condemnation, and forced the annexation of the territory by Belgium in 1908, when it became known as the Belgian Congo. Under Belgian administration and exploitation, the country developed into the richest in Africa, and there was every reason to hope that its future would be bright when independence was achieved and it became the Democratic Republic of the Congo.

These hopes, however, rapidly disappeared when personality conflicts and ethnic tensions flared up soon after independence, and political parties foundered. In addition, there were problems in the armed forces; elements of the army mutinied because of low pay and the Belgian officers declared intentions of retaining their power. The widespread rioting, looting, and atrocities that ensued made headlines around the world, and caused the educated foreign population to flee. Belgian paratroopers occupied a number of Congolese cities, and the United Nations, at the request of the Congolese, who feared Belgium would seize its former colony, sent in troops, police, and other personnel to re-establish order, stability, and government operations. Nevertheless, this did not prevent the mineral-rich provinces of Katanga and South Kasai declaring themselves independent. Conflict continued on a wide scale until 24 November 1965, when some degree of political stability returned with a military *coup d'état*; Mobutu Sese Seko was named head-of-state. By 1967, the new government had reassumed control of most of the country, and embarked on a programme known as 'authenticity', which was aimed at developing a sense of nationalism among its many disparate peoples. Under this programme, which emphasized a return to African origins, the Democratic Republic of the Congo became Zaire in 1971.

However, the dictatorial Mobutu government, now approaching its thirtieth anniversary, has proved disastrous for Zaire. It has led the country to economic ruin, institutions are barely functioning, except those that are religious, ethnic tensions, fostered by the government, are flaring, and although Mobutu remains firmly in power, unrest is growing and has the potential to topple him. Many of the works listed in this bibliography document this transformation from a rich, diverse nation with potential to a fragile country facing a possible return to post-independence chaos.

Zaire, officially known as the Republic of Zaire, is an independent state in the heart of Africa. It is completely landlocked, except for a strip of land connecting it to the Atlantic coast which contains the mouth and lower reaches of the Zaire (Congo) River. It has an area of 905,568 square miles, which means it is roughly the size of the entire United States east of the Mississippi River. On the north, Zaire is bounded by the Central African Republic and the People's Republic of the Congo. Zambia lies to the south, and Angola to the southwest. To the east are Rwanda, Burundi, Uganda, and Tanzania, while the Sudan is to the northeast. Zaire's location has long made it one of the most geo-politically strategic countries in Africa.

According to official 1991 estimates, approximately 36.7 million people live within Zaire's borders. Because of internal migration from rural areas to urban, the periodic arrival and departure of refugees from neighbouring countries, and the absence of a well-developed national data collection system, it is difficult to determine the true number of inhabitants. The population is distributed unevenly, with density highest along the eastern border and in the areas south of the Zaire-Kasai-Sankuru river system. Wildly varying estimates reveal that between twenty per cent and fifty per cent of the population lives in Zaire's urban centres, such as Kinshasa, the capital and largest city, and also the important copper-processing centres of Lubumbashi, Likasi, and Kolwezi, and Kananga and Kisangani, major centres of trade, transport, and administration in the interior.

The central zone of Zaire is an alluvial tableland which rises, on average, some 900 metres above sea level. A chain of uplands, in the southeast and along the eastern border, known as the Mitumba Mountains, climbs to between 1,500 and 5,000 metres. Zaire is drained by the mighty Zaire River, the second-longest river in Africa and second in volume of flowing water only to the Amazon River of South America. Most of the country's eastern border is defined by the

Zaire-Nile and Zaire-Zambezi river watersheds, and touches the lakes of the Great Rift Valley: Lake Albert (Lake Mobutu Sese Seko); Lake Edward; Lake Kivu; Lake Tanganyika; and Lake Mweru.

Zairian territory is largely characterized by the hot, humid, tropical climate of the Zaire Basin, an area with one of the highest rates of rainfall in the world. July is the coolest month, and February the hottest, with only a slight variation in temperature between the two. The average annual temperature is about 27°C. (80°F.), and the average annual rainfall about 150-200 centimetres (60 to 80 inches), most of which falls during the rainy season between October and March. The highlands of Shaba and Kivu have more moderate temperatures and a somewhat lower rainfall.

Generally speaking, Zaire's soil is of poor quality, with the very best found in the flood plains along the middle Zaire River, where sediment is deposited during seasonal flooding. Alluvial deposits are also found along the Kasai River and its numerous tributaries, and there are good volcanic soils in the Great Rift Valley area, especially in the Kivu region. Erosion of Zaire's topsoil is a problem, as is the formation of hard laterite crusts, which often spread over large areas. This means that because good soils are rare fertile areas tend to be overpopulated. Despite its poor soils, and the fact that only two per cent of the land is under cultivation, approximately sixty-five to eighty per cent of the Zairian population is engaged in agriculture, according to various authoritative published sources. Most people produce at the subsistence level. Important food crops include cassava, maize, bananas, rice, sweet potatoes, and peanuts, while the principal cash crops are cocoa, coffee, tea, sugarcane, tobacco, cotton, rubber, and palm products. At the time of independence, Zaire was a net exporter of agricultural products, but today it is a net importer, due to mismanagement and the government's failure to invest in both agriculture itself and the transportation and communications networks required to support it.

Plant and animal life in the country represents some of the richest and most varied in the world. Many species are not found anywhere else, and an extraordinary number have been identified, including approximately 10,000 species of flowering plants. Valuable indigenous trees include ebony and mahogany, with palm trees, plantains, bananas, and resin-yielding trees also growing in Zaire. In addition, the wild rubber trees which grow there were a main attraction for European colonizers during the Free State era. Animals common to Zaire include lions, leopards, and jackals, elephants, chimpanzees and other primates, exotic birds such as parrots, terns, ibises, and herons, and many types of snake. Savannas host antelopes, red buffaloes, and other herbivorous animals, while crocodiles and hippopotamuses inhabit the rivers. As of

1990, Zaire had seven national parks; conservation efforts are considerable, though not without their problems, as evidenced by the fact that only 300 mountain gorillas are thought to exist in Zaire today.

More undesirable forms of Zairian wildlife include malaria-carrying mosquitoes and the tsetse fly, which carries trypanosomiasis, or sleeping sickness, and rendered the Congo Basin unsuitable for cattle-raising until the introduction of trypanotolerant breeds. Other diseases prevalent in Zaire include measles, pneumonia, tuberculosis, leprosy, gastroenteritis, gonorrhea, syphilis, schistosomiasis, and other parasitic diseases. Malnutrition is also common. Like many other sub-Saharan African countries, Zaire faces potential disaster in the form of the human immunodeficiency virus that causes AIDS. In a 1987 report by UNICEF, the average Zairian's life expectancy was estimated at fifty-one years.

Accounts vary, but according to ethnologists, at least 200 different ethnic groups live in Zaire today, the majority of whom speak Bantu languages and share many common traditions, customs, and other cultural traits. A number of major 'clusters', or groupings, have been identified, which include the Kongo, Lulua, Luba, Lunda, Mai-Ndombe, Mongo, and Zande; ethnically, Zaire is more homogeneous than many other African countries. The original inhabitants of what is presently Zaire are believed to be the aboriginal inhabitants of central Africa, the Pygmies, who are found in remote forested areas in only small numbers today. There are over 200 languages and dialects spoken in Zaire, which fall into one of three linguistic categories: Bantu; Nilo-Saharan; and Pygmy. Four 'national' languages are spoken, all of which are related to Bantu and are in themselves regional *lingua francas*: Lingala, spoken in the north and central basin; Swahili, spoken in the east; Kongo, spoken in the west; and Luba (Ciluba), spoken in the south-central area. All are used in radio broadcasting and local trade. Lingala, recognized as the second language of the government, after French, is spreading rapidly and may well become the most important of the four. Zaire is the largest country in the world to use French as its official language; it was brought to the country by Belgian missionaries, traders, and colonial officials in the 1800s. All educated Zairians speak French, and it is used in all formal legal, political, business, diplomatic and academic transactions.

Zaire is officially a secular state, although most Zairians are very religious, and enjoy freedom of religion, with about ninety-five per cent of the population being Christian; approximately fifty per cent are Roman Catholic. The remainder are either Protestant, or adhere to one of the indigenous African churches. Many Christians follow sects which mix their faith with traditional beliefs and practices; Kimbanguism, said to have five per cent of the Zairian population as adherents in the early 1980s, is one example. The number of Muslims is few; there are only about 400,000, most of whom are descendants of 19th-century traders of mixed African and Arab ancestry who were active in eastern Zaire.

Zaire's export trade is dominated by its heavy mineral and energy production, on which it has become increasingly dependent since independence. It is the world's leading producer of cobalt and industrial diamonds, and is one of the main suppliers of copper, which is the foundation of Zaire's economy and is mined exclusively in the Shaba region. Gold, silver, manganese, cadmium, tantalu, tin, zinc, and tungsten are produced, with petroleum and natural gas also exploited. Zaire's chief non-mineral exports include coffee, valuable woods such as teak and ebony, palm products, and rubber whilst the country's principal imports are machinery, foodstuffs, clothing, chemicals, petroleum products, transportation equipment, and primary and fabricated metal. Belgium is Zaire's principal trading partner; it has always purchased most of Zaire's products and has usually been its chief supplier of imports. Other major trading partners, however, include France, West Germany, Italy, Japan, and the United States. Usually, the value of Zaire's yearly exports greatly exceeds that of its imports.

Because it is endowed with such a wealth and variety of natural resources, Zaire has great potential for economic growth, probably the greatest in all of sub-Saharan Africa. The struggles associated with independence wreaked havoc on the economy in the early 1960s, but by 1966 it had rebounded. Since the mid-1970s, however, the Zairian economy has suffered a number of setbacks that have led to severe economic regression, and it is presently in chaos. Zaire's export income shrank because of low world prices for its major exports – diamonds, cobalt, coffee, and copper – while the price for petroleum imports increased dramatically. It was therefore forced to borrow abroad in order to cover the growing cost of imports. This, in turn, meant that aid had to be sought from foreign banks and international agencies to make payments on the debt, which ballooned to more than $5 billion by the end of 1981, and equalled more than ninety per cent of the country's gross domestic product in that year. Agricultural production suffered through neglect, and food had to be imported and purchased with scarce foreign exchange reserves. The economy was further weakened because money was not invested in the maintenance of Zaire's infrastructure, especially its transportation system. In addition, the government ran large budget deficits which, combined with other economic problems, led to very high inflation rates that averaged around sixty per cent per year from 1975 to 1982. Critics maintain that the government was at fault because of its failure to draw up comprehensive development plans, and its fostering of pervasive mismanagement and corruption.

Having previously failed to abide by a series of agreements negotiated with the International Monetary Fund (IMF) and other external forces, under which Zaire rescheduled its foreign debt and promised to adopt economic stabilization programmes, Zaire began to co-operate more seriously in 1981. At that time, large numbers of civil servants and teachers were laid off. In 1983, the Zairian government announced that legal action would be taken against a number of functionaries for embezzlement and fraud, but the most powerful remained unaffected and government monies continued to be lost to mismanagement. Late that year, the government undertook bold and drastic fiscal and monetary reforms, agreeing to devalue its currency by seventy-eight per cent and to liberalize the economy. In response, the IMF rewarded Zaire in the form of yet another economic stabilization agreement and the Paris Club continued to reschedule Zaire's debt in 1985 and 1987.

In spite of its basic compliance with IMF guidelines, economic activity remained stagnant, and living conditions did not improve; they have, in fact, continued to decline. Even if Zaire's export commodities regain their former demand, the majority of the proceeds could not be invested in necessities like health care, transportation, education, and social programmes, but would have to go toward repayment of Zaire's massive foreign debt. The Mobutu government is so riddled with corruption it is incapable of promoting development, and the massive economic, military, and diplomatic aid Zaire has received from the United States and other Western countries has only succeeded in cementing the country's status as a 'basket case' and keeping afloat the régime of a corrupt and increasingly unpopular president. Mobutu, rumoured to have possibly amassed a personal fortune of about $5 billion, is said to be one of the ten wealthiest men in the world, having enriched himself at the expense of the Zairian people and the foreign taxpayer.

Because of the continuing poor state of its economy, Zaire lacks a well-established commercial publishing industry. Although publishing output as a whole is substantial, the bulk of it is produced by the Presses Universitaires du Zaïre, and various research and church-sponsored institutions, such as the Centre Protestant d'Edition et de Diffusion. Development of the publishing industry and trade is hampered by a number of specific factors, including the population's lack of purchasing power, the dearth of skilled, trained publishing staff, little available spare parts and paper for printing operations, as well as the lack of an established publishing association, long-term capital for investment, and a proper system of distribution. Most of the available written material about Zaire is in French, and by non-Zairian authors.

The bibliography

This work was prepared at Northwestern University Library, in Evanston, Illinois, the location of the largest separate collection of Africana materials in the world, the Melville J. Herskovits Library of African Studies. Since this collection is particularly strong in materials either about or from Zaire, it was an ideal location at which to carry out this project. The vast majority of items listed in this bibliography are held by the Library, and may be requested through normal interlibrary loan channels. To our knowledge, no other current general annotated bibliography about Zaire presently exists.

Needless to say, when compiling a bibliography of this size, covering such a large and important country, it is impossible to be comprehensive or exhaustive. Our goal was to create a work that would cover many facets of Zaire's culture, its place in Africa and the world, past and present, and the features and qualities that make it unique. In each subject-based chapter, we have provided a representative sample of the best available literature, most of which contain bibliographies, thereby allowing interested readers to search for further information. Annotations vary in length but are generally substantive and will give readers a good impression of what each title concerns. The chapters vary in length as well, since it was difficult to find materials on certain subjects. For example, much has been published about Zaire's history and politics; in comparison, little can be found on science and technology or transport. To find relevant materials, we have had to search through general reference tools and specialist journals, and have found it necessary to cite some books, journals, and other materials that are not widely available.

Since the Clio *World Bibliographical Series* is primarily aimed at the English speaker, titles selected for inclusion in this volume are typically in that language. It is impossible, however, to undertake extensive research on Zaire without consulting the numerous sources published in French, many of which were included here because of their special importance, or because few or no English sources on a specific topic could be located. Works in Dutch are also plentiful, although we included only a small number of titles in either that language or other Western European languages. Special mention needs to be made of one title that should not be overlooked, and that is the Musée Royal de l'Afrique Centrale's prolific serial publication, *Annales*. Issued since

1898, this title presents the results of important research undertaken within a wide variety of subject areas, and is the source of a wealth of information. See entry number 1 for further information.

A few words of explanation should be given about Zairian personal names. Before independence, they were comprised of African names with Christian forenames but from 1971 onwards, the political ideology of *authenticité* (authenticity) took hold, which celebrated a return to African origins. Zairians were required, by law, to abandon their Christian forenames in favour of those of African inspiration, which had fallen into disuse under the colonial régime. Thus, Norbert Mikanza became Mikanza Mobyem Kidah, Dieudonné Kadima-Nzuji became Kadima-Nzuji Mukala and, an example of an extreme case, Clémentine Nzuji became Clémentine Faïk-Nzuji Madiya, assuming parts of her husband's name. Today, this practice is no longer followed as closely by all Zairians, and Christian forenames have begun to reappear.

Zairian names entirely of African origin do not include a surname, and are always entered under the first element, without any inversion of the name. This presents a problem for those searching for materials on Zaire if they are unaware of this fact. Also, some libraries and research institutions have catalogued materials by Zairian authors under an incorrect form of name, rendering them difficult or impossible to locate. We advise, therefore, when searching in this book for a Zairian author, to check under the various elements of the name, although we have attempted to enter all names we know to be Zairian correctly, under the first element. Zairian names that include a Christian forename have been entered in inverted order, under the African element of the name. Sometimes Zairians living abroad have westernized their names to some extent and should be sought under the inverted form of the name, such as V. Y. Mudimbe, who is indexed under Mudimbe in this bibliography.

Please note that we have not included prefixes as part of the names of Zairian languages and ethnic groups, following the increasingly common anglophone practice. For example, we refer to the Kongo language, not Kikongo, and the Bakongo people are called Kongo. In addition, the reader will notice that the word 'Zairian' is frequently also spelled 'Zairean' throughout this book and both forms are correct. Another important consideration is the name Congo. Do not confuse the present Congo (capital city of Brazzaville), formerly the French or Moyen Congo (Middle Congo), with Zaire's former names of either the Congo Free State, Belgian Congo, or Democratic Republic of the Congo. Because many Zairian geographical names and terms have changed since independence, we advise the reader to refer, whenever necessary, to the *Guide to Former and Present Names* that has been supplied.

The entries in each section of this bibliography are arranged in alphabetical order by title.

Acknowledgements

We would like to express our profound gratitude for the assistance given to us at Northwestern University Library during the course of compiling this bibliography. Mette Shayne and the staff of the Melville J. Herskovits Library of African Studies offered advice and helped us locate materials. Without the assistance of Rita Djuricich, Melissa Jacobi, Gary Strawn, and Robert Trautvetter, we would never have been able to master the intricacies of our indexing software and data manipulation. Finally, the staff of the Interlibrary Loan Department assisted us in obtaining materials not held by the Library.

Chronology

Ca. 2000 BC	First Bantu people, called *proto-Bantu,* arrive in the Congo Basin from Nigeria, and settle in Bas-Zaire and Uele.
1000 BC to 200 AD	Bantu-speaking peoples settle throughout the Congo River Basin.
500 to 1000 AD	Bantu-speaking peoples migrate through what are now the Kasai, Kivu and Shaba regions to the savannas and toward the Indian Ocean.
1200 to 1500 AD	Emergence of the kingdoms of Kongo, Kuba, Luba and Lunda, and the dominions of Zande and Mangbetu.
1483	European penetration of the territory begins with the arrival of Portuguese admiral Diogo Cão at the estuary of the Congo (Zaire) River. In 1485 and 1487 he returns to establish trading posts.
1500	Nilotic people arrive in northeastern Zaire; Zande people migrate into north and central Zaire.
1640	Portuguese power declines in the region toward the end of the 1600s as the English and French establish their presence. The Dutch supplant the Portuguese as the leading traders.
1715-76	The slave trade with the Americas reaches its height.
1789	Portuguese explorer José Lacerda e Almeida discovers copper mines in Katanga as he makes the first scientific exploration of the Congo Basin.
1800	The Afro-Arab trade becomes well-established in eastern Zaire.

Chronology

1816   James Tuckey leads a British expedition up the mouth of the Congo River and inaugurates a continuous period of scientific exploration of central and southern Africa in the 19th century.

1854   David Livingstone, Scottish missionary and explorer, discovers Lake Dilolo in Katanga and crosses the Kasai and Kwango River basins into neighbouring Angola.

1857   British explorers Richard Burton and John Speke discover Lake Tanganyika on Zaire's eastern border.

1864   Explorer Samuel Baker discovers Lake Albert.

1867-71 Livingstone reaches Lakes Mweru and Bangwelu, then Lake Tanganyika in 1869. He sails down the Lualaba River, seeking the headwaters of the Nile River, and reaches the heart of the Congo River at Nyangwe. Stricken by fever, he is rescued by journalist Henry Morton Stanley at Ujiji on Lake Tanganyika in 1871.

1874-77 Stanley, commissioned to continue Livingstone's explorations by the *New York Herald* and *Daily Telegraph* newspapers, navigates the Congo River, partly to prove the Lualaba River is not the headwaters of the Nile, from its upper course to the Atlantic Ocean, which he reaches on 12 March, 1877.

1878-87 Belgium's King Leopold II hires Stanley to establish trading posts and sign protectorate treaties with local chiefs along the Congo River in the name of the International Congo Association.

1884-85 European powers partition Africa at the Berlin Conference, which takes place from 15 November, 1884 to 26 February, 1885. Leopold secures personal sovereignty over the International Association of the Congo, which soon becomes the Congo Free State.

1890-94 Afro-Arab traders are driven from the Congo Free State under a European military campaign and the slave trade with the Middle East is ended. By this time, the major overseas markets for slaves, in Europe and the Americas, have collapsed.

1904-05 Public outcry breaks out in Europe and the United States with reports, made by missionaries and diplomats, of forced labour and brutalities by Congo Free State authorities.

1908   Leopold agrees to relinquish personal control over the Congo Free State as he faces international condemnation for human rights abuses. Belgium annexes the territory as a colony on 9 September, and on 15 November it becomes the Belgian Congo.

1914-45   The Belgian Congo's economy largely imitates that of the world, as it experiences a boom in the 1920s and a depresssion in the 1930s. During the First and Second World Wars, Congolese soldiers fight with the Allies in the African theatre.

1945-55   A class of educated, primarily urban, white collar Congolese workers, known as the *évolués* (the civilized), begins to emerge. African workers seek greater equality and advancement opportunities, and trade unionism springs up.

1958   Hundreds of Congolese are brought to Belgium during the Brussels World Fair. Patrice Lumumba and other Congolese leaders attend the All African-People's Conference in December in newly independent Ghana, and return home inspired with ideas of Congolese independence.

1959   Lumumba calls for independence from Belgium at a rally in Leopoldville (Kinshasa). The announcement of major political reforms comes too late to forestall the eruption of rioting in the capital and other cities and colonial authorities agree to hold local elections; they take place in December but are boycotted by many emerging parties. Continued unrest moves the Belgian government to hold the Round Table Conference in Brussels.

1960   The Round Table Conference is held, with forty-five delegates from various Congolese parties in attendance. The Belgian delegates agree, with reluctance, to set 30 June as the date for independence. Provisions are made for the transfer of power and outlines of future political organizations. Pre-independence elections are held, but no single political party wins a majority. A compromise is struck and Joseph Kasa-Vubu and Patrice Lumumba form a coalition government, becoming President and Premier, respectively, when the Congo becomes independent on 30 June.

Four days later, members of the Force Publique mutiny for higher pay and greater opportunities for promotion. The ensuing violence makes headlines around the world, and leads to the flight of much of the European officers' corps and most European civil servants. Belgian paratroopers occupy a number of cities and fearing a Belgian seizure of their former colony, the Congolese call in the United Nations for military and administrative assistance. Both Katanga, under provisional president Moïse Tshombe, and South Kasai secede on 11 July. Lumumba is dismissed and jailed by Kasa-Vubu on 5 September.

1961   In January Lumumba is murdered in Katanga by his political adversaries, leading to the secession of Orientale and Kivu Provinces. Parliament reconvenes under United Nations protection and Cyrille Adoula is named to head a cabinet of national reconciliation. South Kasai ends its secession.

1963   A United Nations military operation succeeds in forcibly reuniting Katanga with the rest of the country; Tshombe goes into exile.

1964   Adoula is forced to resign his position as premier and is replaced by Tshombe, who returns from self-imposed exile. The country's first constitution is passed on 1 August. The People's Republic of the Congo is proclaimed in Stanleyville (Kisangani) on 7 September and recognized by thirteen foreign countries. Tshombe recalls white mercenaries active in the Katanga secession to regain control of areas where unrest has broken out.

1965   Tshombe is removed from office by President Kasa-Vubu after he fails to establish a national political base. His designated successor, Katanga politician Evariste Kimba, is not accepted by parliament. In an apparent effort to resolve the deadlock, and in the face of more rebellion in the east, General Joseph Mobutu (Mobutu Sese Seko) unseats Kasa-Vubu and is installed as head-of-state by the military, with Léonard Mulamba as prime minister.

1966   The Mouvement Populaire de la Révolution (MPR), or Popular Revolutionary Movement, Zaire's sole legal party, is formed. Mulamba is dismissed and a presidential government established. The mining concession and assets of the Union Minière du Haut Katanga are seized by the government. A state corporation is established, La Générale des Carrières et des Mines du Zaïre (Gécamines), to control activities associated with the mining of copper and other minerals.

1967   The Nsele Manifesto is proclaimed, the outgrowths of which later become the policies of *authenticité* (authenticity), Mobutism, and Zairianization. Rebellion breaks out in the eastern Congo, with the goal of returning Tshombe to power, but is thwarted. A new constitution is promulgated and ratified in a referendum, granting more powers to the president and reducing regional autonomy. Tshombe is kidnapped and imprisoned in Algeria. The last rebellion in the east is quelled, but some territory in Kivu remains under control of the Parti de la Révolution Populaire (PRP), or People's Revolutionary Party.

1969   Kasa-Vubu dies; Tshombe's death in prison is announced by Algeria.

1970   Mobutu, the sole candidate for president, is elected.

1971   Following the concept of authenticity, the Congo becomes the Republic of Zaire.

1973   The Mobutu government seizes some 2,000 foreign-owned economic enterprises (except American ones) and turns them over to Zairians, most of whom are political élites and include Mobutu himself, who profits the most. This 'Zairianization' soon exhibits a negative impact in the form of shortages of goods, tax evasion, and abandonment of businesses.

1974   The pinnacle of centralization of presidential power comes with the third constitution, under which the MPR becomes the 'sole institution' of society, making all other public bodies branches of the party.

1975   Zaire's massive debt crisis is precipitated by a drastic fall in the price of copper and the onset of economic recession.

1976   The government adopts the first of a series of economic stabilization programmes, or 'Mobutu plans', under the guidance of the International Monetary Fund (IMF) and other external groups.

1977   Front National pour la Libération du Congo (FNLC) guerrillas, led by Nathaniel Bumba, hope to spark a general uprising in Zaire by attacking and occupying a series of towns along the railway linking Shaba's mining centres and Angola's Benguela Railway. Most dissidents belong to the Lunda ethnic group, who resent the loss of important positions in government and industry. The Zairian army, backed by Moroccan troops with French logistical support, sucessfully drives them back to their base in Angola. Lunda leaders, including Foreign Minister Nguza Karl-i-Bond, are imprisoned and convicted of complicity; Nguza is later pardoned and returns to the government. Mobutu is elected to a second term as president.

1978   FNLC guerrillas attack again, this time occupying the important mining town of Kolwezi, where work in the mines and other industrial installations comes to a standstill. A looting and killing spree by the guerrillas leads the government to parachute Zairian armed forces, backed by French and Belgian troops, into Kolwezi and the area is retaken after two weeks. Both FNLC invasions, dubbed 'Shaba I' and 'Shaba II,' inspire international criticism of the government's political and economic policies, which leads to enactment of some reforms.

1981   Nguza unexpectedly resigns and goes into exile, charging the Zairian government with corruption, authoritarianism, and abuse of power.

1983   The government launches a series of fiscal and monetary reforms designed to reduce inflation, liberalize the economy, and make Zaire current on foreign debt payments, throwing the country into a recession and causing inflation to sky-rocket to one hundred per cent per annum.

1984   Mobutu is re-elected to a third term as president.

1985   International creditors reward Zaire for remaining current on debt payments and liberalizing its economy by rescheduling Zaire's debt for ten years. The recession is considered ended and annual inflation has dropped to twenty per cent per annum, but the social cost of servicing the debt remains high and the purchasing power of most Zairians low.

1986   The government announces that debt repayment will be limited to twenty per cent of government revenues and ten per cent of export earnings because IMF austerity programmes are adversely affecting the economy.

1987   The Paris Club agrees to reschedule Zaire's debt for fifteen years; payment is deferred on $846 million of debt. Donor nations pledge $1.48 billion in aid over the next two years.

1988   Belgian Prime Minister Maertens' proposition to stagger repayment of Zaire's public and private debt with Belgium, made without the endorsement of his government, precipitates a political crisis and causes a serious deterioration of relations with Kinshasa.

1989   Economic and political dispute between Zaire and Belgium is resolved. After a meeting in Paris between Mobutu and Maertens, Brussels cancels half of its public and commercial debt with Zaire. The United States forgives a portion of Zaire's public debt.

1990   Mobutu announces new austerity measures. He also pledges, in a speech to the nation, the creation of a multi-party system limited to three political groups, the resignation of the present government and a return to democracy; his announcement is greeted with caution and scepticism by the Church and the opposition.

1991   Mobutu declares that 1991 will be the year of democratization. A national conference is held to decide Zaire's future but it collapses amid claims by the *Union Sacrée* (Sacred Union), a coalition of opposition groups, that Mobutu moved to ensure his survival by rigging the proceedings. The opposition galvanizes and renews calls for his removal as economic conditions continue to deteriorate and unpaid soldiers trigger riots in Kinshasa. A new public pronouncement by a standing committee of Zaire's bishops, which has been very critical of Mobutu since the beginning of 1990, denounces the government's blockage of true democratic reforms, and declares itself preoccupied with the explosive situation that reigns in the country, including violent demonstrations against the high cost of living in Kinshasa, and a strike by civil servants.

1992   Prime Minister Nguza, who returned to the government in 1988, accuses the opposition of complicity in an attempted military *coup d'état*. The military continues its night-time pillages in Kinshasa. Ethnic tensions flare and conflict breaks out in the Shaba region.

1993   Ethnic conflicts continue in Shaba. Violent rioting breaks out in Kinshasa when Mobutu insists on paying soldiers with worthless zaire bank notes, which some merchants refuse to honour. Soldiers loot shops and embassy residences, and kill the French ambassador. The United States, Belgium, and France urge Mobutu to step down, which he refuses to do.

Chronology

1994   Refugees pour over the Zairian/Rwandan border as violent ethnic tensions erupt in Rwanda between Hutus and Tutsis immediately following a plane crash that kills the presidents of both Rwanda and Burundi.

Under the auspices of international organizations, refugee camps are established at Goma and Bukavu, where the Rwandan people are plagued by dysentery, cholera, and other diseases. Conflict continues in the camps between Hutu and Tutsi, and civilians and military personnel. Because Zaire and relief agencies are unable to handle such a mass exodus, the United Nations urges the refugees to return to Rwanda, but few comply with its request.

Guide to Current and Former Names

Most of these names were changed between 1966 and 1971.

Former Name	Current Name
Aketi Port-Chaltin	Aketi
Albert, Lake	Mobutu Sese Seko, Lake*
Alberta	Ebonda
Albertville	Kalemie
Bakete	Dibaya
Bakwanga	Mbuji-Mayi
Banningville	Bandundu
Banzyville	Mobaye
Bas-Congo Province	Bas-Zaïre Region
Brabanta	Mapangu
Bomokandi	Bambili
Centime (currency)	Likuta (plural: makuta)
Congo Franc (currency)	Zaire (currency)
Charlesville	Djokopunda
Congo, Republic of	Zaire, Republic of
Congo River	Zaire River**
Coquilhatville	Mbandaka
Costermansville	Bukavu
Cristal Mountains	Mayumbe Mountains
Districts	Sub-Regions
Elisabetha	Lukutu
Elisabethville	Lubumbashi
Jadotville	Likasi
Katanga Province	Shaba Region
Kindu-Port-Empaim	Kindu
Leopold II, Lake	Mai-Ndombe, Lake
Leopoldville	Kinshasa
Leverville	Lusanga

Guide to Current and Former Names

Luluabourg	Kananga
Merode	Tshilundu
Ministries	Departments
Ministers	State Commissioners
Moerbeke	Kwilu-Ngongo
Mopolenge	Bolobo
Orientale Province	Haut-Zaïre Region
Paulis	Isiro
Provinces	Regions
Stanley Pool	Malebo Pool
Stanleyville	Kisangani
Thysville	Mbanza-Ngungu

Lake Albert is the term generally preferred in non-Zairian published sources.
**Zaire River,* the official Zairian name, and *Congo River* are both used, although international cartographers prefer the latter.

The Country and Its People

1 **Annales du Musée Royal de l'Afrique Centrale.** (Annals of the Royal
  Museum of Central Africa.)
  Tervuren, Belgium: Musée Royal de l'Afrique Centrale, 1898- . irreg.
  Published within this series are a great number of sub-series that deal with numerous
  topics as they relate to Zaire; these include history, zoology, botany, economics,
  ethnography, anthropology, geology and linguistics. Articles are mostly in French, with
  some in Dutch and a few in English. For more information about this important series,
  see the introduction.

2 **Les Cahiers du CEDAF.** (CEDAF notebooks.)
  Brussels: Centre d'Etude et de Documentation Africaines, 1971- . monthly.
  Many libraries treat this serial publication as a series in its own right. A serious,
  scholarly study on Zaire is produced on a monthly basis, with each issue usually
  containing only one monograph. The subjects vary widely, covering, for example:
  education; politics; economics; and religion Some of these monographs have been cited
  separately in this bibliography.

3 **Du Congo au Zaïre, 1960-1980: essai de bilan.** (From the Congo to
  Zaire, 1960-1980: attempt at analysis.)
  André Huybrechts, V. Y. Mudimbe, L. Peeters, Jacques Vanderlinden,
  Daniel van der Steen, Benoît Verhaegen, edited by Jacques Vanderlinden.
  Brussels: Centre de Recherche et d'Information Socio-politiques, 1980.
  420p. bibliog.
  For readers of French, this work provides broad coverage of the geography, population,
  economy, politics, and culture of Zaire. Written by a team of six researchers, this
  comprehensive treatment of Zaire is aimed at both a general and an academic audience.

4   **Let's visit Zaire.**
    Noel Carrick.   Basingstoke, England: Macmillan, 1988. 96p.
This is a book prepared for a younger audience. In easy-to-read English, enhanced by
many photographs, Carrick provides a comprehensive treatment of Zaire, covering such
topics as: history; government; people; education; and geography. As with much juvenile
literature, the analysis of the subject is undeveloped: it is uncritical to a fault of Mobutu
Sese Seko, not sufficiently realistic about the economic and political crises facing Zaire,
and contains nothing about human rights violations, violence and crime. This is a
softer style of reportage and is more suitable for children. Alternatively, it could be
used as a point of departure for more realistic discussions about Zaire.

5   **Pile et face: bilan de la coopération belgo-zaïroise.** (Heads and tails:
    analysis of Belgian-Zairian co-operation.)
    Brussels: Revue Nouvelle: CNCD-11.11.11, 1989. 269p. bibliog.
Several well-known authorities on Zaire have contributed chapters to this well-rounded
work on contemporary Zaire. The title indicates a study of the Zairian-Belgian bilateral
relationship, and the essays do indeed reflect this effort at international co-operation.
However, the work maintains a focus on many aspects of Zaire today: economic
development; foreign relations; politics and government; administration; education;
health care; and infrastructure. It is an excellent general introduction to this Central
African nation with a publication date (1989) sufficiently recent to assure the timeliness
of the information. Written in French, the work nonetheless includes contributions by
experts from non-French-speaking countries.

6   **Profils du Zaïre.** (Profiles of Zaire.)
    Kinshasa: Bureau du Président de la République du Zaïre, 1972. 464p. map.
This large general work on Zaire is a publication of the Zairian government. Despite
the obvious political bias of the work, it nonetheless offers very good coverage of the
geography, climate, resources, transportation, industries, economic activity, and
peoples of Zaire. Considerable attention is paid to politics and government and to the
Zairian President Mobutu Sese Seko.

7   **Rapports sur les pays ACP, Zaïre.** (Reports of the ACP countries,
    Zaire.)
    Eurostat.   Luxembourg: Office des Publications Officielles des
    Communautés Européennes pour Office Statistique des Communautés
    Européennes, 1988. 103p. maps. bibliog. (Thème 1, Statistiques Générales.
    Série C, Comptes, Enquêtes et Statistiques).
This short but comprehensive work on Zaire includes a brief analysis of many aspects of
the country such as the physical geography, population, education, public health,
agriculture, foreign trade, industries, resources, and general economic activity. The
author provides abundant statistics to bolster his analysis which, although not current
(1988), certainly reflect the relative strength of each area.

8 **Republic of Zaire.**
Rebecca Stefoff.   Edgemont, Pennsylvania: Chelsea House Publishers,
1987. 92p. map.

A general introduction to Zaire for children, this work is enriched by many brilliant
photographs, illustrating the physical geography, the people, the history, and the culture
and customs of Zaire.

9 **Travaux du Tribunal Permanent des Peuples sur le Zaïre: 18-21
septembre, 1982.** (Papers of the Permanent Peoples' Tribunal: 18-21
September, 1982.)
Tribunal Permanent des Peuples.   Rotterdam, The Netherlands: Tribunal
Permanent des Peuples, 1982. various pagination.

These proceedings of a conference on Zaire include papers on many topics: economics;
politics; social conditions; foreign relations; and government. The emphasis of the
conference was on conditions in Zaire at the time (ca. 1982).

10 **Zaire.**
Series co-ordinated by Patricia S. Kuntz, consultants for Zaire, Thomas
Turner, Margaret Turner.   Gainesville, Florida: University of Florida,
Center for African Studies, 1984. 1 vol. (loose-leaf). bibliog. (Country
Orientation Notebooks for Africa, no. 7).

This general work on Zaire takes the form of a loose-leaf notebook produced and
updated yearly by the Center for African Studies (470 Grinter Hall, University of
Florida, Gainesville, Florida 32611). It is a compilation of previously published articles,
reports, and essays by many authors on most aspects of Zaire: history; society; politics;
current events; agriculture; development; and economy. Chiefly in English, although
some sections are in French, this work could well be one of the most useful resources for
general up-to-date information on Zaire. In some libraries it may be catalogued as part of
a multi-volume set under the series title: Country Orientation Notebooks for Africa.

11 **Zaïre-Afrique.** (Zaire-Africa.)
Kinshasa: Centre d'Etudes pour l'Action Sociale, 1971- . monthly.

Published monthly since 1971, this journal is an excellent source of current information
on Zaire. It contains lengthy, serious articles by Zairian and foreign experts on a wide
variety of topics concerning Zaire today. The subjects of education, politics, government,
social conditions and economics are often discussed, and sometimes an entire issue is
devoted to a single topic.

12 **Zaire: a country study.**
Edited by Irving Kaplan.   Washington, DC: American University,
1979. 3rd ed. 332p. maps. bibliog. (Area Handbook Series).

Produced for the US Army, this American University handbook is an excellent
introduction to Zaire. The political and economic analysis may be slightly dated (1979),
but the analysis of the physical geography, history, ethnic structure, and the social
conditions is still highly accurate. This work would be a fine starting point for both the
general user and the serious scholar.

13 **Zaïre, l'ascension d'une nation engagée.** (Zaire, the rise of a committed nation.)
   Kabongo-Kongo Kola.   Kinshasa: Presses Universitaires du Zaïre, 1983. 257p. bibliog.

Should the user of this bibliography tire of negative or pessimistic analyses of the future of Zaire, this work is the perfect antidote. The praise heaped upon President Mobutu Sese Seko is positively glowing and Zaire is characterized as a nation making considerable national progress, at least up until the time when the international economic slowdown cut the price of mineral exports, thus impeding the country's economic advancement. This alternative analysis might be refreshing if it were not for its sharp contrast with reality; the author of the work, a member of the Central Committee of Mobutu's governing political party (the MPR), is unabashedly and fatuously laudatory of Mobutu and his rule of Zaire. Nevertheless, the reader can learn much about the political and intellectual degradation of Zaire in these elogies. The work also contains several circumstantial poems on the destiny of Zaire and a sycophantic birthday wish by the author on the occasion of Mobutu's fifty-second birthday.

14 **Zaire, what destiny?**
   Edited by Kankwenda Mbaya, translated from the French by Ayi Kwei Armah.   Dakar: CODESRIA; Oxford: Distributed by ABC, 1993. 376p. bibliog. (Codesria Book Series).

This work comprises a translated collection of essays by Zairian researchers and scholars. The topics vary widely, beginning with an analysis of Zaire's prevailing national ideologies: ethnicity; regionalism; and nationalism. The volume continues with an examination of the state structure and the social and political life of the country. The work also covers problems of economic development and devotes considerable attention to education. The economic, financial and agricultural situation of Zaire is discussed under the rubric of 'crisis' and the study ends with an inventory of Zaire's mineral resources and industries. A recent publication, this work gives a comprehensive, general treatment of Zaire.

15 **Zaire, yesterday and today.**
   R. S. Osram.   [N.p.]: [n.p.], 1987 (Boulder City, Nevada: Printing by M. W. Printing & Pub.). 48p. map.

This short, colourful work reflects the author's own impression of Zaire. The book is mainly a travelogue of Osram's journey through Zaire and represents a very personal view of the country.

Le Zaïre: civilisations traditionnelles et culture moderne: archives culturelles d'Afrique centrale.
See item no. 205.

Zaïre: peuples/art/culture.
See item no. 661.

Explorers' Accounts

16   **Across Africa.**
      Verney Lovett Cameron.   New York: Harper, 1877. Reprinted, New
      York: Negro Universities Press, 1969. 508p. map.
Between 1873 and 1876 Scottish Lieutenant Cameron duplicated the Arab
accomplishment of crossing Africa from the east coast at Zanzibar to the west coast of
Africa. Although his primary mission was to locate the missing David Livingstone, he
continued westward through the Congo after meeting up with Livingstone's funeral
procession, crossing several tributaries of the Congo River (Zaire), until he arrived at
Beguela, Angola. His account is particularly noteworthy in its description of ethnic
groups to the west of Lake Tanganyika.

17   **Les Belges dans l'Afrique centrale: voyages, aventures et**
      découvertes d'après les documents et journaux des explorateurs.
      (The Belgians in central Africa: voyages, adventures and discoveries
      from the documents and journals of explorers.)
      Brussels: P. Maes, 1886. 3 vols. maps.
Contained in this three-volume set are: *Le Congo et ses affluents* (The Congo and its
tributaries), by Charles de Martrin-Donos (2 vols.); and *De Zanzibar au Lac Tanganika*
(From Zanzibar to Lake Tanganyika), by Adolphe Burdo (1 vol.). These accounts of
Belgian expeditions from 1876 to 1885 in the Congo region contain valuable information
on ethnology and natural history. The set is also of interest to readers on the history of
Belgian colonialism.

18   **Dark companions: the African contribution to the European**
      exploration of East Africa.
      Donald Simpson.   London: P. Elek, 1975. 228p. maps. bibliog.
Other books in this section of the present bibliography deal with the European explorers
of the Central African region. Simpson turns the tables by examining the rôle of the
Africans who accompanied these European explorers.

19 **Five years with the Congo cannibals.**
Herbert Ward. London: Chatto & Windus, 1891. Reprinted, New
York: Negro University Press, 1969. 3rd ed. 308p. maps.
Ward explored the Congo between 1884 and 1889, just as it became the Congo Free
State. He first served at Vivi, the beginning of the cataract region of the Lower Congo,
and travelled among the Kongo peoples. He was then appointed to the station of the
Bangalas. In 1887, he joined Stanley's Emin Pasha relief expedition and commanded the
Rear Guard at Bolobo, travelling as far as Stanley Falls, but failing to meet up with
Stanley. He relates his experiences with the Kongo, Luba, Mongo, and Ngala people, as
well as numerous other ethnic groups.

20 **From the Congo to the Niger and the Nile: an account of the
German Central African Expedition of 1910-1911.**
Adolf Friedrich, Duke of Mecklenburg. London: Duckworth, 1913.
Reprinted, New York: Negro Universities Press, 1969. 2 vols. map.
This account of German exploration is important for its discussion on northern Zairian
peoples such as the Mangbetu and Manjas. It includes numerous illustrations of coiffure
and dress as well as handicrafts.

21 **Garenganze, or, Seven years' pioneer mission work in Central
Africa.**
Frederick Stanley Arnot. Chicago: Fleming H. Revell, 1889.
Reprinted, London: F. Cass, 1969. 276p. maps. (Cass Library of
African Studies. Missionary Researches and Travels, no. 10).
Arnot was the first missionary to settle in Shaba (then known as Garenganze), among the
Luba, Lunda, Sanga and Yeke peoples. Today he is known for opening up the African
interior to Christian evangelism, rather than as a geographer, scientist, or ethnologist.

22 **The heart of Africa: three years' travels and adventures in the
unexplored regions of central Africa, from 1868 to 1871.**
Georg Schweinfurth, translated from the German by Ellen E. Frewer.
London: S. Low, Marston, Low, & Searle, 1873. Reprinted,
Farnborough, England: Gregg, 1969. 2 vols. map.
Schweinfurth's mission was to determine if Pygmies really existed in the Congo basin.
He discovered that it was possible to gain access to them by travelling from Khartoum
down the Nile and from there, by crossing the Uele River, a tributary of the Congo. His
descriptions of Mangbetu, Zande and Akka Pygmies (northeast Zaire) are noteworthy
and part of his meticulously-collected flora and fauna collections were sent back to
Europe.

23 **In darkest Africa, or, The quest, rescue, and retreat of Emin,
Governor of Equatoria.**
Henry M. Stanley. New York: Scribner's, 1891. 2 vols. maps.
Emin Pasha was a German physician whose real name was Eduard Schnitzer. He was
also governor of Equatoria, the southernmost province of the Sudan, at the time of
General Gordon's murder by fanatical Mahdists in 1886. King Leopold of Belgium

asked Stanley to head the relief expedition to rescue him, with instructions to travel from the west coast of Africa, up the Congo River to Stanley Falls, across the Lualaba through the Ituri Forest, to Lake Albert and along the Nile to Lado, Sudan. The journey took nearly three years, and when Stanley finally located Emin Pasha, he did not want to be rescued. Nevertheless, Stanley forced him to travel to the east coast of Africa. Leopold had failed in his purpose to prove the easy accessability of the southern Sudan via the Congo and this was Stanley's last African expedition. Other editions of this work are available, the latest publication date being 1913.

24 The lake regions of central Africa: a picture of exploration.
Sir Richard F. Burton, introduction by Alan Moorehead. London: Longman, Green & Roberts, 1860. Reprinted, New York: Horizon Press, 1961. 2 vols.

This is the account of British explorers Richard Burton and John Spekes' 1857-59 expedition as they strived to discover the source of the Nile. They followed Arab trade routes from Zanzibar to the eastern shore of Lake Tanganyika, then Speke alone turned northward and arrived at the southern edge of Lake Victoria. Through intuition and the information of Arab slavers he declared that he had discovered the source of the Nile. Since Speke had neither thoroughly explored the area nor found a river to the north of the lake Burton refused to accept his declaration, which was of course correct. Of particular interest to this bibliography are the sections of volume two that discuss the northwestern shores of Lake Tanganyika.

25 The last journals of David Livingstone, in central Africa, from 1865 to his death.
David Livingstone. New York: Harper, 1875. Reprinted, Detroit, Michigan: Negro History Press, 1977. 541p. maps.

Livingstone's account of his expeditions in central Africa from 1866 to 1873 includes a discussion of his journey along the central western shore of Lake Tanganyika from Maniema up to the Lualaba River. His motives in travelling here had been to discover the source of the Nile as well as to expose the Arab slave trade coming from the east African coast. He mentions the Katanga gold supply and malachite mines, and observes numerous ethnic groups. Horace Waller continues the work with a narrative of Livingstone's last moments and sufferings, obtained from his faithful servants Chuma and Susi.

26 Missionary travels and researches in South Africa including a sketch of sixteen years' residence in the interior of Africa.
David Livingstone. New York: Harper, 1858. Reprinted, New York; London: Johnson Reprint, 1971. 732p. maps. (Landmarks in Anthropology).

In this account of his early days (1840-56) as a medical missionary, Livingstone describes his journeys from Cape Town, South Africa to Loanda, Angola, and then into southeastern Zaire, where he met and wrote about numerous ethnic groups such as the Luanda and Chokwe. From there he journeyed down the Zambesi River to Quelimane, Mozambique, making him the first European to cross the African continent from west to east.

27 **My second journey through equatorial Africa from the Congo to the Zambesi in the years 1886 and 1887.**
Hermann von Wissmann, translated from the German by Minna J. A. Bergmann.   London: Chatto & Windus, 1891. Reprinted, Farnborough, England: Gregg, 1971. 326p. map.

Written by German explorer Wissmann, this is an account of his third expedition which was financed by King Leopold of Belgium. It describes his efforts to open the Luba country and make known to the peoples of the south (Kasai) and eastern Congo (Lake Tanganyika region) that in 1885 the Congo Free State had been declared, with King Leopold as its sovereign. The volume includes important ethnographic descriptions of several groups (Luba, Lulua, Kanyok) in these areas. Wissmann's previous African expeditions are described in his German text *Im Innern Afrikas* (In inner Africa) (Nendeln: Kraus Reprint, 1974).

28 **Narrative of an expedition to explore the river Zaire, usually called the Congo in South Africa, in 1816; to which is added, the journal of Professor Smith.**
J. K. Tuckey.   London: John Murray, 1818. Reprinted, London: F. Cass, 1967. 498p. map. (Cass Library of African Studies. Travels and Narratives, no. 23).

This is the account of an expedition which was the precursor of several other expeditions throughout the 19th century to what is now Zaire. In 1815, British Captain James Tuckey was charged with exploring the course of the Congo River, with the aim of discovering a connection between the Congo and the Niger rivers. Here he documents extensively his observations, and reports on the nature and organization of the slave trade. The expedition failed in its primary objective, because Tuckey and a number of his companions died during the journey. Nevertheless, valuable information was gathered during the 300 miles of travel up the Congo to the rapids of Isangila. Chiefly comprised of the journals of Captain Tuckey and Chetien Smith, a botanist, together with observations from the detached notes of three of their companions, this work provides a wealth of information on the expedition itself and its immediate background. An appendix containing information gathered by the expedition on the natural history of the Congo River is included.

29 **Pioneering on the Congo.**
W. Holman Bentley.   London: Religious Tract Society, 1900. Reprinted, New York; London: Johnson Reprint, 1970. 2 vols. map. (Landmarks in Anthropology).

Although the Reverend Bentley describes the 19th-century activities of the Baptist Missionary Society in the Congo, his work is known today as an explorer's account, rich in its ethnographic details. He slowly travelled inland to the upper Congo River, near Stanley Falls. The account includes a history of the area since the earliest Europeans arrived in 1484 through the old slaving days to 1877. The ethnography is noteworthy, as is the chapter on fetishism. Illustrations of fetishes, knives, fauna, currency, postage stamps, and other objects encountered are included.

30   **The quest for Africa: two thousand years of exploration.**
Heinrich Schiffers, translated from the German by Diana Pyke.
London: Odhams Press, 1957. 352p. 3 maps.

This history of the European exploration of Africa does include the basic information on 19th-century exploration of the Congo, but it is scattered in several chapters of the book. Additional maps would have greatly assisted the reader who must unfortunately resort to using the index to locate the relevant text.

31   **A report of the Kingdom of Congo and of the surrounding countries.**
Duarte Lopez, drawn out by Filippo Pigafetta, in Rome, 1591, translated from the Italian, and edited with explanatory notes by Margarite Hutchinson.   London: J. Murray, 1881. Reprinted, London: F. Cass, 1970. 174p. map. (Cass Library of African Studies. Travels and Narratives, no. 66).

This is one of the earliest accounts (1578-89) of the exploration of the Congo. Portuguese explorer Lopez describes the history of the Kongo Kingdom, including the conversion of the King of Sogno. The explanatory notes include the nomenclature of the Congo on maps from 1492 to 1600. The text was also reprinted in 1969 by Negro Universities Press.

32   **The River Congo: the discovery, exploration and exploitation of the world's most dramatic river.**
Peter Forbath.   New York: Harper & Row, 1977. 404p. maps. bibliog.

Forbath offers an excellent introduction to the early voyages and exploration of the nearly 2,000-mile long Congo (Zaire) River and its immense basin. He pays particular attention to the 19th-century contributions of Tuckey, Livingstone, Stanley, and Cameron.

33   **Through the dark continent, or, The sources of the Nile around the great lakes of equatorial Africa and down the Livingstone River to the Atlantic Ocean.**
Henry M. Stanley.   London: G. Newnes, 1899. Reprinted, New York: Dover, 1988. 2 vols. 10 maps.

Stanley's monumental account of his 1874-77 exploration of central Africa is historically important because he assembled what had previously been scattered geographical knowledge of Africa into a cohesive whole. The journey also led to the founding of the Congo Free State. Stanley travelled from Zanzibar around Lakes Victoria and Tanganyika, and was the first European to explore the Congo River, reaching its mouth. In volume two, he describes eastern Zaire and the expedition down the Congo, including significant descriptions of numerous Zairian peoples, flora and fauna. His interesting preface summarizes the rapid increase in the geographical knowledge of Africa obtained by European explorers from 1854-98. Although this journey marked the close of the period of exploration brought on by geographical questions, it also opened the era of political rivalries in which European nations vied to establish their dominance.

34 **Two trips to gorilla land and the cataracts of the Congo.**
Richard F. Burton. London: Sampson Low, Marston, Low & Searle,
1876. Reprinted, New York: Johnson, 1967. 2 vols. 2 maps.
(Landmarks in Anthropology).

In 1863 this notorious British explorer travelled along the lower Congo River from its
mouth to the Yellala – the main rapids near modern-day Kinshasa. He describes the
various people, flora, and fauna he encountered along the way and also routinely refers to
previous explorations, primarily by the Portuguese and French, and corrects the
inaccuracies of their charts and maps.

35 **A voice from the Congo: comprising stories, anecdotes, and
descriptive notes.**
Herbert Ward. New York: Scribners, 1910. 330p.

In this reminiscence of his Congo days, Ward describes some of his experiences with
several ethnic groups, notably the Kongo, Teke, Songye, and Luba. The numerous
illustrations of implements, clothing, weapons, sculpture, collars, and other objects
collected by the author are interspersed with illustrations of his sculptures and drawings
of some of the people he met.

The arts of Central Africa: an annotated bibliography.
See item no. 659.

Travel Guides and Tourism

36   **Adventuring in East Africa: the Sierra Club travel guide to the great**
      safaris of Kenya, Tanzania, Rwanda, Eastern Zaire, and Uganda.
      Allen Bechky.   San Francisco: Sierra Club Books, 1990. 446p. maps.
      bibliog. (The Sierra Club Adventure Travel Series).

Eastern Zaire is covered on pages 384-407 of this travel guide whose focus is, of
course, on nature. The text is helpfully divided into sections on primate safaris
(gorilla and chimpanzee viewing), trekking the Virungas's live volcanoes, climbing
the Ruwenzori mountains, and visiting the Mbuti Pygmies in the Ituri Forest.

37   **Africa's top wildlife countries, with Mauritius and Seychelles.**
      Mark W. Nolting.   Pompano Beach, Florida: Global Travel, 1994.
      4th ed. 532p. maps. bibliog.

For readers interested in wildlife safaris throughout Africa, this excellent up-to-date
guidebook is a must. According to Nolting, although its parks and reserves are among
Africa's finest and rarely visited attractions, 'Zaire is the most difficult country covered
in this book in which to travel' (p. 215). In the chapter on Zaire (p. 209-30), the Great
Lakes Region receives the most attention whilst the Zairian wildlife that are highlighted
are the aquatic hippo, mountain and lowland gorillas, and okapis.

38   **Central Africa: a travel survival kit.**
      Alex Newton.   Hawthorn, Australia: Lonely Planet Publications, 1994.
      2nd ed. 559p. maps.

This volume contains the most current travel information available on Zaire (see pages
452-554). Historical, geographical, political and cultural background information is
followed by a section on practical facts for the visitor and specific locations within Zaire
are described, first by region and then by town. This publication is notable for its
descriptions of national parks, geographical features, and trekking attractions as well as
accommodation and dining recommendations for the budget traveller. If Eastern Zaire is

11

the reader's only interest, Geoff Crowther and Hugh Finlays' *East Africa* (Hawthorn, Australia: Lonely Planet, 1994) should also be consulted.

39 **Cities of the world.**
Edited by Monica M. Hubbard, Beverly Baer.   Detroit, Michigan: Gale Research, 1993. 4th ed. 4 vols. maps. bibliog.

For a ready-reference on Zaire's major cities (see volume 1, pages 930-53) this current source, written with the traveller or foreign resident in mind, provides an excellent overview of Kinshasa, Lubumbashi, and Bukavu as well as a good detailed description of the entire country. The bibliography contains a number of books on recent travel experiences in Zaire.

40 **Lifeline for a nation: Zaire River.**
Robert Caputo.   *National Geographic*, vol. 180 (Nov. 1991), p. 5-35. map.

This is a well-illustrated popular account of the 1,077-mile journey down the Zaire River from Kinshasa to Kisangani. The boat, a microcosm of the country, serves as a floating market, medical clinic, bar, and moving van for the roughly 5,000 passengers willing to spend between twelve and thirty days to reach the end of the line.

41 **Test de fiabilité de l'intégration des circuits touristiques des pays de la communauté. Etude sur la possibilité d'implantation d'un centre régional de formation hôtelière et touristique dans les pays de la communauté, Burundi-Rwanda-Zaïre (Kivu).** (Test of reliability of the integration of tourism circuits in the countries of the communities. Study of the possibility of creating a regional centre for hotels and tourism in the countries of the community, Burundi-Rwanda-Zaire (Kivu).)
Alain Bordier.   Paris: Société Promoteur, 1978. 2 vols. maps. (Division 'Etudes', no. 58).

Northeastern Zaire (the region of Kivu and the city of Kisangani), Burundi and Rwanda cannot sustain a mass tourist trade. However, Zaire has considerable potential to attract international visitors and volume two contains a detailed study of the tourist potential of Zaire's Great Lakes region.

42 **Zaire today.**
Siradiou Diallo, translated from the French by Barbara Shuey.   Paris: Editions JA, 1990. 3rd ed. 263p. 16 maps.

This is an excellent travel guide on Zaire and is amply illustrated with colour photographs. The first 100 pages contain a thorough introduction to modern Zaire (geography, economy, arts and history) whilst the second section describes each of forty-nine towns, from Bandundu to Upemba. The third section provides practical information on travelling to and within Zaire, shopping, sports, dining and accommodation.

Aspects de la conservation de la nature au Zaïre.
See item no. 572.

Geography

43 **Africa's mountains of the moon: journeys to the snowy sources of the Nile.**
Text and photographs by Guy Yeoman, botanical illustrations by Christabel King. New York: Universe Books, 1989. 176p. maps. bibliog.
The natural history and botany of the Ruwenzori Mountains in Zaire and Uganda are documented in this account of the author's 1987 journey.

44 **African boundaries.**
Ian Brownlie. London: Hurst, 1979. 1,355p. maps. bibliog.
The boundaries of Zaire are examined in nine chapters (Angola, Burundi, Central African Empire, Congo-Brazzaville, Rwanda, Sudan, Tanzania, Uganda and Zambia). Current maps, a list of maps which confirm the boundaries, and the texts of treaties are included. Although there are numerous questions of demarcation, no boundary disputes actually exist.

45 **African wetlands and shallow water bodies** = Zones humides et lacs peu profonds d'Afrique.
Edited by M. J. Burgis, J. J. Symoens, B. Davies, F. Gasse. Paris: ORSTOM, 1987-88. 2 vols. maps. bibliog. (Travaux et Documents de L'ORSTOM, no. 211).
A bibliography and directory of African limnology (in English or French) comprise the two volumes. For each volume, the coverage of the Zaire basin is broken down into: Lake Bangweulu; Lake Mweru Wantipa; Lake Mweru of the Lower Luapula; Lake Upemba; swamp forests of the central Zairian depression; Lake Tumba; Lake Mai Ndombe; and Malebo Pool. A third volume on structure, functioning and management proved to be impossible to locate.

46   **Atlas de Kinshasa.** (Atlas of Kinshasa.)
Zaire. Bureau d'Etudes d'Aménagement Urbains.   Paris: Institut
Géographique National, 1975. 44 [i.e. 88] p.

The forty-four plates of colour maps in this folio-size atlas thoroughly document all aspects of Kinshasa, the nation's capital. There is an equal amount of descriptive text on the verso of each plate.

47   **Atlas de la République du Zaïre.** (Atlas of the Republic of Zaire.)
Edited by Georges Laclavère.   Paris: Editions JA, 1978. 72p. maps.
bibliog. (Atlas Jeune Afrique).

Although this French atlas dates from 1978, it is still an excellent popular atlas on Zaire. It covers relief and hydrography, geology, climate, vegetation, soils, history, ethnic groups and languages, administrative divisions, population, cities, agriculture, energy, mines and industry, communications, tourism, teaching and health. Each chapter boasts at least one colour map (agriculture has nine) as well as accompanying descriptive text.

48   **Histoire de la navigation au Congo.** (History of navigation in the
Congo.)
André Lederer, preface by Jean Ghilain.   Tervuren, Belgium: Musée
Royal de l'Afrique Centrale, 1965. 375p. maps. bibliog. (Annales. Série
in-8o, Sciences Historiques, no. 2).

The history of colonial navigation covers eight time periods, starting with European exploration, and moving on to navigation before the railroad, navigation beginning with the inauguration of the railroad, the period of marking the river's channel for dangerous spots, 1914-18 and after the war, the Sonatra transitional period, the Unatra period of organization, and the Otraco period of technical perfection and intensive exploitation.

49   **The inland waters of tropical Africa: an introduction to tropical
limnology.**
L. C. Beadle.   London; New York: Longman, 1981. 2nd ed. 475p.
maps. bibliog.

The Zaire (Congo) River as well as Lakes Mobutu (Albert), Edward, Kivu, and Tanganyika are each discussed at length in this study of the fresh-water ecology of Africa.

50   **The Karisimbi volcano (Virunga).**
M. de Mulder.   Tervuren, Belgium: Musée Royal de l'Afrique
Centrale, 1985. 101p. map. bibliog. (Annales. Série in-8o. Sciences
Géologiques, no. 90).

The inactive Karisimbi volcano is situated precisely on the Rwanda-Zaire border in the Virunga volcanic field. Its geological structure and petrological evolution are examined here.

51 **Natural hazards associated with Lake Kivu and adjoining areas of the Birunga volcanic field, Rwanda and Zaire, central Africa: final report.**
Michele L. Tuttle, John P. Lockwood, William C. Evans. Denver, Colorado: US Geological Survey, 1990. 1 microfiche (37p.) maps. bibliog. (Open File Report, 90-691).

This microfiche describes the hazards of volcanoes and earthquakes associated with the Birunga (or Virunga) volcanic zone in Zaire and Rwanda as well as the harmful dissolved gases in Lake Kivu. Recommendations for remedying the hazards include monitoring the gases, educating the population, establishing a warning system and evacuation plan, and training local scientists.

52 **The Nyiragongo main cone.**
Thure G. Sahama. Tervuren, Belgium: Musée Royal de l'Afrique Centrale, 1978. 88p. map. bibliog. (Annales. Série in-8o. Sciences Géologiques, no. 81).

Sahama examines the petrology and mineralogy of Nyiragongo volcano, located in Zaire in the Virunga volcanic field near the borders of Zaire, Uganda and Rwanda. The data was taken before the 1977 eruption. In addition to the standard bibliography at the end of the work, the author provides a selected bibliography on Nyiragongo, classified into specific geological aspects (p. 3).

53 **Rifts and volcanoes: a study of the east African rift system.**
Celia Nyamweru. Nairobi: Nelson Africa, 1980, 1983 printing. 128p. maps. bibliog.

Written primarily for the secondary school student, this description of the east African rifts and volcanoes is also suitable for the general reader. The geology of the zone is described, followed by chapters on faulting, vulcanicity, and the theory of plate tectonics. Zairian earthquakes and volcanoes are both covered, and many of the illustrations are of Zaire.

54 **Zaire.**
United States. Central Intelligence Agency. Washington, DC: Central Intelligence Agency, 1979. Scale: 1:5,000,000 (Sudocs no. PrEx 3.10/4:Z 1/979).

This single sheet map of Zaire illustrates relief, regional boundaries, towns, roads, railroads, and airports. It also includes small maps showing the population, agriculture, vegetation, minerals and industry as well as the relative size of Zaire and the United States. A small map of Zaire (scale not given) was also published by the CIA in 1983, but it is far less detailed.

Du Congo au Zaïre, 1960-1980: essai de bilan.
See item no. 3.

Cities of the world.
See item no. 39.

Atlas des collectivités du Zaïre.
See item no. 154.

Aménagement du territoire: schéma national, utilisation de l'espace.
See item no. 517.

Atlas de l'agriculture des régions du Bandundu, du Bas-Zaïre et de Kinshasa.
See item no. 518.

Atlas climatique du bassin congolais.
See item no. 573.

Flora and Fauna

55 **Atlas anatomique des bois du Congo belge.** (Anatomic atlas of wood
from the Belgian Congo.)
Lucien Lebacq. Brussels: Institut National pour l'Etude Agronomique
du Congo Belge, 1955. 5 vols. bibliog. (Publications de l'Institut
National pour l'Etude Agronomique du Congo Belge).

This is an encyclopaedic study of the wood of some 500 trees (spermatophytes) in
colonial Zaire. The wood is sliced two ways, transversally and tangentially, and its
anatomy is thoroughly described.

56 **Behavior and ecology of primates in the Lomako Forest, Zaire.**
Suzanne Rebecca Zeeve. PhD thesis, SUNY at Stony Brook, Stony
Brook, New York, 1991. (Available from University Microfilms
International, Ann Arbor, Michigan, order no. 9203007). 238p. maps.
bibliog.

In Lomako Forest, a lowland rain forest of central Zaire, seven primate species (bonobo,
Angolan black-and-white colobus, black mangabey, and four guenons) were studied to
determine their use of habitat, foraging behaviour and formation of groups. Conservation
issues such as the impact of habitat alteration and hunting are also discussed.

57 **Birds of west central and western Africa.**
C. W. Mackworth-Praed, C. H. B. Grant. London: Longman,
1970-73. 2 vols. maps. (African Handbook of Birds. Series III,
vol. 1-2).

This is the best reference source in English on the birds of the Congo basin. Each entry
includes distinguishing characteristics, habits, nest and eggs as well as recorded breeding
and call. Small colour plates of the birds and a map showing their distribution in Africa
are also included.

Flora and Fauna

58 **Butterflies of the Afrotropical region.**
Bernard D'Abrera.   Melbourne: Lansdown Editions in association
with E. W. Classey, 1980. 593p. 2 maps. bibliog.
Sub-Saharan African butterflies are identified in this massive well-illustrated volume,
and in the distribution note those found in Zaire are mentioned specifically. The Latin
names and a brief physical description of the species are also given.

59 **Check-list of the freshwater fishes of Africa** = Catalogue des
poissons d'eau douce d'Afrique.
Edited by J. Daget, J.-P. Gosse, D. F. E. Thys van den Audenaerde.
Paris: ORSTOM; Tervuren, Belgium: Musée Royal de l'Afrique
Centrale, 1984. 3 vols. bibliog.
Arranged by fish family, this set describes the distribution and habitat when known. Its
appearance in the literature is linked in each citation to the bibliography, which is
volume three of this set. There is, unfortunately, no geographical index, such as that
found in A bibliography of African freshwater fish (Rome: Food and Agriculture
Organization of the United Nations, 1973).

60 **Collins photo guide to the wild flowers of East Africa.**
Sir Michael Blundell.   London: W. Collins, 1992. 464p. map. bibliog.
Designed for the general reader as well as the specialist in botany, this field identification
guide is beautifully illustrated with colour photographs. Only grasses and sedges are
excluded from this volume on flowering plants. Although not the primary focus of this
book, eastern Zaire is included in the distribution notes, when applicable.

61 **Contribution à l'étude des plantes toxiques du Katanga.**
(Contribution to the study of toxic plants of Katanga.)
P. Quarre, with the collaboration of A. Mols.   Elisabethville: Comité
Spécial du Katanga, 1945. 72p. bibliog.
Plants from Shaba (Katanga) and poisonous to humans and/or cattle are illustrated and
described.

62 **Contribution à l'étude des poissons de forêt de la cuvette
congolaise.** (Contribution to the study of fish of the forest in the Congo
Basin.)
J. Lambert.   Tervuren, Belgium: Musée Royal de l'Afrique Centrale,
1961. 40p. map. bibliog. (Annales. Série in-8o, Sciences Zoologiques,
no. 93).
This source on the fish of the Congo River is useful, but could have been improved with
more illustrations of the fish described.

63   **Essences forestières du Zaïre.** (Essences of the forests of Zaire.)
      A. Pieters.   Gent, Belgium: Rijksuniversiteit te Gent, Faculteit
      Landbouwwetenschappen, Bosbedrijfsvoering en Bospolitiek,
      Onderzoekscentrum voor Bosbouw, 1977. 349p. map. bibliog.
The first part of this monograph contains the description of tree parts (leaves, flowers,
fruits, for example), including line drawings. The purpose of the book is, however, the
description and identification of 112 Zairian tree species, classified by family.

64   **A field guide to the mammals of Africa, including Madagascar.**
      Theodor Haltenorth, Helmut Diller, translated from the German by
      Robert W. Hayman.   London: Collins, 1980. 400p. maps. bibliog.
This is an excellent African mammal identification guide aimed at the amateur observer.
It describes over 300 species and includes all mammals readily seen in Zaire. Latin
names and common names in English, Afrikaans, French, German and Swahili are
followed by identification, measurements, distribution (accompanied by small
distribution maps), and habitat, as well as habits and reproduction when known. The
multiple paintings on each colour plate permit easy comparison. The scope is similar to
Jean Dorst and Pierre Dandelots' *A field guide to the larger mammals of Africa* (London:
Collins, 1972), but Haltenorth and Diller have been more scrupulous in classification,
and the notes on distribution are considerably more detailed, down to regions within
countries (for example, see the distribution of the okapi, found only in Zaire).

65   **Fishes of Lake Tanganyika.**
      Pierre Brichard.   Neptune City, New Jersey: TFH, 1978. 448p. bibliog.
The fish in Lake Tanganyika, on Zaire's eastern border, are the subject of this
identification guide.

66   **Flore d'Afrique centrale (Zaïre-Rwanda-Burundi).** (Flowers of
      central Africa [Zaire, Rwanda, Burundi].)
      Meise, Belgium: Jardin Botanique National de Belgique, 1972- . irreg.
This exhaustive botanical work is the continuation of *Flore du Congo, du Rwanda et du
Burundi* which began publication in 1948. Each plant is classified and described, and
notes on the precise distribution and habitat accompany black-and-white line drawings.

67   **Flore illustrée des champignons d'Afrique centrale.** (Illustrated flora
      of the mushrooms of central Africa.)
      Brussels: Ministère de l'Agriculture; Jardin Botanique National de
      Belgique, 1972-83. 11 vols. bibliog.
A major study of mushrooms in Zaire, Rwanda and Burundi, this continues but does not
duplicate the eighteen-volume set, *La flore iconographique des champignons du Congo*
(The plant iconography of mushrooms of the Congo) (Brussels: Ministère de
l'Agriculture, Jardin Botanique de l'Etat, 1935-72). Volumes ten and eleven include
English summaries along with the French text. Colour plates and microscopic views are
included, as appropriate.

68 **Gorilla: struggle for survival in the Virungas.**
Photographs by Michael Nichols, essay by George B. Schaller, edited
and with captions by Nan Richardson. New York: Aperture, 1989.
111p. map. bibliog.

This story of the less than 300 remaining mountain gorillas found in Zaire in the
National Park of the Virungas and in Rwanda in the Volcano National Park is a popular
work intended for the general reader. In words and photographs, it describes the struggle
of conservationists to balance the needs of people, gorillas and land. For a more
scholarly work on gorillas, see Schaller's *The mountain gorilla* (q.v.).

69 **A guide to the butterflies of central and southern Africa.**
Elliot C. G. Pinhey. London: J. Causton, 1977. 106p. bibliog.

Pinhey provides the only English-language source for the identification of butterflies
found specifically in Zaire and other central or southern African regions. Some 135
species from nine families are included here and colour illustrations and photographs
accompany brief remarks on physical description, habitat, and distribution.

70 **Handbook of African medicinal plants.**
Maurice M. Iwu. Boca Raton, Florida: CRC Press, 1993. 435p. maps.
bibliog.

Until a monograph on Zairian medicinal plants is published this recent handbook on
African medicinal plants will have to suffice. As it is organized by plant family, and
since there is no geographical index, the reader must look under the habitat and
distribution paragraph of each plant to determine if Zaire is mentioned.

71 **The mountain gorilla: ecology and behavior.**
George B. Schaller. Chicago: University of Chicago Press, 1963.
431p. maps. bibliog.

The mountain gorilla is the subject of this scientific study by Schaller. The behaviour of
the gorilla is completely documented, primarily from Schaller's own research in Kabara,
Zaire (very close to Mount Mikeno and the Rwandan border) and frequently
supplemented by other scientists' research. Schaller's other study, *The year of the gorilla*
(University of Chicago, 1964), is a personal and popularized account of his experiences
with gorillas.

72 **Les oiseaux du Zaïre.** (The birds of Zaire.)
Léon Lippens, Henri Wille, photographs by Hubert Lehaen,
presentation by Mobutu Sese Seko. Tielt, Belgium: Editions Lannoo,
1976. 509p. maps. bibliog.

Contained within this massive volume is a brief physical description of each Zairian bird
and its habitat. The 1,096 birds are each located on a map of Africa and many of the
birds are pictured in accompanying photographs taken from the 1973-74 expedition
ordered by President Mobutu. Useful introductory essays include a summary of the
world interest in Zairian birds as well as a comparison between the birds of Zaire with
other African countries.

73   **Pêche maritime au Congo: possibilités de développement.** (Maritime fisheries in the Congo: possibilities of development.)
Marcel Dormont.   Paris: Mouton, 1970. 282p. maps. bibliog.
(Recherches Africaines, no. 10).

As a country with a diet lacking in animal protein, Zaire must develop both its fishing resources and industry. A major part of this work is an analysis of commercial fishing in the tropical Atlantic Ocean, that is to say, countries along much of the west African coast.

74   **Les poissons du bassin du Congo.** (The fish of the Congo basin.)
G. A. Boulenger.   Brussels: Etat Indépendant du Congo, 1901. 532p. map.

This early work on the fish of the Congo basin is still useful today.

75   **Primates of the world: distribution, abundance, and conservation.**
Jaclyn H. Wolfheim.   Seattle, Washington: University of Washington Press, 1983. 831p. maps. bibliog.

In this handy reference tool to the primates of the world, distribution, abundance, and conservation data are given for each species and Zaire is clearly outlined on each map of Africa. Habitat alteration, human predation, and specific details of the species' collection and capture for export are included. A particularly useful feature is the detailed distribution table for each species, listing the exact location, abundance and bibliographical references if further study is desired; there are thirty sources in the literature on the gorilla in Zaire. It should be noted that this publication does not contain illustrations of the animals described.

76   **Southern, central and east African mammals: a photographic guide.**
Chris Stuart, Tilde Stuart.   London: New Holland, 1992. 144p. maps. bibliog.

This is the most recent popular monograph covering the mammals of Africa. The pocket-sized volume describes each of the 152 representative species in a photograph, a thumbnail description and small distribution map. Since it is designed for the traveller, it conveniently lists sixty specific parks and reserves in which each animal can be found. For Zaire, Garamba, Kahuzi-Biega, Kundelungu, Maiko, Salonga, Upemba, and Virunga are covered.

Africa's top wildlife countries, with Mauritius and Seychelles.
See item no. 37.

Aspects de la conservation de la nature au Zaïre.
See item no. 572.

Island Africa: the evolution of Africa's rare animals and plants.
See item no. 580.

Prehistory and Archaeology

77 **The archaeology of Central Africa.**
Francis Van Noten, contributions by Daniel Cahen, Pierre de Maret, Jan
Moeyersons, Emile Roche.   Graz, Austria: Akademische Druck- und
Verlagsanstalt, 1982. 152, 41p. maps. bibliog.

This work, an attempt to collate all recent information and that found in literature on the
subject, describes Iron and Stone Age archaeological sites that have been systematically
excavated in Zaire and its neighbouring countries. The introduction provides an excellent
analysis of the past and present state of archaeological research in this region and the
difficulties encountered in carrying it out. It also suggests that the contemporary study of
archaeology in Central Africa demands a new approach in order to improve our
understanding of the behaviour of prehistoric man. The text is augmented by numerous
photographs, charts, tables, maps, and lists of radiocarbon dates.

78 **Atlas de préhistoire de la plaine de Kinshasa.** (Atlas of the prehistory
of the Kinshasa plain.)
Hendrik van Moorsel.   Kinshasa: Université Lovanium, Publications
Universitaires, 1968. 287p. maps. bibliog.

The information found in this work summarizes more than thirty years of archaeological
research. Numerous maps and drawings supplement the text, which discusses the
prehistory, geological changes, climatic cycles, antiquities, and succession of prehistoric
cultures associated with the region around Kinshasa.

79 **Evolution of environments and hominidae in the African western Rift Valley.**
Edited by Noel T. Boaz. Martinsville, Virginia: Virginia Museum of Natural History, 1990. 356p. maps. bibliog. (Virginia Museum of Natural History Memoire, no. 1).

Composed of nineteen separate contributions, this volume evolved from preliminary papers presented by members of the Semliki Research Expedition at the University of California, Berkeley, in April 1986. The Expedition, an international multidisciplinary research project formed in 1982, is based at the Virginia Museum of Natural History. The detailed information presented here reflects seven years of work investigating the palaeoanthropology of Miocene-to-Pleistocene sediments of the African Western Rift Valley. It has brought to light considerable new knowledge on the origin and evolution of man, through fieldwork completed in an area which has traditionally been, for a variety of reasons, largely inaccessible to or overlooked by archaeological researchers.

80 **Excavations at Sanga, 1957: the protohistoric necropolis.**
Jacques Nenquin. Tervuren, Belgium: Musée Royal de l'Afrique Centrale, 1963. 277p. (Annales, Série in-8o. Sciences Humaines, no. 45).

This is the first part of a final report, to be complete in three volumes, on the 1957 excavation of approximately fifty graves at Sanga, which contained three pottery groups and metal objects. Descriptions of the excavations, plus notes on and illustrations of artifacts found, comprise the bulk of this work; an analysis of the findings is also included.

81 **Fouilles archéologiques dans la vallée du Haut-Lualaba. I. Sanga, 1958.** (Archaeological excavations in the Upper-Lualaba Valley. I. Sanga, 1958.)
Jean Hiernaux, Emma de Longrée, Josse De Buyst. Tervuren, Belgium: Musée Royal de l'Afrique Centrale, 1971. 148p. maps. (Annales, Série in-8o. Sciences Humaines, no. 73).

Examines the material culture discovered during a second series of excavations of the cemetery at Sanga, undertaken in 1958. An analysis of the skeletal materials found in the graves is also included. This work complements Jacques Nenquin's *Excavations at Sanga, 1957* (q.v.) which is a detailed study of the initial Sanga excavations and the objects exhumed.

82 **Fouilles archéologiques dans la vallée du Haut-Lualaba, Zaïre. II. Sanga et Katongo, 1974.** (Archaeological excavations in the Upper-Lualaba Valley, Zaire. II. Sanga et Katongo, 1974.)
Pierre de Maret. Tervuren, Belgium: Musée Royal de l'Afrique Centrale, 1985. 2 vols. (Annales. Sciences Humaines, vol. 120).

This work, devoted to the results of excavations undertaken at Sanga and Katongo in 1974, is a continuation of Nenquin's *Excavations at Sanga, 1957,* (q.v.) and Hiernaux's *Fouilles archéologiques dans la vallée du Haut-Lualaba, I. Sanga, 1958* (q.v.). The first volume places the two sites in their geographical framework and importance in the history of Central Africa, and provides details of the results of the excavations themselves and a chronology of the two neighbouring sites. The second volume consists of plates of selected items exhumed at both sites.

83   **The Katanga skull.**
Matthew Young, Sir Grafton Elliot Smith.   *Mémoire du Musée Royal d'Histoire Naturelle de Belgique*, 2e Série, fasc. 5 (1936), p. 1-25.
Describes in detail a human skull, approximately five to six hundred years old, found in Zaire in 1918 during mining operations carried out by the Union Minière du Haut-Katanga. The authors attempt to determine which African ethnic group the specimen belongs to by comparing it to some already identified, as well as considering factors such as sex and age.

84   **New survey of archaeological research and dates for West-Central and North-Central Africa.**
Pierre de Maret.   *Journal of African History*, vol. 23 (1982), p. 1-15.
Maret provides a summary of all available radiocarbon dates for West Central Africa at the time this article was published. The scope of the dates includes the Iron Age and the later phase of the Late Stone Age, and much information on Zaire is presented. Also discussed is the state of archaeological research in the region. This updates Maret's previous article in this series, *Radiocarbon dates for West Central Africa: a synthesis,* (q.v.).

85   **The Ngovo group: an industry with polished stone tools and pottery in Lower Zaire.**
Pierre de Maret.   *The African Archaeological Review*, vol. 4 (1986), p. 103-33.
For the first time, Maret places polished stone tools collected throughout Lower Zaire in an exact archaeological context, and associates them with a particular group of pottery previously not thought to be as old as it actually is. The evidence for this, obtained in Lower Zaire during excavations carried out in 1972, 1973, and 1984 is carefully examined in detail in this article.

86   **Notes on Dr. Francis Cabu's collection of stone implements from the Belgian Congo.**
C. van Riet Lowe.   *Transactions of the Royal Society of South Africa*, vol. 30, no. 2 (July 1944), p. 169-74.
The author identifies 331 stone implements collected by archaeologist Francis Cabu as belonging to a series of prehistoric cultures that span Pre-Palaeolithic to Neolithic times. This enables him to conclude that Zaire was definitely not the home of just one single Stone Age culture known as 'Tumbian', as was previously thought.

87   **Notes on some early pottery cultures in northern Katanga.**
Jacques Nenquin.   *Journal of African History*, vol. 4, no. 1 (1963), p. 19-32.
This article, based on a fuller report, *Excavations at Sanga, 1957* (q.v.), summarizes some of the little work that has been done on protohistoric pottery cultures in Zaire. It describes pottery and metal objects discovered during excavations of an Iron Age

cemetery found at Sanga on the northern shore of Kale Kisale in 1957. Three different groups of wares were distinguished, suggesting the pottery traditions belonged to three different cultural groups.

88 **Phases and facies in the archaeology of Central Africa.**
Pierre de Maret. In: *A history of African archaeology.* Edited by
Peter Robertshaw. London: James Currey; Portsmouth, New
Hampshire: Heinemann, 1990, p. 109-34.

An excellent summary and analysis of the archaeological research that has taken place in Central Africa. The information presented is divided by time period and focuses on Zaire, where most research has been undertaken, although comparisons are made to other countries in the region when possible.

89 **Préhistoire et protohistoire de la République démocratique du**
Congo: bibliographie. (Prehistory and protohistory of the Democratic
Republic of the Congo: bibliography.)
Max Liniger-Goumaz. Geneva: Les Editions du Temps, 1969. 64p.

This bibliography contains 336 citations for books, journal articles, and conference proceedings. Most of the material is in French and now dated; however, it is still useful, as more recently published studies on Zairian prehistory are rather sparse, reflecting the lack of research that has been carried out since independence.

90 **Problems of archaeological nomenclature and definition in the**
Congo Basin.
Desmond Clark. *The South African Archaeological Bulletin*, vol. 26
(parts 1-2), nos. 101-02 (Aug. 1971), p. 67-8.

Discusses how a general lack of standardization of nomenclature has contributed to a dearth of knowledge of the archaeology of the Congo Basin region, in comparison to the information available on the surrounding areas. A review and analysis of archaeological discoveries made in the Congo Basin from 1899 to approximately the time this article was published reveals how the terminology developed and why it was often inadequate in defining the prehistory of this part of Africa.

91 **Radiocarbon dates from West Central Africa: a synthesis.**
Pierre de Maret, Francis Van Noten, Daniel Cahen. *Journal of African*
History, vol. 18, no. 4 (1977), p. 481-505.

This article is part of a series on radiocarbon dates begun by B. M. Fagan in 1961. Previously, it focused on two areas: northern and western Africa; and eastern and southern Africa. Because of a revival of archaeological activity in west central Africa, the authors thought it appropriate to finally present the over 160 radiocarbon dates that had been obtained for this region. The first part of the article presents a country-by-country survey of datable evidence from each site; the second provides a chronological outline of the prehistory of this important region. Information on Zaire is generous, due to extensive research undertaken in certain areas.

92 **Recent archaeological research and dates from Central Africa.**
Pierre de Maret. *Journal of African History*, vol. 26 (1985),
p. 129-48.

Updates Maret's article, 'New survey of archaeological research and dates for
West-Central and North-Central Africa' (q.v.), on the same topic from 1982. This survey
covers archaeological research and dates from mid-1981 to mid-1984, and considers
some older results which were previously overlooked. Maret notes a cessation of
excavation of Early and Middle Stone Age sites, and a migration of prehistorians out of
the area, as well as the renewed study of material culture already collected.

93 **Report on the Likasi skeleton.**
M. R. Drennan. *Transactions of the Royal Society of South Africa*,
vol. 29, pt. 2 (1942), p. 81-89.

Drennan describes and analyses the specific features of a fossilized skeleton found at
Likasi in Zaire's Katanga province in 1935. Comparisons are made with other fossil
bones found within the same region and other parts of Africa in an attempt to suggest the
origins of this particular specimen. At the time of this article's publication, very few
studies had been made on skeletons from this part of Africa.

94 **Rude stone implements from the Congo Free State.**
Frederick Starr. *Wisconsin Archaeologist*, vol. 7, no. 3 (1915),
p. 111-15.

The author, a professor emeritis of anthropology at the University of Chicago, describes
a visit to a Stone Age site in Zaire and the subsequent discovery of a number of artifacts.

95 **Sanga: new excavations, more data, and some related problems.**
Pierre de Maret. *Journal of African History*, vol. 18, no. 3 (1977),
p. 321-37.

This article begins with a summary of the 1957-58 excavation results from the Iron Age
cemetery at Sanga. It then presents the main results of the excavations undertaken in
1974-75, and concludes with a discussion of possible relationships between the evidence
found at the Sanga site and the history of Central Africa, in the light of other research
completed elsewhere in Africa on archaeology, linguistic history, and oral traditions.

96 **Some aspects of the Stone Age in the Belgian Congo.**
Francis Cabu. In: *Proceedings of the Pan-African Congress on
Prehistory, 1947*. Edited by L. S. B. Leakey, assisted by Sonia Cole.
Oxford: Basil Blackwell, 1952, p. 195-201.

A description of the prehistoric periods of Zaire and the different cultures associated
with them.

History

General

97 **Chronologie générale de l'histoire du Zaïre: des origines à 1988.**
(General chronology of the history of Zaire: from its origins to 1988.)
Mandjumba Mwanyimi-Mbomba.   Kinshasa: Centre de Recherches
Pédagogiques, 1989. 2nd ed., corrected and augmented. 191p. maps.
bibliog. (D. P., no. 4).
This is an invaluable guide to the history of Zaire, from the prehistoric period to 1988,
presented in chronological form. Also included are a number of appendices, such as a list
of prime ministers, provincial governors, commanders-in-chief of the army and other
important people, a glossary, brief bibliography, list of present and former place names,
and other useful information.

98 **The Congo.**
Edouard Bustin.   In: *Five African states: responses to diversity.*
Edited by Gwendolen M. Carter.   Ithaca, New York: Cornell
University Press, 1963, p. 1-159.
A general history of Zaire up to 1961 is followed by an analysis of some of its
component elements, including economic and social conditions, the population, and the
political situation. A critical bibliographical essay is found at the end of the chapter.

99 **Congo-Zaïre: la colonisation, l'indépendence, le régime Mobutu, et demain?** (Congo-Zaire: colonization, independence, the Mobutu regime, and tomorrow?)
Colette Braeckman. Brussels: GRIP, 1989. 166p. (Collection GRIP-Informations).

Consists of essays by several authors, chiefly on Zairian history, including the period of Belgian colonization and independence, plus the turbulent period that followed, up to and including the present Mobutu régime. Included also are some contributions that discuss Zaire's economic situation, position within the international scene, and the country's future.

100 **Guide de l'étudiant en histoire du Zaïre.** (Guide to the study of the history of Zaire.)
Jean-Luc Vellut. Kinshasa: Editions du Mont Noir, 1974. 207p. bibliog. (Collection 'Objectif 80', Série 'Essais', no. 8).

This useful work is divided into three parts. The first is a discussion of the collected knowledge of Africa's past, including how it was gathered, how it developed, and the problems associated with African history as documented by non-Africans. The second presents the principal categories of written classical, Muslim, and European sources useful to the study of Africa, particularly Central Africa. The last part is intended to serve as a guide for the researcher working in Zaire; it locates, describes and evaluates available Zairian archival material, and includes a 545 citation bibliography of works on Zaire.

101 **Histoire du Zaïre.** (History of Zaire.)
Robert Cornevin. Brussels: Hayez, 1989. 4th edition. 635p. maps. bibliog.

Following an initial chapter describing the country and its resources, the author presents a complete history of Zaire.

102 **Historical dictionary of Zaire.**
F. Scott Bobb. Metuchen, New Jersey; London: Scarecrow Press, 1988. 349p. map. bibliog. (African Historical Dictionaries, no. 43).

One of the last volumes to be published in Scarecrow Press's *African Historical Dictionaries* series, this reference work is a comprehensive guide to Zairian history in dictionary-entry form. It provides the user with a broad understanding of a large, wealthy and important African country that remains relatively unknown despite its significant rôle in recent African and US history. An extensive subject-oriented bibliography is included.

Pre-colonial (to 1885)

103 Britain and the Congo in the nineteenth century.
Roger Anstey.   Oxford: Clarendon Press, 1962. 260p. maps.

A survey of British expansion into Congo River territory from Tuckey's 1816 expedition to the formation of the Congo Railway Company in the 1880s. Includes extensive discussion of Britain's expansionist policies and British relations with other European powers interested in the area at the time, specifically the Belgians and the Portuguese.

104 The fall of the Congo Arabs.
Sidney Langford Hinde.   London; New York: Methuen, Thomas Whittaker, 1897. Reprinted, New York: Negro Universities Press, 1969. 308p. map.

During the last century, a body of Arab traders from Zanzibar had long been making attempts to control the trade of Central Africa, while Belgians of the Congo Free State, arriving in the area later, sought to divert this commerce to the mouth of the Congo River and, ultimately, Europe. The Arabs, recognizing that a clash with the Europeans was inevitable, took the initiative and attacked the Europeans attached to the area, thereby opening the successful campaign against them described by Captain Hinde in this work.

105 The kingdom of Kongo.
Anne Hilton.   Oxford: Clarendon Press, 1985. 319p. maps. bibliog.

A history of the Kongo Kingdom is presented here, from the first contact with Europeans in 1483 to the early 20th century, by which time the kingdom had become a concept used to legitimize national movements and political and social structures. Contemporary documents form the primary basis for this study.

106 Kingdoms of the savanna.
Jan Vansina.   Madison; Milwaukee, Wisconsin: University of Wisconsin Press, 1966. 364p. maps. bibliog.

The political history of the states of Central Africa from their pre-colonial origins to their fall around 1900 is presented here. A number of states that included all or part of what is now Zaire are covered, including the kingdom of Kongo, the Luba and Lunda empires, and others.

107 Power and prestige: the rise and fall of the Kongo Kingdom.
Kajsa Ekholm.   Uppsala, Sweden: Skriv Service AB, 1972. 196p. maps. bibliog.

This history of the Kongo kingdom focuses extensively on the structure of its society, economy, and politics.

108 **The rainbow and the kings: a history of the Luba Empire to 1891.**
Thomas Q. Reefe.   Berkeley, California: University of California
Press, 1981. 286p. maps. bibliog.

Based on oral data as well as published material, this work chronicles the rise and evolution of the famed Luba Empire, from its earliest origins, which can be traced back over a thousand years, to 1891, when it ceased to exist as a large state dictating events in this part of Africa.

109 **River of wealth, river of sorrow: the central Zaire basin in the era of the slave and ivory trade, 1500-1891.**
Robert W. Harms.   New Haven, Connecticut; London: Yale
University Press, 1981. 277p. maps. bibliog.

Through extensive archival research and field work in Zaire, the author has constructed a history of how expanding international trade impacted on the economy and societies of the central Congo River basin between 1500 and 1891. Three particular changes are analysed: the expansion of commerce in the basin area; changes in investment strategies among traders and fishermen; and a shift in the structure of political units and ethnic identity of the river people.

110 **Tippu Tip and the East African slave trade.**
Leda Farrant.   London: Hamish Hamilton, 1975. 162p. bibliog.

A biography of one of the last great slave traders of the 19th century, this work includes details of Tip's contacts with famous explorers such as Stanley, Livingstone, and Cameron, his tenure as Governor of the Congo Free State, and his treacherous career as a trader in human flesh.

Congo Free State (1885-1908)

111 **Britain and the Congo question, 1885-1913.**
S. J. S. Cookey.   New York: Humanities Press, 1968. 340p. bibliog.
(Ibadan History Series).

A study of the Congo Reform Movement, this is the first published work to utilize the abundance of existing documents, previously inaccessible, on this subject, especially the archives of the Foreign Office at the Public Records Office in London. Reviewed in detail is the state of British diplomacy and Anglo-Belgian relations as influenced by the re-awakening of British humanitarian and commercial interests in the Congo, sparked by the barbarities inflicted upon the native Congolese under King Leopold's personal management. Also examined is the Belgian government's policy toward the Congo after its formal annexation in 1908, and why Britain refused to recognize the annexation until 1913.

112 **The Congo: a brief history and appraisal.**
Maurice N. Hennessy. New York: Praeger, 1961. 148p. map.
bibliog.
A concise analysis of major historical events in the history of Zaire, this studies the
period of the Congo Free State in 1885 to the independence crisis of 1960. The last half
of the book, including the appendices, is devoted to this crisis, including the tumultuous
events leading up to and immediately succeeding the intervention of United Nations
peacekeeping forces.

113 **E. D. Morel's history of the Congo Reform Movement.**
E. D. Morel, edited by William Roger Louis, Jean Stengers. Oxford:
Clarendon Press, 1968. 289p. map. bibliog.
In 1904, at the age of thirty, Morel founded the Congo Reform Association as part of his
campaign to end human rights abuses in Zaire when it was personally ruled by King
Leopold of Belgium. This book constitutes his autobiographical account of the events
which led to the founding of the Association. The work was never completed; hence, the
editors' addition of supplementary chapters relating to the history of the Congo reform
movement to the end of the Association's work in 1913.

114 **The ending of slavery in the eastern Belgian Congo.**
David Northrup. In: *The end of slavery in Africa*. Edited by
Suzanne Miers, Richard Roberts. Madison, Wisconsin: University of
Wisconsin Press, 1988, p. 462-82.
This chapter examines the problems linked with instituting alternatives to the system of
slavery which emerged in Zaire in the latter half of the 19th century, and King Leopold's
failure to create, during the Free State era, anything resembling a free-labour system in
its place.

115 **Europeans in Katanga, 1877-1923: the effects of their policies and
actions upon Katanga's people.**
Edgar M. W. Boyd. PhD thesis, Indiana University, Bloomington,
Indiana, 1982. 341p. maps. bibliog. (Available from University
Microfilms, Ann Arbor, Michigan, order no. 8300841).
Boyd examines the causes and effects of Belgian policies on Zairians in the Katanga
province during the formative period of Belgian colonialism. The study considers how
different regions within the area were affected in their own particular way by the
European presence.

116 **The King incorporated: Leopold II in the age of trusts.**
Neil Ascherson. London: G. Allen & Unwin, 1963. 310p. maps.
bibliog.
This biography is a portrayal of the Belgian king who, seeing the rôle of grand financier
as the way to liberate himself from conflicts with politicians and the middle classes,
became the founder, owner and exploiter of the Congo Free State. By the author's
admission, most of the material is not new, but the work is an example of one of the few
attempts, in English, to present Leopold as someone other than the person of extreme
positive and negative character which was created by his apologists and critics.

117 **King Leopold's Congo: aspects of the development of race relations in the Congo Independent State.**
Ruth M. Slade. London; New York: Oxford University Press, 1962. 230p. maps. bibliog.

In this study the author discusses particular aspects of the development of race relations within Zaire from 1885 to 1908, when, as King Leopold's African colony, it was known as the Congo Independent State. It attempts to show how relations developed between Africans and Europeans within Zaire itself as well as from Europe through Belgian colonial and diplomatic policy. An account of African/European relations from the time when the Portuguese first arrived on the Congo coast in 1482 to the 1880s is included.

118 **King Leopold's soliloquy.**
Mark Twain. Boston: P. R. Warren, 1905. Reprinted, New York: International Publishers, 1970. 87p.

Twain, known best for his novels and humorous writings, also penned works with a political slant which remain largely unknown in comparison. This title, a biting, scathing indictment of Leopold the man, written to expose the abuses that took place in Zaire under his personal rule, is but one example, fuelled by Twain's hate of injustice. When first published, this work caused a great outcry, especially among American business interests that were benefitting from exploitation of Zaire's resources.

119 **Leopold II of the Belgians: king of colonialism.**
Barbara Emerson. London: Weidenfeld & Nicolson, 1979. 324p. maps.

A well-written, balanced, and detailed biography of King Leopold.

120 **Red rubber: the story of the rubber slave trade flourishing on the Congo in the year of grace 1906.**
E. D. Morel. New York: Nassau Print, 1906. 2nd ed. Reprinted, New York: Negro Universities Press, 1969. 213p. maps.

Written with the aim of informing the British public, this narrative details the human rights abuses of the rubber-collection system that took place in Zaire under King Leopold's personal rule.

121 **Roger Casement and the Congo.**
William Roger Louis. *Journal of African History*, vol. 5, no. 1 (1964), p. 99-120.

This article discusses the activities of Irish patriot and Congo reformer Roger Casement, who, as British consul, travelled in Zaire's interior in 1903 and gathered evidence of King Leopold's maladministration of the territory. Casement inspired E. D. Morel, who penned *Red rubber: the story of the rubber slave trade flourishing on the Congo in the year of grace 1906* (q.v.) to found the Congo Reform Association. Casement was greatly influential in bringing about Belgium's annexation of the Congo in 1908.

Belgian Congo (1908-60)

122 **Belgian historiography since 1945.**
Jean Stengers. In: *Reappraisals in overseas history.* Edited by
P. C. Emmer, H. L. Wesseling. Leiden: Leiden University Press,
1979, p. 161-81. (Comparative Studies in Overseas History, vol. 2).
Investigates important developments in Belgian historiography, particularly after 1960. It
is limited to those works which discuss the history of Belgian colonization in Zaire.

123 **Belgisch Congo in oude prentkaarten = Le Congo belge en cartes
postales anciennes.** (The Belgian Congo in Old Post Cards.)
Marcel Luwel. Zaltbommel, Netherlands: Europese
Bibliotheek-Zaltbommel, 1972. 158p.
One hundred and fifty-six post cards, each with captions in Dutch and French, provide a
sketch of life in Zaire during the late 19th and early 20th centuries. The illustrations were
carefully selected for their various depictions of Zaire's colonial past, and include the
following subjects: indigenous life in its traditional form and in its relations with
Europeans; transport; commerce; missions; medical services and hospitals; the activities
of the colonial armed forces, the Force Publique; scientific research; the daily life of the
whites; and others.

124 **Biographie coloniale belge = Belgische koloniale biografie.**
(Colonial Belgian biography.)
Institut Royal Colonial Belge. Brussels: Librairie Falk Fils, 1948- .
7 vols.
Entries in this biographical dictionary include deceased Belgians and others who played
a prominent rôle in the history and development of Zaire. Examples of persons found are
territorial administrators, missionaries, doctors, military officers and agents, engineers,
directors of corporations, members of the Force Publique, journalists, diplomats and
explorers. Arrangement is alphabetical within each volume; the publication of this
dictionary was taken over, with the sixth volume, by the Academie Royale des Sciences
d'Outre-Mer. Volumes six and seven are entitled *Biographie belge d'outre mer* and
entries are in French or Dutch; each volume has a cumulative index to earlier ones.

125 **Force Publique, force unique: the military in the Belgian Congo,
1914-1939.**
Bryant P. Shaw. PhD thesis, University of Wisconsin-Madison,
Madison, Wisconsin, 1984. 348p. map. bibliog. (Available from
University Microfilms, Ann Arbor, Michigan, order no. 84-15580).
Focusing on the period between the two world wars, this thesis examines the character
and rôle of the military arm of Zaire when it was known as the Congo Free State and the
Belgian Congo. The author examines how the Force Publique's dual rôle as colonial
army and police force undermined its strength as a trained, disciplined institution of
coherence and strength.

126 **King Leopold's legacy: the Congo under Belgian rule, 1908-1960.**
Roger Anstey. London; New York: Oxford University Press, 1966.
293p. map. bibliog.

This work analyses why Belgium assumed formal control of the Congo Independent
State in 1908, what she sought to accomplish there, and how Belgian rule impacted on
the Congolese economy and society. It serves as a companion volume to R. Slade's *King
Leopold's Congo* (q.v.).

127 **Leopold to Lumumba: a history of the Belgian Congo, 1877-1960.**
George Martelli. London: Chapman & Hall, 1962. 259p. maps.

The first attempt, by an English author, to create a single-volume account of the
colonization of what became the richest country in central Africa. Martelli does not
intend for this to be a complete history of Zaire as a Belgian colony, but a work that
examines some of the controversial and thought-provoking questions that were raised
after Zaire gained international notoriety following independence: how was the colony
acquired by Belgium; how did the Belgians treat it; why were they really there; and what
went wrong after independence?

128 **Lunda under Belgian rule: the politics of ethnicity.**
Edouard Bustin. Cambridge, Massachusetts: Harvard University
Press, 1975. 303p. maps.

This is an extensive study of the impact of the effects of Belgian colonial rule on Lunda
social and political institutions.

Independence (1960-65)

129 **The bloody Congo.**
David Logan. Downsview, Ontario: Unit Nine, 1979. 130p. maps.

Some of the major conflicts and political upheavals in the history of Zaire from 1960 to
1978 are summarized here. Also documented are some of the numerous atrocities
inflicted on Zairians and Europeans alike during this tumultuous period.

130 **Challenge of the Congo.**
Kwame Nkrumah. London: Thomas Nelson; New York:
International Publishers, 1967. 304p. map.

A critical analysis of the political influences and intrigues which took place in the Congo
immediately after independence forms the substance of this work, from the Katanga
secession crisis to Mobutu's takeover of the government. The work is interesting in its
own right because the situation is presented through the eyes of an African statesman
serving as Ghana's president after her own liberation from colonialism.

131 **Congo: background of conflict.**
Alan P. Merriam.   Evanston, Illinois: Northwestern University Press,
1961. 368p. bibliog. (Northwestern University African Studies, no. 6).
This very early work analyses the rising political tide of nationalism which led the
Belgian Congo toward independence and the early stages of Zairian independence. The
author sets the political scene by discussing the parties and politicians who dominated
the political life of the newly independent country.

132 **The Congo mercenary: a history and analysis.**
Stephen John Gordon Clarke.   Braamfontein, Johannesburg: South
African Institute of International Affairs, 1968. 104p. maps.
The practice of 'seconding' skilled soldiers by both the Katanga régime during its
secession crisis, and the central Congolese government after Katanga was reintegrated is
assessed in this work. At the same time, it attempts to create a broader picture of the
modern mercenary, both as a military professional and social phenomenon.

133 **The Congo since independence, January 1960-December, 1961.**
Catherine Hoskyns.   London; New York: Oxford University Press,
1965. 518p. maps. bibliog.
This analysis of Zairian political life was published in 1965 and is limited to the
movement toward independence and the early years of self rule. Hoskyns is very
interested in the formal structure of government and emphasizes public statements,
speeches, documents, statutes and the legal structure of the state. She discusses the basic
organization of government and administration under the Belgians and the
institutionalization of the independent government under Zairian leadership. The
personalities and events of the early independence years are analysed in depth.

134 **Congo, the birth of a new nation.**
Jules Archer.   New York: Julian Messner, 1970. 190p. map. bibliog.
Discusses the bloody strife and near anarchy that plagued Zaire as it emerged as an
independent nation.

135 **Crisis in the Congo: a United Nations force in action.**
Ernest W. Lefever.   Washington, DC: Brookings Institution, 1965.
215p. bibliog. (Studies of US Policy and the UN).
This 1965 analysis of Zairian politics and government details the public events of the
early independence period. There is considerable discussion of the 'Katanga problem',
offering a rich analysis of the national and international politics surrounding this
attempted secession.

136 **Footnotes to the Congo story.**
Edited by Helen Kitchen.   New York: Walker & Co., 1967. 175p.
Kitchen has put together a collection of essays which consider some of the accepted
stereotypes associated with what came to be known as 'the Congo story.' All except two
were taken from the widely-read *Africa Report,* and cover events that occurred between
1960 and 1966. Thirteen different American, British, Belgian, and Congolese scholars,

journalists, and government officials are the authors of these essays; it is interesting to compare and contrast their analyses of the events discussed.

137 The Katanga circus: a detailed account of three UN wars.
Mugur Valahu. New York: R. Speller, 1964. 1st ed. 364p.

Presented in this book are the author's unbiased impressions of the political intrigues that took place in Katanga during the secession crisis of 1960-62. At the time, he was a foreign correspondent there and a first-hand witness of the greed, corruption, and betrayal that existed among all factions involved, enabling him to lace this work with fascinating anecdotes and accounts. For a true insider's view of UN activities during the Katanga secession crisis, see diplomat Conor Cruise O'Brien's classic work *To Katanga and back* (New York: Grosset & Dunlap, 1966).

138 Katanga report.
Smith Hempstone. London: Faber & Faber, 1962. 212p. maps.

This volume is an attempt to place the Katanga secession crisis of 1960-62 in perspective, by reviewing and analysing the area and its history. Hempstone's premise is that it was inevitable that the province became a literal and ideological battleground. The work is also a scathing indictment of US and UN policy in Katanga during this period.

139 Lumumba: the last fifty days.
G. Heinz, H. Donnay, translated from the French by Jane Clark Seitz. New York: Grove Press, 1969. 210p.

Patrice Lumumba's last days are chronicled in this book and the political turmoil that surrounded him in a country torn by strife is demonstrated.

140 The province of the Katanga and Congolese independence.
Republic of the Congo, Ministère des Affaires Etrangères. Leopoldville: Document Division of the Ministry of Foreign Affairs, 1962. 62p.

A history of Katanga Province, this focuses on the secession crisis of 1960-62. It is highly critical of Moise Tshombe and his rôle in precipitating this chaotic situation.

141 The road to Kalamata: a Congo mercenary's personal memoir.
Mike Hoare. London: Leo Cooper, 1989. 132p. map.

Between 1960 and 1961 the president of the newly-formed independent state of Katanga, Moise Tshombe, recruited a force of mercenary soldiers to assist his army in quelling an uprising by one of Katanga's two great ethnic groups, the Luba. *The road to Kalamata* is an account of the author's experiences as commander of a unit of those soldiers, the 4 Commando, and the true story of a tragic accident that occurred during the Katanga campaign.

Post-independence and Mobutism (1965-)

142   An African horror story.
Bill Berkeley. *The Atlantic Monthly*, vol. 272 (Aug. 1993), p. 20-28.
The author describes how, deserted by his Western backers and in conflict with pro-democracy forces and rebellious troops, Mobutu continues to maintain power in Zaire and deflect the people's resentment of his régime toward others. Through a 'divide and rule' strategy he exploits ethnic rivalries and resentments, particularly in Shaba Province, a traditionally troublesome region for Mobutu and where violence and what some term 'ethnic cleansing' has broken out.

143   Un avenir pour le Zaïre. (A future for Zaire.)
Nguza Karl-i-Bond.   Brussels: Vie Ouvrière, 1985. 159p. bibliog.
Nguza Karl-i-Bond is a major figure on the Zairian political scene. He served as foreign minister and prime minister under President Mobutu but resigned the latter position in 1981 and became active in the opposition to the Mobutu régime. In 1982 he assumed the presidency of the Front Congolais pour la Restauration de la Démocratie (Congolese Front for the Restoration of Democracy), a blanket organization which includes many political parties and groups of the opposition. This book begins with an analysis of the current political, economic, and social conditions of Zaire. The author goes on to set out his political plans for the restoration of civil liberties, public morality and democracy, basing this on the participation of greater numbers of Zairians and the creation of a new, enlarged national concensus. In the event of an important political shift in Zaire, Nguza Karl-i-Bond and his ideas could easily have major influence in the constitution of a new political order in Zaire.

144   The causes of Shaba I and Shaba II rebellions in Zaire during the Second Republic.
Jacques Vangu Dinavo.   PhD thesis, University of Denver, 1984. 310p. bibliog. (Available from University Microfilms, Ann Arbor, Michigan, order no. 8509514).
Several causes are proposed for the rebellions that took place in the towns and copper mining installations of Shaba in March 1977 and May 1978; the primary one was the resentment of the Lunda people at losing important positions in government and industry.

145   Decline or recovery in Zaire?
Thomas Turner.   *Current History*, vol. 87 (May 1988), p. 213-16, 230.
Turner considers that, despite the official US line on Zaire, which states that the Zairian government has heeded Western advice and implemented key economic reforms since 1983, the truth is that President Mobutu has continued to preside over a régime that is riddled with corruption and pays lip service to true reform. Since the firmly-entrenched system is incapable of promoting development, and the social and economic situation has declined so much, access to high office is the only hope for a decent life for a member of the Zairian élite. In addition, Zaire continues to be plagued by a high level of AIDS infection.

146   **The rise and decline of the Zairian state.**
Crawford Young, Thomas Turner.   Madison, Wisconsin: University
of Wisconsin Press, 1985. 500p. bibliog.

Crawford Young is a frequent writer on Zaire. In this work, he and co-author Thomas
Turner show the conceptual framework of the Zairian state and the nature of the civil
society that the state represents. Since most political life in Zaire has been co-opted by
the Mobutu régime, much is said of the policies and programmes of the Zairian
president. Although mainly concerned with the development of the state and political
life, the work also considers economic conditions and foreign affairs.

147   **The state-society struggle: Zaire in comparative perspective.**
Thomas M. Callaghy.   New York: Columbia University Press, 1984.
515p. bibliog.

Many African studies scholars analyse politics in the newly freed continent of the 1960s
and 1970s as a phenomenon isolated from the history and experience of other parts of the
world. In this work Thomas Callaghy looks at state formation in Zaire as part of a
universal political phenomenon, typical of similar processes in Europe in the early
modern period and in Latin America in its post-independence period. He looks at the
theoretical paradigms of state development and applies this to the Zaire of Mobutu Sese
Seko. In the first part of his study Callaghy examines the Mobutu régime as an
authoritarian, early modern, patrimonial administrative state on the model of other
historical examples. Much attention is paid to the theoretical political and sociological
underpinnings of state development. Proceeding from the abstract to the specific, the
author gives a thorough analysis of the political and social development of Zaire as an
absolutist state, examining its national politics, outside interventions, and public
administration on the national and local level. This is one of the chief studies on politics
and government in Zaire, and anyone wishing to have a thorough grasp of government in
this country will need to read it.

148   **Zaire: stalemate and compromise.**
Thomas Turner.   *Current History* (April 1985), p. 179-83.

Provides an assessment of the political and economic situation in Zaire in 1984. At this
point in time Mobutu was still firmly entrenched in power after two decades despite great
potential opposition, the economy was stagnant despite measures taken to improve it,
and foreign supporters continued to keep the régime afloat through economic,
diplomatic, and military aid, prolonging the country's status as a 'basket case'.

149   **Zaire: the roots of the continuing crisis.**
Ghislain C. Kabwit.   *Journal of Modern African Studies*, vol. 17,
no. 3 (1979), p. 381-407.

During a second civil war in 1978 – dubbed 'Shaba II' – Mobutu's corrupt and tottering
régime was once again saved by Western intervention, leaving him firmly entrenched in
power and a lingering, bitter resentment on the part of many. This article measures the
scope of the political crisis, evaluates the great problems that faced the régime in the
aftermath of Shaba II and examines the policies that led to great disenchantment with
Mobutu's rule in Zaire.

Zaire.
See item no. 10.

Demography and history in the Kingdom of Kongo, 1550-1750.
See item no. 156.

The native problem in Africa.
See item no. 292.

The sociology of black Africa.
See item no. 299.

La vie des belges au Congo.
See item no. 302.

Population and Demography

150 **African historical demography: a multidisciplinary bibliography.**
Joel W. Gregory, Dennis D. Cordell, Raymond Gervais. Los
Angeles: Crossroads Press, 1984. 248p. (The Archival and
Bibliographic Series).

This bibliography on historical demography is divided geographically (Central Africa,
for example) and then further subdivided by broad studies and methodology, fertility and
nuptiality, mortality and morbidity, and migration and urbanization.

151 **African population and capitalism: historical perspectives.**
Edited by Dennis D. Cordell, Joel W. Gregory. Boulder, Colorado;
London: Westview Press, 1987. 302p. maps. bibliog. (African
Modernization and Development).

The two chapters which discuss population in Zaire are: Lututala Mumpasi's 'Les
origines des migrations modernes dans l'ouest du Zaïre' (The origins of modern
migrations in western Zaire) (p. 153-169) and Bogumil Jewsiewicki's 'Toward a
historical sociology of population in Zaire: proposals for the analysis of the demographic
régime' (p. 271-279).

152 **Angolan refugees in Shaba, Zaire 1984-1990: a case study of
management imbroglio.**
Katherine Hilderbrand, Jan van Erps, Bernard Hody, Marc Arbijn.
Journal of Refugee Studies, vol. 5, no. 3/4 (1992), p. 336-42.

Because of the Angolan civil war, some 35,000 refugees fled to Shaba at the beginning
of 1984. A long-term strategy was adopted to assist them in health and agriculture
although conflicting policies on settlement and repatriation caused the deterioration of
the refugees' health and nutritional situation.

153 **Approche ethnique des phénomènes démographiques: le cas du Zaïre.** (Ethnic approach to demographic phenomena: the case of Zaire.)
Mpembele Sala-Diakanda. Louvain-la-Neuve: CABAY, Département de Démographie, 1980. 433p. maps. bibliog. (Recherches Démographiques, cahier no. 4).

What is the rôle of ethnicity in determining fertility? In this study of western Zairian demography, issues such as age, nuptiality, mortality, and fertility are thoroughly examined in an attempt to answer this question. Statistical tables comprise pages 311-409.

154 **Atlas des collectivités du Zaïre.** (Atlas of the communities of Zaire.)
Léon de Saint Moulin. Kinshasa: Presses Universitaires du Zaïre, 1976. 65p. 16 maps.

Using data from the 1970 census, this atlas of population densities includes two maps of the whole country as well as fourteen maps of *'collectivités'* (the fourth level of administrative division in Zaire, down from region, subregion, and zone). Statistical population tables and foreign population by region are appended.

155 **Le courrier d'un réfugié africain: le bilan d'une révolte socialiste zaïroise en métropole impérialiste.** (Letters from an African refugee: the experience of a Zairian socialist revolt in an imperialist metropolis.)
Mabaya ma Mbongo. Sartrouville, France: Editions Kolwezi, 1984. 72p.

The author, a Zairian political refugee living in France, discusses the social conditions of Zairians living in France, and exhorts his fellow countrymen not to be exploited by 'imperialist' societies. Africans must regain their dignity by confronting the problems they encounter when living in industrialist countries.

156 **Demography and history in the Kingdom of Kongo, 1550-1750.**
John Thornton. *Journal of African History*, vol. 18, no. 4 (1977), p. 507-30. 2 maps. bibliog.

Thornton refutes the commonly-held view that the population of the Kongo Kingdom suffered a severe decline due to the civil wars of the 17th century and the slave trade. His calculations of 1.5 million people (1650-1700), however, are a half million people less than the commonly accepted figure.

157 **EDOZA: étude démographique de l'ouest du Zaïre, 1975-1976.** (EDOZA: demographic study of western Zaire, 1975-1976.)
Louvain-la-Neuve, Belgium: République du Zaïre, 1977-78. 7 vols. maps.

This demographic survey of western Zaire consists of three bibliographical parts published in six physical volumes plus a separate synthesis *(Synthèse des études démographiques de l'ouest du Zaïre, 1974-1977)*. Methodology, population structures, and population movement (marriage, fertility, mortality, migration) are described in the text and accompanying statistical tables.

158 **Perspectives démographiques du Zaïre, 1984-1999 & population d'âge électoral en 1993 et 1994.** (Demographic perspectives of Zaire, 1984-1999 & voting-age population in 1993 and 1994.)
S. Ngondo a Pisthandenge, L. de Saint Moulin, B. Tambashe Oleko.
Kinshasa: Centre d'Etudes pour l'Action Sociale, 1992. 72p. bibliog.

The methodology used to determine regional and subregional data is discussed in this demographic study of Zaire. It also contains statistical tables of the projected population and voting-age population by administrative units throughout Zaire. Earlier publications of interest include: *Perspectives démographiques régionales, 1975-1985* (Kinshasa, Département du Plan, 1978) and *Perspectives démographiques provisoires pour la République du Zaïre, 1970-1980* (Kinshasa: Planification du Développement, 1972).

159 **Population and worker mortality in western Zaire, ca. 1900-1935.**
Sabakinu Kivilu. In: *Demography from scanty evidence: Central Africa in the colonial era.* Boulder, Colorado; London: L. Rienner, 1990, p. 327-47. bibliog.

Using Catholic colonial missionary records from Matadi, Zaire as a basis for an historical demographic study, the author analyses trends in population formation and worker mortality. By comparing Catholic sources to administrative census data, he adjusts the data and Matadi's African and non-African populations. High worker mortality is due to poor living conditions and epidemics such as smallpox, yellow fever, and typhoid.

160 **A race with death.**
Russell Watson, James Schofield, Robin Sparkman, Laurance N'Kaoua, Katharine Chubbuck, John Barry. *Newsweek*, vol. 124, no. 5 (Aug. 1, 1994), p. 26-31. map.

Because of the Rwandan civil war, 2 million people, nearly one fourth of the population of Rwanda, have fled the country to the eastern border of Zaire. It is estimated that 1.2 million refugees were in Goma, Zaire, and 400,000 additional Rwandans are in Bukavu, Zaire. The refugees are dying by the thousands (estimated at one a minute) of cholera, dysentery, bubonic plague and measles. This article explains how, since Zaire and various relief agencies are unable to handle this mass migration, the United Nations has urged the refugees to return to Rwanda, although, to date, few have done so. Other articles on this situation can be found in further issues of *Newsweek, Time* and other contemporary periodical literature.

161 **Recensement pilote, août 1982: rapport.** (Pilot census, August 1982: report.)
Kinshasa: Commissariat Général au Plan, 1983. 20p. map.

A pilot census of the Zairian population was taken in 1982 of which this is the report. The purpose was to test the methodology and evaluate results in preparation for the official census to be taken in 1983, that is to say 1984.

162   **Recensement scientifique de la population, juillet, 1984.** (Scientific census of the population, July 1984.)
Kinshasa: République du Zaïre, Ministère du Plan et Aménagement du Territoire, Institut National de la Statistique, 1991-94. 14 vols. maps.

A number of key publications have resulted from the most recent Zairian census taken in 1984. As of late 1994, they are still being published, and they include: Totaux définitifs (3 vols.); Caractéristiques démographiques (6 vols.); Projections démographiques: Zaïre et régions, 1984-2000; Profil de la femme au Zaïre; Zaïre, un aperçu démographique 1984; Combien sommes-nous?; and Résultats provisoires.

163   **Recueil des rapports et totaux: calculés à partir des résultats officiels du Recensement de la population de la R. D. C. en 1970.**
(Collection of reports and totals: calculated from the official results of the Census of the population of the D.R.C. in 1970.)
Kinshasa: Institut National de la Statistique, 1973. 94p.

This volume contains data from the official 1970 census including statistical tables on the population of Zaire (excluding foreigners) by sex and age, totals of population for each year between the 1959 and 1970 censuses, and population density by administrative entity.

164   **Refugee participation case study: the Shaba settlements in Zaire.**
Lance Clark.   Washington, DC: Refugee Policy Group, 1987. 21p.
map.

Over 300,000 Angolan refugees were residing in Zaire when this publication was written. The settlement sites of Tshimbumbulu and Kisenge in Shaba are the subject of this study which analyses settlement design, refugee representation in decision-making and management of the settlement, and the integration of refugees into the area.

165   **Résultats officiels du recensement général de la population de la République démocratique du Congo: proclamés par arrêté no. 1236 du 31 juillet 1970 du Ministère d'Etat Chargé de l'Intérieur.**
(Official results of the general census of the population of the Democratic Republic of the Congo: proclaimed by order no. 1236 of 31 July, 1970 by the Minister of State in Charge of the Interior.)
Kinshasa: Ministère de l'Intérieur et des Affaires Coutumières, 1970. 14p.

The official statistical results of the 1970 census of the Zairian population (Zairians and foreigners) are included here in fourteen tables.

166   **Social science research for population policy design: case study of Zaïre.**
Mpembele Sala-Diakanda, Louis Lohlé-Tart, edited by James McCarthy.   Liege: IUSSP, 1982. 55p. maps. bibliog. (IUSSP Papers, no. 24).

This analysis of fertility histories is taken from the *EDOZA: étude démographique ouest Zaïre* (q.v.) survey from 1975-77. Although further research is needed to determine a population policy, fertility trends appear in the conclusion of this study.

167   **Village, ville et migration au Zaïre: enquête pschyo-sociologique sur le mouvement des populations de la sous-région de la Tshopo à la ville de Kisangani.** (Village, city and migration in Zaire: psycho-sociological study on the movement of population from the sub-region of Tshopo to the city of Kisangani.)
Friedhelm Streiffeler, Mbaya Mudimba.   Paris: L'Harmattan, 1986. 178p. bibliog. (Collection Alternatives Paysannes).

Kisangani (formerly Stanleyville), in the region of Haut-Zaïre, continues to experience a rural exodus. This psycho-sociological study of the causes of rural-urban migration is based on interviews with migrants, potential migrants and people who have chosen not to leave their villages.

168   **What is known of the demographic history of Zaire since 1885?**
Leon de St. Moulin.   In: *Demography from scanty evidence: Central Africa in the colonial era.*   Boulder, Colorado; London: L. Rienner, 1990, p. 299-325. maps. bibliog.

This important historical look at Zaire's population spans the 20th century. Using current statistical methodology, St. Moulin amends historical population and census data. He demonstrates the fallacies of using the raw census data; in the 1984 census, for example, the data does not show the return of East Kasai former refugees soon after 1960. He reconstructs the evolution of population at the sub-regional level between 1938 and 1984 and also estimates birth and mortality rates as well as migration by region.

169   **World Refugee Survey.**
New York: US Committee for Refugees, 1980- . annual.

The latest volume available at the time of publication was the 1993 issue. In the section on Africa, in addition to the discussion under Zaire itself, Angolan refugees in Zaire, and Zairian refugees in Uganda and Zambia are also highlighted. Because of the recent civil war in Rwanda, when the refugees fled in their millions to Goma, Zaire, the 1994 volume should be consulted when available.

Du Congo au Zaïre, 1960-1980: essai de bilan.
See item no. 3.

De la nuptialité et fécundité des polygames: le cas des Yaka de Popokabaka (Zaïre).
See item no. 180.

Les ethnies en démographie: l'exemple du Zaïre.
See item no. 184.

Kasongo: child mortality and growth in a small African town.
See item no. 314.

Techniques for collection and analysis of data on perinatal mortality in Kinshasa, Zaire = Techniques de collecte et d'analyse de données sur la mortalité périnatale à Kinshasa, Zaïre.
See item no. 321.

Bulletin Trimestriel des Statistiques Générales.
See item no. 564.

Kisangani, 1876-1976: histoire d'une ville. Tome 1: la population.
See item no. 585.

Ethnic Groups

170   African divination systems: ways of knowing.
Edited by Philip M. Peek.   Bloomington, Indiana: Indiana University
Press, 1991. 230p. map. bibliog. (African Systems of Thought).

Two chapters in this recent book concentrate on Zairian divination systems. Alden
Almquist's 'Divination and the hunt in Pagibeti ideology' (p. 101-11) discusses the
variations within the divinatory practices of these hunters/agriculturalists of northcentral
Zaire. René Devisch's 'Mediumistic divination among the northern Yaka of Zaire'
(p. 112-32) demonstrates how the Yaka system of divination maintains their social
structure.

171   An African world: the Basongye village of Lupupa Ngye.
Alan P. Merriam.   Bloomington, Indiana: Indiana University Press,
1974. 347p. maps. bibliog.

The Songye are the subject of this ethnography of Lupupa Ngye in Eastern Kasai, Zaire.

172   Azande.
New Haven, Connecticut: HRAF, 1976. 186 microfiches. maps.
bibliog. (HRAF Microfiles. Series 16, F07).

The ethnographic texts on the Azande (Zande) reproduced here are from sixty-eight
sources published between 1860 and 1950, and include 3,264 pages of text. Hardcopy
paper files have also been published, but may not be as complete as the microfiche
collection. HRAF files have also been published on the Mongo (29 microfiches; 9
sources from 1910-1950 in 773 pages of text) and Pygmies (56 microfiches; 4 sources
from 1930-1960 in 1,285 pages of text).

173 **The behavioral ecology of Efe Pygmy men in the Ituri Forest, Zaire.**
Robert C. Bailey, foreword by John D. Speth.   Ann Arbor, Michigan: University of Michigan, Museum of Anthropology, 1991. 143p. map. bibliog. (Anthropological Papers, Museum of Anthropology, University of Michigan, no. 86).

This study of time allocation and subsistence patterns among the Efe in the Ituri Forest uses the approach of behavioural ecology to describe Efe hunting and gathering activities, food production, and the relationship of hunting success to marital success and wealth. The relationship of the Efe to the Lese, slash-and-burn horticulturalists, with whom the Efe trade, is also discussed.

174 **Carte ethnique de la République du Zaïre: quart sud-ouest.** (Map of ethnic groups of the Republic of Zaire: south-west quarter.)
Olga Boone.   Tervuren, Belgium: Musée Royal de l'Afrique Centrale, 1973. 406p. maps. bibliog. (Annales. Série in-8o, Sciences Humaines, no. 78).

This is the author's second and final completed atlas of Zairian ethnic groups. For each of the fifty-five peoples studied in southwest Zaire, it includes information on the name and language (including variants) of the ethnic group and their geographical location, plus a map. The demography is also studied and a bibliography provided.

175 **Carte ethnique du Congo: quart sud-est.** (Map of ethnic groups of the Congo: south-east quarter.)
Olga Boone.   Tervuren, Belgium: Musée Royal de l'Afrique Centrale, 1961. 271p. maps. bibliog. (Annales. Série in-8o, Sciences Humaines, no. 37).

The southeast region of Zaire is the subject of this volume, the first of two completed maps on the ethnic groups of Zaire. In this volume, fifty-six ethnic groups are discussed, and the Kongo are divided into Western, Central and Eastern Kongo, and then further subdivided. A map of the entire region is also included.

176 **Catastrophe and creation: the transformation of an African culture.**
Kajsa Ekholm Friedman.   Chur, Switzerland: Harwood Academic Publishers, 1991. 271p. maps. bibliog. (Studies in Anthropology and History, vol. 5).

The Kongo people of the Lower Congo (Bas-Zaïre, Congo-Brazzaville and northern Angola) are the subject of this book on cultural change. A description of the pre-colonial society (1860-85) is followed by the effects of colonization on society. The psychological aspects of colonization are analysed and the author concludes with an analysis of the transformation of Kongo society through religion, witchcraft and cannibalism.

177   **The children of woot: a history of the Kuba peoples.**
Jan Vansina.   Madison, Wisconsin: University of Wisconsin Press;
Kent, England: Dawson, 1978. 394p. maps. bibliog.
In this political history of the Kuba Kingdom, Vansina delineates two separate
approaches to history: first, the past as it is perceived by the Kuba themselves; second,
the historian's interpretation of Kuba oral traditions. 'Lexical comparisons' (p. 249-318)
between Bushoong terms and neighbouring Bantu languages results in an interesting
appendix.

178   **Collection de monographies ethnographiques: sociologie
descriptive.** (Collection of ethnographic monographs: descriptive
sociology.)
Published by Cyr. van Overbergh.   Brussels: Albert de Wit; Institut
International de Bibliographie, 1907-13. 11 vols. maps. bibliog.
The ethnographic studies in this early colonial set are still considered to be of great value
today. The ethnic groups covered are Zairian except where noted: Bangala, by C. Van
Overbergh; Mayombe, by C. Van Overbergh; Basonge, by C. Van Overbergh;
Mangbetu, by C. Van Overbergh; Warega, by Le commandant Delhaise; Kuku
(Anglo-Egyptian possessions), by J. Vanden Plas; Ababua, by J. Halkin; Mandja (French
Congo), by F. Gand; Baholoholo, by R. Schmitz; and Baluba, by Le R. P. Colle (2 vols.).

179   **The dangerous journey: symbolic aspects of boys' initiation among
the Wagenia of Kisangani, Zaire.**
André Droogers, foreword by J. Vansina.   The Hague, Netherlands;
New York: Mouton, 1980. 416p. maps. bibliog. (Change and
Continuity in Africa).
This is an excellent in-depth study of initiation rites and their symbolism among the
Wagenia (Genya) people of Haut-Zaïre.

180   **De la nuptialité et fécundité des polygames: le cas des Yaka de
Popokabaka (Zaïre).** (Of the nuptiality and fertility of polygamous
marriages: the case of the Yaka of Popokabaka [Zaire].)
I. Ngondo a Pitshandenge.   Tervuren, Belgium: Musée Royal de
l'Afrique Centrale, 1982. 340p. maps. bibliog. (Annales. Série in-8o,
Sciences Humaines, no. 109).
The subject of this excellent study is the relationship between polygamy and fertility in
marriages of the Yaka of western Zaire. In his conclusion, the author confirms that on
average, fertility in polygamous marriages is less than fertility in monogamous
marriages.

181 **The dietary repertory of the Ngandu people of the tropical rain forest: an ecological and anthropological study of the subsistence activities and food procurement technology of a slash-and-burn agriculturist in the Zaire River basin.**
Jun Takeda. Kyoto: Kyoto University, Center for African Area Studies, 1990. 75p. map. bibliog. (African Study Monographs. Supplementary Issue, no. 11).
The food acquisition and consumption patterns of the Ngandu are analysed. They are nearly self-sufficient people, utilizing the plant and animal resources of the Ituri Forest, and cultivating cassava.

182 **Dreams among the Yansi.**
Mubuy Mubay Mpier. In: *Dreaming, religion, and society in Africa.* Edited by M. C. Jedrej, Rosalind Shaw. Leiden, Netherlands; New York: Brill, 1992, p. 100-10. bibliog. (Studies on Religion in Africa, no. 7).
Dream interpretation among the Yansi of Bandundu is an important aspect of their belief system and an integral part of their everyday lives.

183 **The ecological basis of hunter-gatherer subsistence in African rain forests: the Mbuti of eastern Zaire.**
Terese B. Hart, John A. Hart. *Human Ecology*, vol. 14, no. 1 (1986), p. 29-75. maps. bibliog.
By assessing the plant and animal food resources of the Ituri Forest the authors determined that the Mbuti pygmies did not live independently from their cultivator-neighbours on the forest-savanna border.

184 **Les ethnies en démographie: l'exemple du Zaïre.** (Ethnic groups in demography: the example of Zaire.)
Tshiswaka Lumembo. Paris: AMIRA, 1985. 16p. bibliog. (Brochure, no. 47).
The problems posed by using the idea of 'ethnic groups' in ethno-demographic studies of Black Africa are presented by this Zairian author. The ethnological work of colonial authors is characterized by studies full of prejudices. This methodological study uses as examples Olga Boone's two *Carte ethniques* (q.v.), Jan Vansina's *Introduction à l'ethnographie du Congo* (q.v.), and B. Crine-Mavar's 'Ethnies et langues du Zaire' in the *Atlas de la République du Zaïre* (q.v.).

185 **Ethnobotany of the Lega in the tropical rain forest of eastern Zaire: part one, Zone de Mwenga.**
Hideaki Terashima, Seya Kalala, Ngandu Malasi. Kyoto: Kyoto University, Center for African Area Studies, 1991. 61p. map. bibliog. (African Study Monographs. Supplementary Issue, no. 15).
The southeastern Lega of Mwenga, who are slash-and-burn agriculturalists, are the subject of this ethnobotanical and ecological study of plant utilization.

186 **Ethnographic survey of Africa: Central Africa: Belgian Congo.**
London: International African Institute, 1954-60. 5 vols. maps.
bibliog.

This French language ethnographic set continues in the vein of the *Collection de monographies ethnographiques* (q.v.). It covers: Les tribus Ba-Kuba et les peuplades apparentées (The BaKuba and related tribes), by J. Vansina; Les Bira et les peuplades limitrophées (The Bira and neighbouring tribes), by H. Van Geluwe; Mamvu-Mangutu et Balese-Mvuba (The Mamvu-Mangutu and Balese-Mvuba), by H. Van Geluwe; Les peuplades de l'entre Congo-Ubangi (Ngbandi, Ngbaka, Mbandja, Ngombe et gens de l'est) (The tribes between the Congo-Ubangi), by H. Burssens; and Les Bali et les peuplades apparentées (Ndaka, Mbo, Beke, Lika, Budu, Nyari) (The Bali and related tribes), by H. Van Geluwe. This set was also published as: *Annales du Musée Royal du Congo Belge, sciences de l'homme, monographies ethnographiques*, vol. 1-5.

187 **Ethnographische Notizen aus den Jahren 1905 und 1906.**
(Ethnographic notes from the years 1905 and 1906.)
Leo Frobenius, edited by Hildegard Klein.   Stuttgart, Germany:
F. Steiner Verlag Wiesbaden, 1985-90. 4 vols. maps. (Studien zur
Kulturkunde, Band 80, 84, 87, 97).

Leo Frobenius' pioneering ethnographic notebooks include over 1,900 drawings of his field sketches as well as those of expedition artist Hans Martin Lemme. Frobenius' notes are arranged by type of material culture such as clothing, housing, handicrafts, and musical instruments. The following ethnic groups are covered: the Kwilu and Lower Kasai; Kuba, Lele and Kete; Luluwa, South Kete, Bena Mai, Pende, Chokwe; and the Kanyok, Luba, Songye, Tetela, Songo Meno/Nkutu. This major work is of interest to historians, anthropologists and art historians.

188 **Folk knowledge of fish among the Songola and the Bwari:
comparative ethnoichthyology of the Lualaba River and Lake
Tanganyika fishermen.**
Yuji Ankei.   Kyoto:Kyoto University, Center for African Area
Studies, 1989. 88p. maps. bibliog. (African Study Monographs.
Supplementary Issue, no. 9).

Freshwater fish are classified according to the Songola fishermen along the Lualaba River and the Bwari fishermen of northern Lake Tanganyika. The difference in the folk knowledge can be attributed to the difference in the occurrence of the fish populations in the two bodies of water.

189 **The forest people.**
Colin Turnbull, with a new introduction by the author.   London:
Pimlico, 1993. 256p. maps. (Pimlico, no. 114).

This classic ethnographical study of the Mbuti (pygmies) of the Ituri forest was first published in 1961, and it is still capturing imaginations today. The Mbutis love the forest and believe that it is better than the outside world which rapidly encroaches upon them today.

190 **Houses in the rain forest: ethnicity and inequality among farmers and foragers in Central Africa.**
Roy Richard Grinker. Berkeley, California: University of California Press, 1994. 225p. 1 map. bibliog.
Much has been written about forager (Efe or pygmy)-farmer (Lese) relations from the Efe perspective. Grinker's work at last concentrates on the Lese. He also takes a critical look at Colin Turnbull's *The forest people* (q.v.). Grinker uses the 'house' as a model for society and the economy as well as social institutions.

191 **Initiation dans les sociétés traditionnelles africaines: le cas Kongo.**
(Initiation in traditional African societies: the Kongo case.)
Ngoma Ngambu. Kinshasa: Presses Universitaires du Zaïre, 1981. 227p. maps. bibliog.
In this examination of Kongo initiation rites, the author follows descriptions of the various ceremonies by region with an analysis of their differences and similarities.

192 **Introduction à l'ethnographie du Congo.** (Introduction to the ethnography of the Congo.)
Jan Vansina. Kinshasa: Université Lovanium; Brussels: CRISP, 1966. 227p. maps. bibliog.
Arranged by cultural regions and designed to reach non-ethnologists, this comprehensive ethnological study of Zaire describes the principal characteristics and profile of each of its important peoples. Chapters are divided into the following components: history; languages; economics; social structure; political structure; religion; and artistic life.

193 **The Kanyok of Zaire: an institutional and ideological history to 1895.**
John C. Yoder. Cambridge, England; New York: Cambridge University Press, 1992. 213p. maps. bibliog. (African Studies Series, no. 74).
Yoder analyses Kanyok myths and legends that comment on their activities and institutions in order to record Kanyok intellectual history up until the end of the 19th century.

194 **Kings and clans: Ijwi Island and the Kale Kivu Rift, 1780-1840.**
David S. Newbury. Madison, Wisconsin: University of Wisconsin Press, 1991. 371p. maps. bibliog.
Ijwi Island is located literally in Lake Kivu, on the Zairian side of the Zaire/Rwanda border. This history of the Havu people in the 18th and 19th centuries details the creation of their society and how a new kingdom emerged.

195 **Legends and history of the Luba.**
Harold Womersley. Los Angeles: Crossroads Press, 1984. 102p.
maps. bibliog. (African Primary Texts).

The oral dynastic histories and genesis tales of the Luba Empire in Shaba were collected
by the Reverend Womersley and are presented here.

196 **Luba religion and magic in custom and belief.**
W. F. P. Burton. Tervuren, Belgium: Musée Royal de l'Afrique
Centrale, 1961. 193p. map. (Annales. Série in-8o, Sciences Humaines,
no. 35).

The Luba's death and burial customs, spirit possession, and secret societies are the major
topics described in this monograph.

197 **La parenté égyptienne des peuples du Zaïre: racines millénaires
d'une vie socio-culturelle commune.** (The kinship of the Egyptian
people to the people of Zaire: thousand year old roots of a common
socio-cultural life.)
Tshimpaka Yanga. Lubumbashi: Edition Cactus, 1989. 204p. map.
bibliog.

The author's thesis is that, despite the great cultural diversity of modern Zaire, its
cultural heritage has at its foundation the people of Pharonic Egypt. He uses established
cultural, historical and linguistic facts to support his controversial argument.

198 **Les peuplades de la République du Congo, du Rwanda et du
Burundi.** (The peoples of the Republic of the Congo, of Rwanda and
of Burundi.)
A. Dorsinfang-Smets. In: *Ethnologie régionale.* Edited by Jean
Poirier. Paris: Gallimard, 1972, vol. 1, p. 566-661. maps. bibliog.

The chapter on the Congo, Rwanda and Burundi concentrates on the peoples of the
Congo. Topics covered include: geography; prehistory; history; languages; hunting;
agriculture; social and political organization; religion and art. The chapter on pygmies,
which follows immediately after, and is written by Lucien Demesse, also contains
significant material on the three pygmy populations of Zaire (Babinga, Mbuti, and
Batwa) (p. 662-693).

199 **Les peuplades du Congo belge: nom et situation géographique.**
(The tribes of the Belgian Congo: name and geographical situation.)
J. Maes, O. Boone. Brussels: Musée du Congo Belge, 1935. 379p.
map. bibliog. (Publications du Bureau de Documentation
Ethnographique. Série 2, Monographies Idéologiques, vol. 1).

This is Boone's earliest work of classification of the people of Zaire. The name and
variant names, the geographical location and a map are provided for each of the 178
ethnic groups listed. This work differs from Boone's two later works, the *Carte ethnique
du Congo* (q.v.), by quoting the various names of each ethnic group from passages in
previously published works.

200 **Pouvoir et parenté chez les Kongo-Dinga du Zaïre.** (Power and
kinship among the Kongo-Dinga of Zaire.)
Joseph Henri Cecil Ceyssens.   Meppel, Netherlands: Krips Repro,
1984. 528p. maps. bibliog.

The Kongo-Dinga live on the Zairian-Angolan border and form the subject matter of this
doctoral dissertation (Katholieke Universiteit te Nijmegen, 1984). After a cultural
analysis of the various ethnic groups of Haut-Kasayi, the author discusses Kongo-Dinga
kinship, particularly their matrimonial alliances. The last part covers descent groups, and
leads to a discussion of power and authority. An English summary is included.

201 **Power and performance: ethnographic explorations through
proverbial wisdom and theater in Shaba, Zaire.**
Johannes Fabian.   Madison, Wisconsin: University of Wisconsin
Press, 1990. 314p. maps. bibliog. (New Directions in Anthropological
Writing).

In this innovative anthropological study of popular culture, the theatre serves as the
vehicle to research power and performance. Fabian discovered 'performative
ethnography' while discussing the axiom 'Le pouvoir se mange entier' (Power is eaten
whole) with the Luba theatrical group Mufwankolo, of Lubumbashi. This record of the
making of a popular play includes the texts in Shaba Swahili and English translation. It is
intended for a rather sophisticated reader.

202 **Red-white-black as a mode of thought: a study of triadic
classification by colours in the ritual symbolism and cognitive
thought of the peoples of the Lower Congo.**
Anita Jacobson-Widding.   Uppsala, Sweden: Uppsala University,
1979. 396p. map. bibliog. (Acta Universitatis Upsaliensis. Uppsala
Studies in Cultural Anthropology, no. 1).

The Kongo-speaking peoples of the Lower Congo (in this study, Congo-Brazzaville and
Zaire) are the basis of this structural approach to the system of colour symbols used in
ritual and profane situations (such as in grave, shrine, and *nkisi* or 'fetish' cults).

203 **Traditions verbales et rituelles chez les Lele, Kuba, Ding, Lulua,
Luba, Komo et Yira (Rép. du Zaïre).** (Oral and ritual traditions of
the Lele, Kuba, Ding, Lulua, Luba, Komo and Yira [Rep. of Zaire].)
Minga Shanga, Makutu Nym.   Bandundu, Zaire: Ceeba, 1984. 180p.
map. bibliog. (Publications CEEBA. Série II, vol. 92).

Religion, death rites, initiation rites, spiritual possession, and an essay on the symbolism
of Lulua tales are included in this volume covering the various ethnic groups cited in the
title.

204 **Wild plant utilization of the Balese and the Efe of the Ituri Forest, the Republic of Zaire.**
Hideaki Terashima, Mitsuo Ichikawa, Masato Sawada. Kyoto: Kyoto University, Center for African Area Studies, 1988. 78p. map. bibliog. (African Study Monographs. Supplementary Issue, no. 8).
The subject of this comparative study is the ethnobotanical and ecological utilization of plants by the Lese cultivators and the Efe hunter-gatherers in the Ituri Forest.

205 **Le Zaïre: civilisations traditionnelles et culture moderne: archives culturelles d'Afrique centrale.** (Zaire: traditional civilizations and modern culture: cultural archives of central Africa.)
Théophile Obenga.   Paris: Présence Africaine, 1977. 270p. map.
This handbook represents an introduction to the Zairian people and includes chapters on Zairian geography, prehistory, languages, and ethnic groups. The last chapter on modern Zairian culture is by now dated, but includes excellent summaries of Zairian intellectual life up to the mid-1970s.

Demography and history in the Kingdom of Kongo, 1550-1750.
See item no. 156.

Cultural roots of Kongo prophetism.
See item no. 253.

Death and the invisible powers: the world of Kongo belief.
See item no. 254.

Religion and society in Central Africa: the BaKongo of Lower Zaire.
See item no. 278.

A socio-religious and political analysis of the Judeo-Christian concept of prophetism and modern Bakongo and Zulu African prophet movements.
See item no. 281.

Ethnic politics in Zaire.
See item no. 342.

African agrarian systems.
See item no. 513.

Shifting cultivation in Africa.
See item no. 527.

Kisangani, 1876-1976: histoire d'une ville. Tome 1: la population.
See item no. 585.

The arts of Central Africa: an annotated bibliography.
See item no. 659.

Zaïre: peuples/art/culture.
See item no. 661.

African reflections: art from Northeastern Zaire.
See item no. 662.

Art of Africa: treasures from the Congo.
See item no. 670.

The arts of Zaire.
See item no. 674.

100 peoples of Zaire and their sculpture: the handbook.
See item no. 684.

Languages and Dialects

General

206 The classification of the Bantu languages.
Malcolm Guthrie.   London; New York: Oxford University Press, 1948. 91p.

Although the world's languages have seen newer classification schemes such as C. F. and F. M. Voegelin's *Classification and index of the world's languages* (New York: Elsevier, 1977), Guthrie is still considered a recognizable authority in both the United States and in the United Kingdom. His work is, in fact, still the basis of language classification in two of the world's important library classification systems: the Dewey Decimal Classification (DDC) and the Universal Decimal Classification (UDC). A recent article which refers to his classification is I. C. McIlwaine's 'UDC: the present state and future developments', in *International Cataloguing and Bibliographical Control* (vol. 23, no. 2 [April/June 1994], p. 29-33), which shows on a map of Africa the seven linguistic zones Guthrie assigned to Zaire.

207 Comparative handbook of Congo languages.
Walter Henry Stapleton.   Yakusu: [n.p.], 1903. 326p.

This early comparative grammar of the languages spoken along the Congo River up to Stanley Falls (Kongo, Bangi, Lolo, Ngala, Poto, Ngombe, Soko and Kele) also includes Swahili. A comparative vocabulary of 800 words from these languages also appears with their English equivalents.

208 **Introduction à l'étude des langues bantoues du Congo belge.**
(Introduction to the Bantu languages of the Belgian Congo.)
Amaat Burssens.   Anvers, Belgium: De Sikkel, 1954. 152p. maps.
bibliog. (Kongo-Overzee Bibliotheek, no. 8).

In this introduction to the languages of the Belgian Congo the author offers an overview
of the Bantu languages, but concentrates on a basic grammar of Swahili, Luba, Mongo,
and Lingala.

209 **Language map of Africa and the adjacent islands.**
David Dalby.   London: International African Institute, 1977.
Provisional ed. 63p. map. bibliog.

In this detailed linguistic map of Africa (scale 1:5,000,000) Dalby updates Greenberg's
classification, mapping and classifying African languages. The accompanying booklet,
which clarifies the languages spoken in Zaire, is difficult for the layman to use, but still
provides valuable information.

210 **Language situation, language planning and nationhood: the case of
Zaire.**
Menayame Ndolo.   DA thesis, State University of New York at Stony
Brook, 1992. 193p. 5 maps. bibliog. (Available from University
Microfilms International, Ann Arbor, Michigan, order no. 9322296).

This dissertation reviews the various pre-independence language policies, describes
educational reform and the impact on language policies from 1960 to 1990, and
examines the impact of language policies on the development of a sense of nationhood.
The concept of national language is also thoroughly analysed. Among the four national
languages (Ciluba [Luba], Kikongo [Kongo], Lingala and Swahili), Lingala appears to
be spreading the most rapidly because of several factors. For example, it is the language
spoken in the capital and the language of the Mobutu régime. The status of French as the
'official' language of Zaire is also discussed.

211 **Les langues au Zaïre à l'horizon 2000.** (Languages in Zaire in the
perspective of the year 2000.)
Mutombo Huta-Mukana.   In: *Les langues en Afrique à l'horizon
2000.*   Brussels: Académie Royale des Sciences d'Outre-Mer, 1991,
p. 85-107. bibliog.

The current thinking on Zaire's linguistic situation is summarized in this paper, dividing
Zaire's languages into Bantu and non-Bantu. The author then discusses the linguistic
politics of Zaire. The four *lingua francas* (Kongo, Swahili, Luba, and Lingala) are
caught between the other ethnic languages and French and the State must intervene and
decide the future of languages in Zaire.

212 **Lexicography in Central Africa: the user perspective, with special reference to Zaire.**
Masidake Busane. In: *Lexicography in Africa.* Edited by R. R. K. Hartmann. Exeter: University of Exeter Press, 1990, p. 19-35. bibliog. (Exeter Linguistic Studies, vol. 15).

This chapter focuses on the intended uses of language dictionaries in Central Africa. Most of the dictionaries in Zaire cannot be easily used by Africans because of the presentation of grammatical information and the arrangement of the entries. The author urges lexicographers to adopt an African user perspective.

213 **Situation linguistique de l'Afrique centrale: inventaire préliminaire, le Zaïre.** (Linguistic situation of central Africa: preliminary inventory, Zaire.)
Paris: Agence de Coopération Culturelle et Technique; Centre Régional de Recherche et de Documentation Sur les Traditions Orales et Pour le Développement des Langues Africaines, Equipe Nationale Zaïroise, 1983. 161p. maps. bibliog. (Atlas Linguistique de l'Afrique Centrale) (Atlas Linguistique du Zaïre).

Consisting primarily of text, this atlas of languages in Zaire, contains the following chapters: an inventory of languages; the state of research on languages; tables of classification and maps of where the languages are spoken; and an alphabetical index of languages. The bibliography contains 843 citations.

214 **Talking drums of Africa.**
John F. Carrington. London: Carey Kingsgate Press, 1949. Reprinted, New York: Negro Universities Press, 1969. 96p. bibliog.

The author, a missionary in the Stanleyville (Kisangani) area of the Belgian Congo, describes how all-wooden and skin-topped Central African drums are made. The bulk of the text explores the use of drums as a language, with illustrations from Lokele drums, using the Kele language.

French, the official language

215 **Documents pour une étude des particularités lexico-sémantiques du français au Zaïre.** (Documents on a study of the lexico-semantic peculiarities of the French language in Zaire.)
Sumaili N'gaye Lussa. Lubumbashi, Zaire: Centre de Linguistique Théorique et Appliquée, 1974. 57p. (Collection 'Textes et Documents').

The French language spoken in Zaire is a product of languages in contact. Some of the terms come from Bantu languages, others come from French, English, Portuguese or Arab languages (but are 'bantuisized' before returning to French), while others are a hybrid or of uncertain origin.

216 **La francophonie au Zaïre.** (The speaking of French in Zaire.)
Sully Faïk, Kilanga Musinde, Ngirabakunzi Kaberuka, Nyembwe
Ntita, Max Pierre, Sesep Nsial.   Lubumbashi, Zaire: Editions Impala,
1988. 240p. bibliog.
The history, use, study, and impact of the French language in Zaire forms the subject of
the eight essays contained in this volume.

National languages

217 **L'arabe et le swahili dans la République du Zaïre: études
islamiques: histoire et linguistique.** (Arabic and Swahili in the
Republic of Zaire: Islamic studies: history and linguistics.)
Adnan Haddad.   Paris: SEDES, 1983. 262p. maps. bibliog.
This study of Zairian Swahili begins with the origins of the Swahili language, then
discusses the penetration of Swahili into pre-colonial and colonial Zaire. The history and
influence of the Arab slave traders and Islam are followed by a section on Swahili and
Arabic linguistics, including a glossary of Arabic loan words in Swahili.

218 **Bukavu Swahili: a sociolinguistic study of language change.**
Timothy Lloyd Wilt.   PhD thesis, Michigan State University, 1988.
300p. bibliog. (Available from University Microfilms International,
order no. 8900125).
In his thesis, the author examines language contact and change by researching the
historical and social factors that influenced the development of Swahili, as spoken in
Bukavu. Appendix A is a comparison of standard coastal Swahili, standard Zairian
Swahili, and Bukavu Swahili.

219 **Le contexte historique de la naissance et de la diffusion du
kingwana.** (The historical context of the birth and diffusion of
Kingwana.)
D. L. Goyvaerts, A. Kabemba.   In: *Language and history in central
Africa.*   Wilrijk, Belgium: Universiteit Antwerpen, 1986, p. 197-244.
bibliog. (Antwerp Papers in Linguistics, no. 44).
The authors ignore the linguistic aspects of Kingwana, an Eastern Zairian dialect of
Swahili, and concentrate on the historical context of its emergence in Maniema.
Kingwana spoken in Maniema was influenced by the people who lived in their
households, Koranic schools, markets, and Koranic tribunals.

220   **Deux milles phrases de Swahili tel qu'il se parle au Zaïre.** (Two
      thousand sentences of Swahili such as it is spoken in Zaire.)
      Shigeki Kaji.   Tokyo: Institute for the Study of Languages and
      Cultures of Asia and Africa, 1985. 395p. (African Languages and
      Ethnography, no. 19).
      Two thousand French sentences are translated into Zairian Swahili using as a basis Henri
      Frei's standard French text of *Le livre des deux mille phrases* (Geneva: Droz, 1953).

221   **Dictionary and grammar of the Kongo language.**
      W. Holman Bentley.   London: Baptist Missionary Society; Trubner,
      1887-95. Reprinted, Farnborough, England: Gregg Press, 1967 (1984
      printing). 2 vols.
      Bentley, an English missionary, wrote this still well-regarded two-way dictionary and
      grammar of the Kongo language. The second volume is the appendix which contains
      some 4,000 new words as well as updates on grammar and syntax.

222   **Dictionnaire français-tshiluba.** (French-Luba dictionary.)
      Emile Willems.   Kananga, Zaire: Editions de l'Archidiocèse, 1986.
      342p.
      Willem's French-Luba dictionary is quite comprehensive; he published a Luba-French
      dictionary when he revised Auguste de Clercq's *Dictionnaire tshiluba-français*
      (Leopoldville: Société Missionnaire de St. Paul, 1960).

223   **Dictionnaire kikongo-français: avec une étude phonétique
      décrivant les dialectes les plus importants de la langue dite
      kikongo.** (Kikongo-French dictionary: with a phonetic study
      describing the most important dialects of the language called
      Kikongo.)
      K. E. Laman.   Brussels: Institut Royal Colonial Belge, 1936.
      Reprinted, Ridgewood, New Jersey: Gregg Press, 1964. 2 vols. map.
      bibliog. (Mémoires, Collection in-8o, t. 2).
      This excellent one-way dictionary, from Kongo to French, includes a phonetic analysis
      of the Kongo language and its regional variants.

224   **Dictionnaire kiluba-français.** (Luba-French dictionary.)
      E. van Avermaet, in collaboration with Benoît Mbuya.   Tervuren,
      Belgium: Musée Royal du Congo Belge, 1954. 838p. (Annales.
      Sciences de l'Homme. Linguistique, vol. 7).
      This is the most comprehensive Luba-French dictionary, even though it was written
      some time ago, and does not include a French-Luba section.

225 **Dictionnaire luba: luba-français, français-luba.** (Luba dictionary: Luba-French, French-Luba.)
Auguste de Clercq.   Brussels: A. Dewit, 1914. 583p.
This early two-way dictionary of Luba and French was written by Father de Clercq, a pioneer in recording the Luba language.

226 **Emprunts français en kikongo: essai sémantique et phonétique.** (French loan words in Kikongo: semantic and phonetic essay.)
Mayaka Makanda.   Kinshasa: Université Nationale du Zaïre, Institut Pédagogique National, 1974. 43p. map. bibliog. (Collection 'Sciences et Lettres', no. 6).
A brief semantic classification of French loan words in the Kintandu dialect of the Kongo language family is followed by a phonetic study of vowel and consonant transformations.

227 **English-Congo and Congo-English dictionary.**
Henry Craven, John Barfield.   London: Harley House, Bow, 1883.
Reprinted, Freeport, New York: Books for Libraries Press, 1971. 248p.
This dictionary is generally regarded as the definitive early Kongo dictionary.

228 **English-Lingala manual.**
John D. Odhner.   Washington, DC: University Press of America, 1981. 187p. maps.
This text contains a combination of Lingala grammar, exercises and practical sentences. It also includes several anecdotes in Lingala and English as well as brief vocabularies. Although the manual was issued with audio cassette recordings of the exercises and anecdotes, they are difficult to locate, and the text can be used without them.

229 **Esquisse grammaticale de la langue luba-shaba (parler de Kasongo Nyembo).** (Grammatical outline of the Luba-Shaba language [dialect of Kasongo Nyembo].)
Nkiko Munya Rugero.   Lubumbashi: Université Nationale du Zaïre, Faculté des Lettres, Centre de Linguistique Théorique et Appliquée, 1975. 95p. (Collection 'Travaux et Recherches').
A native speaker of the Kasongo Nyembo dialect wrote this grammar of the Luba language.

230 **Grammaire pratique lingala.** (Practical Lingala grammar.)
Matumele Maliya, Ayibite Pela Asey, Epanga Pombo, under the direction of Kazadi Ntole.   Kinshasa: Centre de Linguistique Théorique et Appliquée, 1988. 74p. (Collection 'Enseignement des Langues Zaïroises').
The stated audience for this Lingala grammar in French is not scholarly but the *'grand public'* (the masses).

231 **Grammar and dictionary of the Buluba-Lulua language as spoken in the upper Kasai and Congo basin.**
W. M. Morrison. New York: American Tract Society, 1906. 417p.
Pioneering missionary Morrison wrote this standard grammar and two-way dictionary of the Luba language, which was the trade language used in the area at that time.

232 **History from below: the 'Vocabulary of Elisabethville' by André Yav.**
Johannes Fabian, with assistance from Kalundi Mango, with linguistic notes by Walter Schicho. Amsterdam; Philadelphia: John Benjamins, 1990. 236p. maps. bibliog. (Creole Language Library, no. 7).
The *Vocabulary of Elisabethville* appears here in its original Shaba Swahili text, in a new Shaba Swahili transcription, and in English translation. The authors place the text in its socio-linguistic, historical and cultural contexts.

233 **Indoubil: a Swahili hybrid in Bukavu.**
Didier L. Goyvaerts, with comments on Indu Bill by K. Kabongo-Mianda. *Language in Society*, vol. 17, no. 2 (1988), p. 231-42.
Indoubil, the language of Bukavu's younger generation, exists today in all the larger Zairian cities, but has marked differences from city to city. While the Indoubil of Kinshasa is based on Lingala, the Indoubil of Bukavu is based on Swahili. Bukavu's version is characterized by borrowing European words and giving new meanings to Swahili words as well as creating neologisms, all having the effect of confusing the uninitiated. It also neutralizes the ill-effects of ethnicity in this pluralistic society.

234 **Jifunze-yekola Lingala-Kiswahili.** (Learn Lingala-Kiswahili.)
Kahombo Mateene. Kampala: Edition Bureau Linguistique de l'OUA, 1981. 3rd ed. 136p. (Publication, OAU Inter-African Bureau of Languages, no. 1).
This unusual instruction manual in parallel Lingala and Swahili texts, is designed for an African learning a new African language without needing to have knowledge of a European language.

235 **Language and colonial power: the appropriation of Swahili in the former Belgian Congo, 1880-1938.**
Johannes Fabian. Cambridge, England; New York: Cambridge University Press, 1986. 206p. bibliog. (African Studies Series, no. 48).
Fabian discusses the rôle of Swahili in the colonial Belgian Congo and its evolution from the language of choice of colonial policy-makers, to *lingua franca*. Particular attention is paid to variants of Swahili such as missionary Swahili, company-town Swahili of the Union Minière/Gécamines and the pidginized Swahili of Katanga, in the context of historical events, political decisions and socio-economic conditions. The text was also published in 1991 by the University of California Press with a foreword by Edward Said.

236 **Lingala: basic course.**
James Redden, F. Bongo, et al. Washington, DC: Foreign Service
Institute, Department of State, 1963. 293p. (Basic Course Series).
Dialogues and grammatical drills are used in the course to provide basic structures and
vocabulary of the trade language, Lingala.

237 **Lingala grammar and dictionary.**
Malcolm Guthrie, John F. Carrington. London: Baptist Missionary
Society, 1988. 238p.
This is the revised edition of Guthrie's important work first published in 1935, and
completed by Carrington after Guthrie's death in 1973.

238 **Maloba ma lokota lingala = Dictionnaire lingala: lingala-français,
français-lingala.** (Lingala dictionary: Lingala-French,
French-Lingala.)
René van Everbroeck. Limete, Kinshasa: Editions l'Epiphanie, 1985.
358p.
This is the most recent general two-way Lingala-French dictionary available.

239 **A textbook of the Tshiluba language.**
Virginia Gray Pruitt, Winifred Kellersberger Vass. Luebo, Congo:
American Presbyterian Congo Mission, 1965. 304p.
For the English-language speaker, this Luba textbook is an excellent introduction. It is
based on three of W. M. Morrison's works: *Grammar of the Buluba-Lulua language*
(Luebo, 1930. 189p.), *Exercise book on the Buluba-Lulua grammar* (publication details
unknown), and *Dictionary of the Tshiluba language* (Luebo, 1939. 173p.).

240 **Le tshiluba du Kasayi.** (Tshiluba of Kasai.)
Emile Willems. Luluabourg, Zaire: Mission de Scheut, 1970. 4th ed.
221p.
Willems wrote this post-independence Luba textbook for French speakers.

241 **Vocabulaire tshiluba-français et français-tshiluba.** (Luba-French
and French-Luba vocabulary.)
Emile Willems. Kananga, Zaire: Editions de l'Archidiocèse, 1989.
2nd ed., revised and enlarged. 103p.
This slender two-way dictionary is the most recent Luba dictionary published.

Le Groupe Mufwankolo.
See item no. 726.

Religion

242 African traditional religions in contemporary society.
Edited by Jacob K. Olupona. New York: International Religious Foundation, 1991. 204p. bibliog. (New ERA Book).

This consists of a collection of essays on traditional African religion and is not specifically a study of religion in Zaire. In the introduction the editor proclaims the important rôle of African religion in shaping the character of African society and culture, despite the fact that the majority of Africans have formally converted to Islam or Christianity. Some of the essays deal with the revitalization of traditional religion, the relationship of traditional religion and Christianity, and the continuity of African religious life, despite the inroads of outside religions. This is a good general introduction to traditional religion in Africa.

243 The birth of the Kimbanguist movement in the Bas-Zaire 1921.
Cecilia Irvine. *Journal of Religion in Africa*, vol. 6, fasc. 1 (1974), p. 23-76.

Irvine reviews the religious and political environment and the events surrounding the emergence of Kimbanguism and the imprisonment of Simon Kimbangu, 1921-22. The Belgian authorities at first viewed Kimbanguism as a Protestant cabal, for Protestant missionaries were already regarded with great suspicion by the Belgian colonial régime of the period. The political implications of these events still greatly influence the relationship of Kimbanguism, Catholicism, and Protestantism in Zaire to this day. The author includes an extensive chronology of the events of 1921-22 as well as other documents.

244 **Charisma and cultural change: a study of the Jamaa movement in Katanga.**
Johannes Fabian. PhD thesis, University of Chicago, Chicago, Illinois, 1969. 439p. bibliog. (Available from the Department of Photoduplication, University of Chicago Library, Chicago, Illinois, thesis no. T17568).
This 1969 PhD dissertation focuses on the origins of the Jamaa movement – a charismatic spiritual movement within the Roman Catholic Church – in Shaba Province, Zaire. The author discusses the early proponents of the movement, the socio-economic background of the early followers, the development of the movement, and its doctrine.

245 **Le chrétien et le développement de la nation: exhortation pastorale des évêques du Zaïre.** (The Christian and the development of the nation: pastoral exhortation by the bishops of Zaire.)
Catholic Church. Conférence Episcopale du Zaïre. Kinshasa: Secrétariat Général de la CEZ, 1988. 92p. bibliog.
The Roman Catholic Church plays an enormous social rôle in Zaire. This work demonstrates the social mission of the Church, and more specifically the rôle of the Christian in the economic development of Zaire. It is issued to the faithful by the Roman Catholic Episcopal Conference of Zaire and represents the official teachings of the Church on social and economic matters.

246 **Christian missionizing and social transformation: a history of conflict and change in Eastern Zaire.**
Jack E. Nelson. New York; Westport, Connecticut; London: Praeger, 1992. 209p. map. bibliog.
Available through University Microfilms International, order no. 9007369, this publication is a re-written version of the author's 1989 PhD dissertation. The work is a history of the missionary effort of Paul Hurlburt, a Protestant, who founded the Katwa mission station near Butembo in Eastern Zaire in 1929. It provides a very good coverage of the social and political environment of this missionary society, which would reflect the development of missionary work throughout all of Zaire. Also covered is the impact of Christianity on African culture.

247 **The Church in Congo and in Ruanda-Urundi.**
Brussels: Pontifical Missionary Works, 1950. 63p. maps.
This is a history of the implantation, growth, and development of the Roman Catholic Church in Zaire as well as in Rwanda and Burundi. Published in 1950, it presents a very colonial perspective on missionary activity and the evangelization of the Zairian masses. There is extensive coverage of the institutional development of Catholicism in Zaire. The work is also available in French under the title: *L'Eglise au Congo et au Ruanda-Urundi.*

248 **The Church of Christ in Zaire: a handbook of Protestant
churches, missions, and communities, 1878-1978.**
Cecilia Irvine.   Indianapolis, Indiana: Christian Church (Disciples of
Christ), Division of Overseas Ministries, Department of Africa, 1978.
161p. maps. bibliog.

This work is a handbook of various Protestant missions, missionary societies, and
religious organizations in Zaire. There is an extensive listing of individual organizations,
referenced to short descriptions of the history and work of the organization. This
handbook would be most useful to a scholar studying Protestantism in Zaire or to a more
casual reader who requires information on specific Protestant activities in Zaire.

249 **The Church-State conflict in Zaire, 1969-1974.**
Kenneth Lee Adelman.   *African Studies Review*, vol. 18, no. 1 (April
1975), p. 102-16. bibliog.

Adelman reviews the events of the Church-State conflict in Zaire. The authoritarian
Zairian President Mobutu Sese Seko has sought to extend the control of the State to
religious organizations whilst the churches, resisting this political pressure, have in turn
been critical of the lack of justice and arbitrary decision-making in the Zairian
government. This is a short but comprehensive analysis of the Church-State conflict from
1969 to 1974.

250 **Concepts of God in Africa.**
John S. Mbiti.   New York; Washington, DC: Praeger, 1970. 348p.
bibliog.

Examines the concept of the divinity in traditional African religion. The work looks at
the moral, spiritual, psychological, and ritualistic universe, which is the heritage of
African religion, and considerable space is devoted to eschatology (the history of salva-
tion), which underlies the profusion of prophetic or messianic movements throughout
Africa. The author does not discuss the specifics of individual local practices, but he
paints the concepts of African religion in broad, abstract strokes. The study is not limited
to Zaire but serves as an excellent general introduction to traditional African religion.

251 **Congo crisis and Christian mission.**
Robert G. Nelson.   St. Louis, Missouri: Bethany Press, 1961. 112p.

The author, an American Protestant missionary, presents the history of missions in Zaire
under Belgian rule. The major focus is on how the independence crisis impacted Christian,
largely Protestant, institutions and their function within the country. During the upheaval of
independence, many missionaries fled the new state, greatly affecting the institutions that
they supported. The author speculates on the future of Christianity in Zaire.

252 **Cross and sword: the political role of Christian missions in the
Belgian Congo, 1908-1960.**
Marvin D. Markowitz.   Stanford, California: Stanford University,
Hoover Institution Press, 1973. 223p. (Hoover Institution Publications,
no. 114).

Catholic missions were greatly favoured by the Belgian colonial government of Zaire,
and they were encouraged in their evangelization effort by authorities who often viewed

their Christianizing and Europeanizing efforts as a branch of public policy. Consequently, there was great co-operation between the administration and the missions in such areas as education. The author traces this political entente between the Church and State from its original community of purpose to an increasing distance as secularization and anticlericalism become the trend in government circles. Markowitz does not ignore the other religious groups; he chronicles the rivalry of Catholic and Protestant missions, and the efforts by Protestants to establish their school system with the same state subsidies that the Catholics enjoyed. The author also discusses the messianic and syncretistic cults, such as Kimbanguism, which grew up as an adaptation of Christianity to local custom and culture, and he analyses their political relationship to the state.

253   **Cultural roots of Kongo prophetism.**
      Wyatt MacGaffey. *History of Religions*, vol. 17, no. 2 (Nov. 1977), p. 177-93. bibliog.
This is a short review of the cultural and spiritual foundations of the messianic and prophetic movements centred in the Bas-Zaire Province. MacGaffey talks about the indigenous belief that the spirits conferred special powers on chosen individuals, supporting the prophetic ideal.

254   **Death and the invisible powers: the world of Kongo belief.**
      Simon Bockie.   Bloomington, Indiana; Indianapolis, Indiana: Indiana University Press, 1993. 157p. bibliog.
A study of the spirituality of the Kongo people, living chiefly in Bas-Zaire (the western part of Zaire), as well as in neighbouring Angola and the Congo (Brazzaville). The author does not deal with the formal religious establishment or belief systems but rather analyses the spiritual universe and cosmology of the Kongo people. Although limited to a small portion of the country, it is an excellent introduction to the religious anthropology of Zaire.

255   **L'Eglise du Christ au Zaïre: formation et adaptation d'un protestantisme en situation de dictature.** (The Church of Christ in Zaire: formation and adaptation of a Protestantism in a situation of dictatorship.)
      Philippe B. Kabongo-Mbaya.   Paris: Karthala, 1992. 467p. maps. bibliog. (Collection Hommes et Sociétés).
This is a very up-to-date study of Protestantism in Zaire. It includes a history of the non-Catholic Christian missionaries during the colonial period, when there was official government discouragement of their efforts. The major focus of the work is the post-independence state of the Protestant churches, their nature and institutional structure, and their relationship to the dictatorial Mobutu régime, which has endeavoured to impose its ideology and political control on most aspects of institutional life in contemporary Zaire.

256 **L'église du prophète Kimbangu: de ses origines à son rôle actuel au Zaïre (1921-1981).** (The Church of the prophet Kimbangu: from its origins to its current rôle in Zaire [1921-1981].)
Susan Asch.   Paris: Karthala, 1983. 342p. map. bibliog. (Collection Hommes et Sociétés).

Asch's serious but highly readable study of Kimbanguism is an objective and comprehensive analysis of the founder, the spontaneous religious movement, and the organizational structure of the Kimbanguist Church. She includes discussion of Kimbangu beliefs, political and social bases, and its regional implantation within Zaire. This is perhaps the most authoritative and thorough study of Kimbanguism.

257 **Eglise et développement: rapport du 3e séminaire national, Kinshasa, 15-22 novembre 1981.** (Church and development: report of the 3rd national seminar, Kinshasa, 15-22 November, 1981.)
Roman Catholic Church. Commission Episcopale pour le Développement.   Kinshasa/Gombe: Commission Episcopale pour le Développement, 1982. 502p.

This work comprises the proceedings of a conference on the Church and development, organized by the Catholic Episcopal Conference of Zaire. There is a wide variety of papers on topics dealing with economic, social, and political issues from a religious, or more specifically Catholic perspective.

258 **L'église zaïroise au service de quelle nation?** (The Zairian church in the service of what nation?)
Rob Buyseniers.   Brussels: Association pour la Formation, la Recherche et l'Information sur le Centre de l'Afrique, 1980. 77p. bibliog. (Cahier AFRICA, no. 2).

Contains chapters on various aspects of Church/State relations in Zaire. The relationship of President Mobutu and the Roman Catholic Church has been rocky; Mobutu Sese Seko has been very sensitive to Catholic criticism of his policies and régime, and he has chafed at the refusal of complete subservience on the part of the Church. The Church, for its part, has followed a policy of withdrawing from any rôle in national politics, protecting its own vital interests and maintaining its independence. The question of the title is unanswered: is there a nation, beyond the Mobutu state structure, which the Church can serve?

259 **Eglises nouvelles et mouvements religieux: l'exemple zaïrois.** (New churches and religious movements: the Zairian example.)
Pius Ngandu Nkashama.   Paris: L'Harmattan, 1990. 257p. (Médiations Religieuses).

The author attempts to capture the beliefs, the customs, and the social and psychological circumstances of the Zairian masses that have given rise to a quest for spiritual fulfilment and a ferment of new religious movements and organizations. Given their neo-colonial character, the established Catholic and Protestant churches have proved incapable of incorporating this native Zairian spiritualism. New churches, springing from entirely spontaneous popular beliefs, have arisen to fill the spiritual aspirations of many Zairians in truly Zairian adaptations of Christianity to local conditions.

260   **English-speaking missions in the Congo Independent State**
       (1879-1908).
       Ruth M. Slade.   Brussels: Académie Royale des Sciences Coloniales,
       1969. 432p. maps. bibliog. (Mémoires in-8o. [Classe des Sciences
       Morales et Politiques], nouv. sér., t. 16).

Ruth Slade's history of English-speaking missions in the early colonial period of Zaire
(1879-1908) is the seminal work on the subject and is cited in many other sources. An
original impetus behind this missionary effort was to dry up the sources of the slave
trade. The first Europeans, slave traders and exploiters of human misery, made the
missionary effort difficult as did the abusive officials of the Congo Free State. The
establishment of stable, law-based government by the Belgians, however, improved
conditions for the English-speaking missionaries.

261   **Face à l'avenir: l'Eglise au Congo belge et au Ruanda-Urundi.**
       (Facing the future: the Church in the Belgian Congo and in
       Ruanda-Urundi.)
       Marie Joseph Lory.   Tournai, Belgium; Paris: Casterman, 1958. 210p.

This work examines the rôle of Christianity (or more specifically Roman Catholicism) in
the social, economic, and political development of Zaire. The style of the narrative is
conversational and epistolary and may appeal to those who prefer a more personalized
account to an objective study. Published in 1958 by a Belgian national, it gives an
interesting and not uncritical perspective of Belgian rule in Zaire from a religious angle.

262   **Histoire du kimbanguisme.** (History of Kimbanguism.)
       Diangienda Kuntima.   Kinshasa: Editions Kimbanguistes, 1984.
       343p. bibliog.

Simon Kimbangu launched his Christian spiritual awakening in 1921. Despite strong
repression by the colonial régime and the long imprisonment of Kimbangu himself, by
1984 this religious movement had grown into a church of five million members, spread
throughout Central Africa beyond the borders of Zaire. Today the Kimbangu Church is
an organized ecclesiastical structure and a member of the World Council of Churches.
Although theologically Christian, Kimbanguism represents an inclusion of African
attitudes, customs, and culture combined with a strong spiritual and human commitment
to the church community. The author of this work is the spiritual head of the Kimbangu
Church, and his account of the history of the movement is that of an insider.

263   **Histoire du protestantisme au Congo.** (History of Protestantism in
       the Congo.)
       E. M. Braekman.   Brussels: Editions de la Librairie des Eclaireurs
       Unionistes, 1961. 391p. bibliog. (Collection Histoire du
       Protestantisme en Belgique et au Congo Belge, vol. 5).

Despite discouragement by Belgian authorities, a large number of Protestant missionary
societies made colonial Zaire their field of activity. This work reviews the evangelization
efforts and history of early Protestant explorers, missionary societies, and individual
denominations during the colonial period. Although very exact and detailed, the study is
weak in presenting a conceptual whole of the religious activities of Zairian
Protestantism. Since the work was published in 1961, readers seeking more up-to-date
information should consult later works.

264   **Indigenization in the African church.**
William H. Crane.   *International Review of Missions*, vol. 53, no. 212
(Oct. 1964), p. 408-22.

Written by a Presbyterian missionary in Africa, this article talks about the need to adapt
Christian practices and rituals to African cultural, psychological, and spiritual realities.
The author also discusses other problems of Christianity in Africa: replacing the
European personnel with Africans; the denominational divisions of the African churches;
and the need for increased financial resources.

265   **Introduction to African religion.**
John S. Mbiti.   Oxford; Portsmouth, New Hampshire: Heinemann
Educational, 1991. 2nd rev. ed. 216p. bibliog.

Although not specifically about Zaire, this work serves as a general introduction to
traditional African religion, which flourished in Zaire before the arrival of the Christian
missionaries. Although the Zairian masses have been profoundly affected by Christian
evangelization, the customs, rites, rituals, and mind-set represent the substratum of
African religion and greatly influence current religious practices in Zaire. The study
examines the cosmology of African religions, the place of man in the religious universe,
the concept of God and spirits, the value of art, myth, and oral tradition in religion,
superstitions, medicine, healing, and the importance of individual rituals, such as
initiation rites. The author acknowledges the inroads of Islam and Christianity within
Africa and estimates that in 1972 only twelve per cent of Africans practised traditional
religions although many times that number are influenced by them.

266   **Jamaa: a charismatic movement in Katanga.**
Johannes Fabian.   Evanston, Illinois: Northwestern University Press,
1971. 284p. bibliog.

This study is the most extensive English work to analyse the origins, development,
doctrines, and beliefs of the Jamaa, a charismatic spiritual movement within the Roman
Catholic Church. The work also includes extensive discussion of the social and cultural
factors that have moulded Jamaa into a dynamic, transforming spiritual force in
contemporary Zaire. Included are original texts, illuminating Jamaa doctrine, in Swahili,
with English translation.

267   **The Jamaa and the Church: a Bantu Catholic movement in Zaire.**
Willy de Craemer.   Oxford: Clarendon Press, 1977. 192p. bibliog.
(Oxford Studies in African Affairs).

Contemporary Zaire has been a birthplace of many cults and religious movements. One
of these, Jamaa, distinguishes itself from the others on several points. Launched by
Flemish missionary-priests in 1953, Jamaa is a charismatic movement of intense spiritual
experience. As with other spiritual movements, it is an adaptation of Christianity to local
social and cultural realities, but unlike other new religious expressions, it has remained
within the organizational framework of the Roman Catholic Church. Jamaa has a strong
regional base in the Shaba and Kasai Provinces, and it is strongly represented among the
educated élite of the most industrially advanced region of Zaire. This work is a highly
objective and analytical account of the history of the Jamaa movement, its beliefs, rites,
rituals, and the sometimes tenuous relationship with the Roman Catholic Church.

268 **Kimbangu, fondateur d'église.** (Kimbangu, church founder.)
Charles-André Gilis. Brussels: Librairie Encyclopédique, 1960.
123p. bibliog.
This is an account of the life and mission of Simon Kimbangu by an author who is very sympathetic to Kimbanguism although he is not a follower. The work covers the rites, rituals, beliefs, and customs of the Kimbanguists.

269 **Kimbanguism at the grass roots.**
André Droogers. *Journal of Religion in Africa*, vol. 11, fasc. 3, 1980, p. 188-211. bibliog.
The rudimentary beliefs and moral attitudes of ordinary Kimbangu believers are studied in this article. This sociological examination of Kimbanguism is an excellent complement to more theological and abstract treatises.

270 **The Kimbanguists and the Bapostolo: a study of two African independent churches in Luluabourg, Congo, in relation to similar churches and in the context of Lulua traditional culture and religion.**
Haldor Eugene Heimer. PhD thesis, Hartford Seminary, Hartford, Connecticut, 1971. 478p. maps. (Available from University Microfilms International, Ann Arbor, Michigan, order no. 7212816).
This PhD dissertation is a study of two Christian movements (Kimbanguism and Bapostolo) in a specific region, Luluabourg (Kananga), Zaire. In investigating these two movements, the author largely covers the history of Christianity in Zaire and many other Christian groups are discussed as well as the social and cultural background of the Zairian people.

271 **Messianic popular movements in the Lower Congo.**
Efraim Andersson. Uppsala, Sweden: Almqvist & Wiksells Boktryckeri, 1958. 287p. bibliog. (Studia Ethnographica Upsaliensia, no. 14).
An important early analysis of the prophetic and messianic popular religious movements that have arisen in the Bas-Zaire region of this Central African nation. The author discusses the cultural and religious environment that gave rise to prophetism, the early efforts of Protestant and Catholic evangelization, and the most outstanding individual and movement of prophetism: Simon Kimbangu and Kimbanguism. The study demonstrates the historical continuity of prophetism with the earlier religious life of the Bas-Zaire.

272 **Mission and state in the Congo: a study of the relations between Protestant missions and the Congo Independent State authorities with special reference to the Equator District, 1885-1903.**
David Lagergren. Uppsala, Sweden: Gleerup, 1970. 365p. maps. bibliog. (Studia Missionalia Upsaliensia, no. 13).

This history of early Protestant missionary efforts in Zaire emphasizes the tenuous relationship between Church and State. Protestant missionaries found much to criticize in the government of Leopold II's Congo Free State, and this often resulted in church/state conflict in the early colonial period. The Belgian régime favoured Catholic missionary efforts, and this also led to conflict with Protestant missionaries. Individual early missionary societies and organizations are discussed but the work is limited to the 19th century.

273 **Modern Kongo prophets: religion in a plural society.**
Wyatt MacGaffey. Bloomington, Indiana: Indiana University Press, 1983. 285p. bibliog. (American Systems of Thought).

Prophetism is not limited to Zaire; it is a popular religious expression in many parts of Africa. Nevertheless, MacGaffey restricts his study of the prophet movement to the Bas-Zaire Province of Zaire, an area occupied by the Kongo people. The most widely recognized figure of prophetism is Simon Kimbangu, who emerged as the first great modern prophet in 1921. Kimbanguism is very strong in Zaire today, and the movement's leaders now head the largest 'independent' church in the country. The author notes that the prophetism of this region from pre-colonial days into the present displays a remarkable degree of continuity with earlier religious patterns, both within the region and in all of Central Africa. The Bas-Zaire is depicted as a pluralistic society, where the formal elements of European institutions and religion flourish alongside the popular customs and religious practices of the masses, which have little formal organization.

274 **Ombres et clairières: histoire de l'implantation de l'Eglise Catholique dans le Diocèse de Sakania, Zaïre (1910-1970).**
(Shadows and clearings: history of the implantation of the Catholic Church in the Diocese of Sakania, Zaire [1910-1970].)
Léon Verbeek. Rome: LAS, 1987. 422p. bibliog. (Studi [Istituto Storico Salesiano], no. 4).

This work traces the history of Roman Catholicism in a single diocese of Shaba Province, Zaire, from its beginnings until 1970. Although limited to a single region, the study may be generalized to represent the evangelization experience throughout Zaire. In conjunction with Church history, much is said about the social, economic, and spiritual conditions of the region.

275 **Out of Africa: Kimbanguism.**
Joseph Diangienda. London: Christian Education Movement, 1979. 66p. (CEM Student Theology Series).

Kimbanguism, the prophetic movement that has become one of the three major church groupings in Zaire, is treated comprehensively in this brief account of its history, rituals, and beliefs. The point of view is very sympathetic to the Kimbangu Church.

276　The political role of Christian missions in the Belgian Congo, 1908-1960.
Marvin D. Markowitz.　PhD thesis, Columbia University, New York, 1968. 515p. bibliog. (Available from University Microfilms International, Ann Arbor, Michigan, order no. 6909205).
This PhD dissertation contains much of the same information included in the author's work entitled: *Cross and sword* (q.v.), and it is easily obtainable through University Microfilms International. In this work the author enters into greater detail about the political relationship between organized religion (Catholicism, Protestantism, and Kimbanguism) and the state. At the beginning of the colonial period, the state, the Church, and the great capitalist interests were considered the 'trinity', the three great supports of the colonial régime. The author notes the radical change in the church/state relationship in the late colonial period as the state tries to free itself from its alliance with the missions.

277　Prophetic Christianity in the Congo: the Church of Christ on Earth through the prophet Simon Kimbangu.
Marie-Louise Martin.　Braamfontein, South Africa; Johannesburg: Christian Institute of Southern Africa, 1968. 40p. bibliog.
This short work traces the life of Simon Kimbangu and his religious teachings and mission. It continues with the history of his movement and the structure of the Kimbanguist Church. The beliefs, rituals, and practices are discussed as well as the political and social stance of the Church. Several documents outlining some key elements of Kimbanguism are included. The analysis is objective and, though brief, the coverage is quite comprehensive.

278　Religion and society in Central Africa: the BaKongo of Lower Zaire.
Wyatt MacGaffey.　Chicago: University of Chicago Press, 1986. 295p. map. bibliog.
In an earlier work, *Modern Kongo Prophets*, (1983) (q.v.), the author analyses the Kimbangu religious movement. In this study, MacGaffey delves into the social, spiritual and ethnic basis of popular religious expression of the Kongo people. Although the focus is on an individual ethnic group, much of MacGaffey's conclusions can be generalized to apply to all of Central Africa. He endeavours to describe the cosmology, the spiritual universe of the masses, which forms the basis of the prophetic phenomenon in Africa today.

279 **Religions et développement social: les sectes aujourd'hui: actes du Troisième Week-end Moral des Intellectuels Chrétiens de Matadi du 6 au 10 mars 1993.** (Religions and social development: the sects today: proceedings of the Third Moral Week-end of Christian Intellectuals of Matadi from March 6 to 10, 1993.)
Catholic Church. Archdiocese of Matadi (Zaire). Commission des Intellectuels Catholiques de Matadi. Matadi, Zaire: Evêché de Matadi, 1993. 157p. bibliog. (Etudes du Laïcat Chrétien, no. 3).

These are the proceedings of a recent conference on the themes of religion, national economic development, and the religious sects which flourish in Zaire today. There are also papers on Christian (Roman Catholic) spirituality, mysticism, and the past and present evangelization of Zaire. Despite the sponsorship by an individual diocese, the scope of the conference is truly national.

280 **Simon Kimbangu, prophète et martyr zaïrois.** (Simon Kimbangu, Zairian prophet and martyr.)
Martial Sinda. Paris: ABC; Dakar; Abidjan: NEA, 1977. 111p. map. bibliog. (Grandes Figures Africaines).

Simon Kimbangu was the most important religious figure in 20th-century Zaire and this work is a devotional biography of his life. The objective of the biography is to illuminate the life's mission and beliefs of Kimbangu as an inspirational message to the reader.

281 **A socio-religious and political analysis of the Judeo-Christian concept of prophetism and modern Bakongo and Zulu African prophet movements.**
Samuel S. Simbandumwe. Lewiston, New York; Queenston, Ontario; Lampeter, Wales: Mellen, 1992. 434p. bibliog.

Analyses the social and religious bases of prophetic teaching, which have given rise to numerous messianic religious movements throughout Africa. The study is limited to two ethnic groups: the Zulus in Southern Africa; and the Kongo people in Western Zaire and the neighbouring countries. There is an extensive examination of Kimbanguism, and it is placed in the context of other prophetic and charismatic movements.

282 **A truly African Church.**
Salvatore Coppo. Eldoret, Kenya: Gaba Publications, AMECEA, 1987. 32p. bibliog. (Spearhead, no. 99).

The mission and ministry of the Roman Catholic Church in Zaire are discussed in this short work. Given the endemic shortage of priests in all of Africa, increasing involvement of the laity, particularly at the parish level, is necessary to strengthen the ecclesiastical structure and carry on the mission of spreading the faith. This book discusses the implementation of programmes to increase lay participation and to co-ordinate their efforts with the clergy and the hierarchy.

Garenganze, or, Seven years' pioneer mission work in Central Africa.
See item no. 21.

Pioneering on the Congo.
See item no. 29.

Dreams among the Yansi.
See item no. 182.

Luba religion and magic in custom and belief.
See item no. 196.

Eglise et éducation: histoire de l'enseignement protestant au Zaïre, 1878-1978.
See item no. 607.

Chants de cultes du Zaïre: chants et possession dans les cultes du Butembo et des Mikendi chez les Bahemba et les Baluba: essai d'étude ethnolinguistique.
See item no. 735.

Social Conditions

283 **African peasants in the totalitarian colonial society of the Belgian Congo.**
Bogumil Jewsiewicki. In: *Peasants in Africa: historical and contemporary perspectives.* Edited by Martin A. Klein. Beverly Hills, California; London: Sage Publications, 1980, p. 45-75. (Sage Series on African Modernization and Development, vol. 4).
Analyses the evolution of Congolese peasants under the regimental and paternalistic colonial policies established by the Belgians.

284 **Analyses Sociales.** (Social Analyses.)
Kinshasa: Laboratoire d'Analyses Sociales de Kinshasa, 1984- . bimonthly.
This publication considers, analyses, and offers solutions to social problems in Zairian society from a scientific point of view. It is the official journal of the Laboratoire d'Analyses Sociales de Kinshasa.

285 **Class relations in a dependent economy: businessmen and businesswomen in Kisangani, Zaire.**
Janet MacGaffey. PhD thesis, Bryn Mawr College, Bryn Mawr, Pennsylvania, 1981. 328p. map. bibliog. (Available from University Microfilms, Ann Arbor, Michigan, order no. 82-02570).
A study of the patterns of stratification of social groups in Kisangani during the post-colonial period. Specifically, the author explains the rise of a small middle class of both male and female entrepreneurs, all of whom are business owners and some of whom are investors in productive property and real estate. What is notable about the members of this class is the fact that they do not necessarily owe their achievements to political connections.

286 **Food crisis and agrarian change in the Eastern Highlands of Zaire.**
Brooke Grundfest Schoepf, Claude Schoepf. *Urban Anthropology and Studies of Cultural Systems and World Economic Development*, vol. 16, no. 1 (Spring 1987), p. 5-37.
This study relates how, in three different areas in Zaire, institutions such as marketing boards, and co-operatives, plus the local social organization, affect the efforts of men and women to produce and market food crops. In addition, their impact on rural agricultural development, women's income, and family nutrition is examined. The study concludes that women's status and access to resources in society and community directly relate to their ability to reap the benefits from increased agricultural production.

287 **The free women of Kinshasa: prostitution in a city in Zaire.**
Jean S. La Fontaine. In: *Choice and change: essays in honour of Lucy Mair*. Edited by J. Davis. London: Athlone; New York: Humanities Press, 1974, p. 89-113. bibliog. (Monographs on Social Anthropology, no. 50).
An ethnographic study of prostitution as it existed in Zaire's capital city between 1962 and 1963. The author discusses the social and economic conditions that caused women to become one of three different classes of prostitute: *femmes libres* (free women), *chambres d'hotel* (hotel room prostitutes), or *vedettes* (film star prostitutes). She describes the different lives they led, plus Zairian attitudes toward prostitutes and prostitution.

288 **Freire's concept of critical consciousness and social structure in rural Zaire.**
David Merrill Ewert. PhD thesis, University of Wisconsin-Madison, 1977. 317p. maps. bibliog. (Available from University Microfilms, Ann Arbor, Michigan, order no. 77-23707).
This dissertation considers Brazilian adult educator Paulo Freire's concept of critical consciousness, in which he suggests that through critical thinking people can change perceptions about themselves and, in turn, their lives. The author examines the applicability of Freire's theory to a rural Zairian community, and analyses the extent to which the people there perceive their problems as a function of social structure.

289 **God and man in Zaire.**
Hesh Kestin. *Forbes*, vol. 136 (Nov. 18, 1985), p. 100-110.
Discusses the horrific social and economic situation in Zaire, presided over by a corrupt president who has amassed a personal fortune that possibly exceeds four billion dollars. A sidebar features short interviews with President Mobutu and a former close political advisor, now living in voluntary exile, on such topics as political corruption and foreign investment in Zaire.

290 **"I'm sick ... I'm coming": illness among Zairian élite women.**
Ruth Kornfield. East Lansing, Michigan: Michigan State University,
1985. 15p. bibliog. (Working Paper, no. 101).
In this paper Kornfield analyses three case studies of illness episodes among urban élite
Zairian women, and how their social networks, based on friendship, offer the support to
the sick person that the kin networks do in rural Zaire.

291 **Naître et mourir au Zaïre: un demi-siècle d'histoire au quotidien.**
(Birth and death in Zaire: a half-century of history in daily life.)
Bogumil Jewsiewicki, with the collaboration of Elikia M'Bokolo,
Ndaywel 'e Nziem, Sabakinu Kivilu. Paris: Editions Karthala, 1993.
253p. bibliog. (Afriques).
Obtaining source material on daily life in Zaire which is not usually available to
researchers was the aim of the project undertaken by the editor, the results of which are
presented in this book. Chosen from a large collection of interviews, gathered as part of
this project, it is a compilation of life histories, introduced by Elikia M'Bokolo, of eight
ordinary Zairians, one claiming to be born around 1880, the others between 1920 and
1932. The fact that these people are 'ordinary' is what makes this work particularly
interesting and noteworthy.

292 **The native problem in Africa.**
Raymond Leslie Buell. London: Archon Books, 1965. 1,101p.
2 vols.
This book is a report based upon the author's fifteen-month-long investigation, in
French, British, and Belgian colonies and Liberia during 1925-26, of 'the problems
which have arisen out of the impact of primitive peoples with an industrial civilization'.
It constitutes a somewhat racist look at native peoples, race relations, and the effects of
colonization in the above-mentioned areas but it includes a wealth of information on the
Belgian Congo.

293 **Older persons and their families in a changing village society: a
perspective from Zaire.**
Masamba ma Mpolo. Washington, DC: International Federation on
Ageing; Geneva: World Council of Churches, Office of Family
Education, 1984. 49p. maps. bibliog.
In the words of the author, this work presents 'a microcosm of those who still live and
grow old in remote and unknown villages around the world'. It uses biographical case
studies and data to illuminate how the elderly and their families, living in a Zairian
village, attempt to cope with social and cultural changes resulting from such phenonema
as widespread urbanization and migration.

294 **The policy of national integration in Zaire.**
Wyatt MacGaffey. *Journal of Modern African Studies*, vol. 20, no. 1
(March 1982), p. 87-105.
Discusses the policy of 'national integration,' which refers to the suppression of social
pluralism, or, *le régime dualiste* (the dualist régime), a legacy of Belgian colonial rule.

National integration was intended to abolish, in four domains, the uncomfortable condition whereby the lives of Zairians were regulated by both statutory and customary rules in four areas: marriage and inheritance; the legal system; administration; and access to land.

295   **The role of women in rural Zaire and Upper Volta: improving methods of skill acquisition.**
David A. Mitchnik.   Geneva: International Labour Organisation, 1977. 36p.
Mitchnik discusses the intertwining social and economic patterns of work and production in rural families, which affect the rôle and status of women. He argues how women in these two countries need access to greater opportunities and income through skill acquisition, which is limited because of both men and womens' attitudes and the structure of training and rural development policies.

296   **Social action in the Belgian Congo and Ruanda-Urundi.**
Centre d'Information et de Documentation du Congo Belge et du Ruanda-Urundi.   New York: Belgian Government Information Center, 1954. 128p.
A review of social conditions, social policy and public welfare in post-Second World War Belgian Africa.

297   **Social classes in Zaire today.**
T. K. Biaya, Omasombo Tshonda.   In: *Zaire, what destiny?*   Edited by Kankwenda Mbaya.   Dakar: CODESRIA, 1993, p. 97-127. (Codesria Book Series).
An overview of Zaire's social classes and the environment in which they exist. The authors focus on social stratification in Zairian society, and consider the use of state power in the light of Zairian social dynamics.

298   **Social structure, women's status and sex differential nutrition in the Zairian Copperbelt.**
Brooke Grundfest Schoepf.   *Urban Anthropology and Studies of Cultural Systems and World Economic Development*, vol. 16, no. 1 (Spring 1987), p. 73-102.
Examines how the high social value of women among the Lemba of the Shaba region is linked to greater nutritional equality among men and women than among other ethnic groups nearby that have a different social organization and lower status of women. The article also considers how changing social relations cast doubt upon continued community equality and the elevated status of women in Lemba culture.

299   **The sociology of black Africa.**
Georges Balandier.   London: André Deutsch, 1970. 540p. maps. bibliog.
A translation of the author's *Sociologie Actuelle de l'Afrique Noire* (Paris: Presses Universitaires de France, 1963), this work compares Kongo and Fang society as they

developed and faced situations arising first from a slave economy, then colonialism, and finally decolonization.

300 **The story of a Congo victim.**
Bokwala, a Congo resident, with a preface by H. Grattan Guinness.
London: Religious Tract Society, 1910. 124p.
In a direct and simple style, Bokwala, a Congolese native and victim of forced labour under Belgian rule, tells of his early life before Europeans came to the country and how their arrival profoundly changed life and society in his village.

301 **Value conflict and development: the struggle of the professional Zairian woman.**
Terri F. Gould.   *Journal of Modern African Studies*, vol. 16, no. 1 (March 1978), p. 133-39.
Discusses how Zairian women struggle, in their consciousness and their everyday lives, with attitudes toward work, marriage, motherhood, and the extended family.

302 **La vie des belges au Congo.** (Belgian life in the Congo.)
Jean-Louis Gillot.   Brussels: D. Van Eeckhoudt, 1983. 228p. maps.
Arranged by province, this album constitutes a photographic record of Belgian life in Zaire during the colonial period. Most images date from the 1950s, and include homes, churches, schools, hospitals, administrative and industrial installations, patriotic and sporting events, visits of VIPs, and other events.

Zaire.
See item no. 10.

Zaïre-Afrique.
See item no. 11.

Zaire, what destiny?
See item no. 14.

Decline or recovery in Zaire?
See item no. 145.

The emerging physician: a sociological approach to the development of a Congolese medical profession.
See item no. 308.

Le Congo de la colonisation belge à l'indépendance.
See item no. 333.

Les origines sociales du sous-développement politique au Congo belge: 'de padroado à la loi fondamentale,' 1482-1960.
See item no. 354.

1er plan quinquennal de développement économique et social, 1986-1990.
See item no. 464.

Reinventing the past and circumscribing the future: authenticité and the negative image of women's work in Zaire.
See item no. 549.

La condition de la femme à travers la musique zaïroise moderne de 1964 à 1984.
See item no. 703.

Health and Medicine

303 **Child health in the tropics: a practical handbook for health personnel.**
Edited by D. B. Jelliffe.   Baltimore: Edward Arnold, 1985. 5th ed. 290p. bibliog.

An introduction to the main aspects of child health – clinical, social, and preventive – as seen mostly in tropical areas such as Zaire. Designed to be used by medical and paramedical personnel, especially those responsible for instructing and training primary health care service workers, this edition has been revised to include newer ideas and developments in medicine. Authorship has been broadened to include experts from around the world to increase the book's international perspective.

304 **The colonial disease: sleeping sickness in the social history of northern Zaire, 1903-1930.**
Maryinez Lyons.   PhD thesis, University of California, Los Angeles, 1987. 467p. maps. bibliog. (Available from University Microfilms, Ann Arbor, Michigan, order no. 87-19966).

The disruption and dislocation of the Zairian people during the Belgian colonial conquest led to the outbreak of epidemics of sleeping sickness and this is examined here. Also considered are the responses of both Europeans and Africans to the ravages of the disease, and how their concepts of health, disease and medicine conflicted.

305 **Disease and illness among Cokwe: an ethnomedical perspective.**
Paul Stanley Yoder.   PhD thesis, University of California, Los Angeles, Los Angeles, California, 1981. 343p. maps. bibliog. (Available from University Microfilms, Ann Arbor, Michigan, order no. 82-06092).

Discusses, within the framework of Cokwe medical theory, how the Cokwe people respond to specific episodes of illness. The structure and content of their ethnomedical system is revealed, which includes the use of herbal medicines, cleansing rituals organized by healers, and visits to biomedical practitioners.

306   **The ecology of malnutrition in middle Africa: Ghana, Nigeria, Republic of the Congo, Rwanda, Burundi and the former French Equatorial Africa.**
Jacques M. May.   New York: Hafner Publishing, 1965. 255p. maps. bibliog. (Studies in Medical Geography, vol. 5).
A detailed analysis of food production and consumption, diet, and malnutrition in countries of equatorial Africa, including Zaire. This book also touches upon the problems associated with the change from a subsistence-level way-of-life to a money economy in which mechanical technology is dominant.

307   **The economic impact on families of children with AIDS in Kinshasa, Zaire.**
Farzin Davachi, Paola Baudoux, Ndoko Kabote, B. N'Galy, Jonathan Mann.   In: *The global impact of AIDS: proceedings of the First International Conference on the Global Impact of AIDS.*   Edited by Alan F. Fleming.   New York: Alan R. Liss, 1988, p. 167-69.
The authors present the results of a study of thirty-three families of children with AIDS, undertaken in order to determine the economic impact of the disease on these families, plus their employers and the State. The impact is indeed severe, especially on the family, not only because of the cost of treatment but because of the dictates of African funerary traditions.

308   **The emerging physician: a sociological approach to the development of a Congolese medical profession.**
Willy De Craemer, Renee C. Fox.   Stanford, California: Stanford University, Hoover Institution on War, Revolution and Peace, 1968. 99p. bibliog. (Hoover Institution Studies, no. 19).
This essay is an in-depth study of Zairian medical students who have become or were studying to become physicians and how their professional careers were shaped by historical events and social processes. The study analyses such aspects as: why the students became interested in medicine; their training, problems, satisfactions, and achievements; how the students felt about their country's struggle to become independent; the conditions under which they practiced medicine and how they felt about them. According to the authors, this book can be described as 'one of the few attempts to analyse sociologically an important subgroup of an emerging professional class in a contemporary African society'.

309   **Finding the causes of child malnutrition: a community handbook.**
Judith E. Brown, Richard C. Brown.   Mayombe, Zaire: Bureau of Study and Research for the Promotion of Health, 1984. 2nd ed. 87p.
Those who wish to solve the problem of protein-energy malnutrition in young children in their own communities should consult this handbook. It offers guidance on obtaining answers to the following questions: how should community malnutrition be measured; what food problems exist in your community; what problems should be attacked?

Information is also provided on how to establish community centres to deal with malnutrition prevention and those children already affected by this condition. The authors were previously involved in health and nutrition projects in Zaire and elsewhere in Africa.

310 **Health in Belgian Africa.**
Belgium. Ministère des Affaires Africaines. Groupe Hygiène et Santé.
Brussels: INFOR CONGO, 1958. 78p. bibliog.

Contains information and statistics on the organization of the medical system in late 1950s Zaire which, at the time, was one of the most extensive health care systems in Africa. A discussion of the medical system in Burundi and Rwanda is also included and a final section considers the major public health problems of the three countries.

311 **HIVs and AIDS in Central Africa.**
Helene D. Gayle, William L. Heyward, Nzilambi Nzila.   In: *AIDS in Africa*.   Edited by Max Essex, Souleymane Mboup, Phyllis J. Kanki, Mbowa R. Kalengayi.   New York: Raven Press, 1994, p. 651-67.

This chapter summarizes the incidence, distribution and control of the HIV epidemic in Zaire and the other countries of Central Africa. National programmes for the prevention and control of HIV and AIDS are briefly described as well.

312 **In the shade of an acacia tree: memoirs of a health officer in Africa, 1945-1959.**
Frank L. Lambrecht.   Philadelphia: American Philosophical Society, 1991. 418p. (Memoirs of the American Philosophical Society, vol. 194).

Lambrecht, a Welsh health officer who became a noted expert on the tsetse fly and trypanosomiasis, was employed by the Belgian government in what is now Zaire, Rwanda, and Burundi. Drawing heavily on his diaries and letters, his memoirs document Belgian colonial life during the years immediately after the Second World War to just prior to independence. Also of value are his descriptions of health conditions in the area, as well as the extensive material on the tsetse fly and trypanosomiasis. His thoughts are certainly presented from the colonial perspective and at times they are somewhat racist and paternalistic, but he and his wife, Dora, are to be commended for their efforts to improve public health in Belgian Africa.

313 **An inquiry into the effects of health policy on health underdevelopment in Zaire: problems and prospects for change.**
Tshiabukole Mukendi.   PhD thesis, University of Pittsburgh, Pittsburgh, Pennsylvania, 1986. 289p. bibliog. (Available from University Microfilms, Ann Arbor, Michigan, order no. 74-16828).

This study asserts that the bureaucratic and institutional nature of Zairian health policy, and not a scarcity of resources, is the primary impediment to an improvement of infant morbidity and mortality in Zaire. It demonstrates that structural factors in society are projected into the area of health care, with the result being a series of misdirected priorities, mismanagement of the few resources available in the interest of a small segment of the population, and a gap between community health needs and the allocation and organization of health care resources.

314   **Kasongo: child mortality and growth in a small African town.**
Wim Van Lerberghe.   London: Smith-Gordon, 1989. 159p. bibliog.
(Monographs on Human Growth, no. 1).
Presents the findings of a community survey, carried out between 1974 and 1977, in
which mortality levels and causes in 6,228 children were considered for an average
period of more than eighteen months.

315   **Médecine et hygiène en Afrique centrale de 1885 à nos jours.**
(Medicine and hygiene in Central Africa from 1885 to the present.)
Edited by P. G. Janssens, M. Kivits, J. Vuylsteke.   Brussels:
Fondation Roi Baudouin, 1992. 2 vols. maps. bibliog.
Consisting of separate contributions by forty-eight specialists and experts, this is a
comprehensive synthesis of the knowledge gained, work accomplished, and foundation
laid in the field of medicine in Central Africa by Belgium, both past and present.
Although Rwanda and Burundi are discussed, the primary focus is on Zaire. Chapters are
arranged under four subheadings: context, organization, and research; sanitary problems,
specific means of fighting illness and disease, and prevention; urban afflictions and
maladies of tropical regions; and tropical ailments. Bibliographical references are
generous and can be found at the end of each chapter.

316   **Nutrition and the fertility of younger women in Kinshasa, Zaire.**
Barbara A. Anderson, James L. McCabe.   *Journal of Development
Economics*, vol. 4 (1977), p. 343-63.
This paper examines the relationship between nutrition and fertility in Zaire, which
suffers from substantial malnutrition. Specifically, it is an analysis of individual
household data gathered in Kinshasa, which indicates a significant positive link between
fertility and purchased calories per adult equivalent, among those households with no
child deaths to wives aged between twenty and twenty-four.

317   **Onchocerciasis in Zaire: a new approach to the problem of river
blindness.**
Edited by F. C. Rodger.   Oxford; New York: Pergamon Press, 1977.
195p. map. bibliog.
Presents the results of an intensive study, carried out by a team of doctors and scientists,
on people of the Kasai region harbouring the onchocerciasis-causing parasite. The object
of the study was to examine each subject closely and determine what factors
(socio-economic and nutritional for example) contributed to the incidence of the disease.

318   **The quest for therapy in Lower Zaire.**
John M. Janzen, with the collaboration of William Arkinstall.
Berkeley; Los Angeles; London: University of California Press, 1978.
266p. maps. bibliog.
Janzen describes a regional medical system that exists among the Kongo in Lower Zaire.
Patients are administered a combination of traditional and Western medical techniques
and practices as their health care providers determine illnesses, choose therapies and
evaluate treatments, a process long-familiar to Central Africans and known as 'therapy
management'.

319   **Revue de Médecines et Pharmacopées Africaines.** (Review of
      African Medicine and Pharmacology.)
      Eysines, France: ACCT, GRIPT, 1987- . semi-annual.

Intended to serve as a link between specialists and the francophone world, this periodical frequently contains articles about traditional medicine and pharmacology as these topics relate to Zaire. Its title has changed; from 1987-90 it was called *Médecine Traditionnelle et Pharmacopée;* the present title dates from vol. 5, no. 1 (1991).

320   **The sustainability of U.S.-supported health, population, and
      nutrition programs in Zaire: 1972-1988.**
      Nancy B. Mock, Thomas Bossert, Miatudila Milanga.   Washington,
      DC: US Agency for International Development, 1990. [58p.] bibliog.
      (AID Evaluation Occasional Paper, no. 38).

This report is part of a series of studies implemented by the Agency for International Development's Center for Development Information and Evaluation (CDIE), which were designed to assess sustainability of health development assistance programmes in foreign countries after AID financial support ends. Specifically, this work focuses on four projects, dealing with maternal and child health and family planning, health system development, malaria control, and community health-integrated rural development. The characteristics of these projects are evaluated, as are contextual factors that would affect their success and sustainability, including the Zairian economy, political environment, socio-cultural conditions and US Zairian relations.

321   **Techniques for collection and analysis of data on perinatal
      mortality in Kinshasa, Zaire = Techniques de collecte et d'analyse
      de données sur la mortalité périnatale à Kinshasa, Zaïre.**
      D. Nzita Kikhela.   Ottawa: International Development Research
      Centre, 1989. 84p. map. bibliog. (Technical Study, 61e, Infant
      Mortality and Health Studies).

The findings are presented of a study that took place in Kinshasa from 1981 to 1986 to determine how to conduct more accurate research on mortality in the young. Three topics are considered: the gathering of data, creating and/or applying a conceptual framework, and determining which families are at risk.

322   **Traditional medicine in Zaire: present and potential contribution
      to the health services.**
      Ottawa: International Development Research Centre, 1980. 39p.
      (IDRC, 137e).

A report on trends in traditional medicine in Zaire's rural areas, towns, and capital city. Included are suggestions on how traditional medical services could be integrated into the formal health care system.

323   **Women, AIDS, and economic crisis in Central Africa.**
Brooke Grundfest Schoepf. *Canadian Journal of African Studies*,
vol. 22, no. 3 (1988), p. 625-44.
A detailed report on the CONNAISSIDA Project's research on the risks that AIDS
presents for women, and gender perceptions of this disease. The Project, an
interdisciplinary group which began in 1985, was specifically formed to study the social
construction of and response to AIDS in Zaire; Schoepf is its director.

324   **Zaire.**
Karen E. Lashman.   Washington, DC: US Department of Health,
Education, and Welfare, Office of International Health, Division of
Program Analysis, 1975. 178p. bibliog. map. (Syncrisis, the Dynamics
of Health, no. 14) (DHEW Publication, no (OS) 75-50,019).
Lashman provides a detailed picture of the state of health and health care in Zaire in
1974. While every effort was made to be accurate and comprehensive in gathering the
information contained in this book, it must be remembered that in the absence of a
well-developed national data collection system, some of the data synthesized was often
dated, incomplete, or otherwise unreliable. In spite of this shortcoming, the book
presents a generally accurate picture of the problems with health and the delivery of
health care that plagued Zaire in 1974, the same problems which still exist today.

Handbook of African medicinal plants.
See item no. 70.

"I'm sick . . . I'm coming": illness among Zairian élite women.
See item no. 290.

Politics

325 African politics in Congo-Kinshasa to independence.
John Masare.   In: *Aspects of Central African history*.   Edited by
T. O. Ranger.   Evanston, Illinois: Northwestern University Press,
1968, p. 246-72. maps. bibliog. (Third World Histories).

John Masare discusses the popular basis for Zairian politics and nationalism. He traces
Zairian nationalism to the resistance of the people to Belgian rule in various regions and
in diverse manners. Simon Kimbangu, the messianic religious figure who emerged in the
1920s, is named as a nationalist leader. Kimbanguism and other religious sects were the
object of Belgian repression since they were independent organizations and strongly
represented the traditions and aspirations of their people. In a country where direct
political activity was forbidden, many pre-political community or fraternal organizations
arose to fill the void. Masare also analyses the rising discontent among Zairians in the
1950s, which fed the growth of nationalism and the creation of an authentic national
political life for the country.

326 Agony of the Congo.
Ritchie Calder.   London: V. Gollancz, 1961. 160p. maps.

This work is dated (1961), but it tells in a very urgent, compelling fashion of the political
crisis of decolonization in Zaire, treating: the Zairian state under Belgian rule; the
gathering political crisis; the panic abandonment of Zaire by the Belgians; the
governmental and political reorganization of the independent state; and the UN
intervention. This is a brief recounting of this troubled period by an author who himself
witnessed the events.

327 **L'appareil gouvernemental du Zaïre (1960-1987): des
restructurations pour quelles finalités?** (The government apparatus
of Zaire [1960-1987]: restructuring for what ends?)
Nkuku Khonde, Meso Ma-Bisudia. *Enquêtes d'Histoire Zaïroise*,
vol. 9 no. 1 (1989), p. 34-54.

The authors examine in detail the structure of government represented in the various
ministries. The analysis begins in late colonial times and proceeds through the divided
authority structure of government under the First Republic to the 'monocratic executive'
of the Second Republic, gathering all the powers in the hands of the President, Mobutu
Sese Seko. The authors remark upon the frequent 'cabinet reshufflings', which are often
accompanied by changes in the institutional structure of the government. Far from
depicting government instability, these surface changes do not affect the exercise of
Presidential authority. A system of sub-cabinet level bureaus, many of them
interministerial, assures the normal workings of the government. This article provides an
overall conceptual structure of the upper level of government in Zaire, which could be
very helpful for diplomats or private individuals who must deal directly with these
various ministries.

328 **L'ascension de Mobutu: du Sergent Désiré Joseph au Général Sese
Seko.** (The rise of Mobutu: from Sergeant Désiré Joseph to General
Sese Seko.)
Jules Chomé. Paris: Maspéro, 1979. New enlarged ed. 202p. bibliog.
(Petite Collection Maspéro, no. 224).

Jules Chomé paints the picture of the political repression of the late colonial period, the
unconscionable lack of preparation by the Belgians for Zairian independence and their
sabotage of the new state. The chaos and the political void created by the Belgians set
the stage for the rise of a strongman, who could bring some order to this turbulent land.
Describing the origins and early career of Joseph Désiré Mobutu, the author studies the
personality and the political ruthlessness that allowed this one-time army sergeant to rise
to supreme power in Zaire and maintain himself at the helm. Mobutu eliminates his
political rivals: first Lumumba, then Kasavubu and Mulele. Then, with the support of
foreign powers, he assures the establishment of his neo-colonial dictatorship. The story
of his rise is clearly and analytically presented in this work, which was forbidden in
France by the Minister of the Interior and caused great consternation in the author's
native Belgium, where authorities took measures to prevent its wide distribution.

329 **L'automne d'un despotisme: pouvoir, argent et obéissance dans le
Zaïre des années quatre-vingt.** (Autumn of a despotism: power,
money and loyalty in the Zaire of the 1980s.)
Jean-Claude Willame. Paris: Editions Karthala, 1992. 226p. map.
bibliog. (Les Afriques).

Willame has written extensively on Zaire and in this recently published work, he traces
the decline of the autocratic state of Mobutu Sese Seko. He focuses upon the Mobutu
régime, the political opposition, and the national decline under Mobutu and also writes
about the economic conditions of Zaire under Mobutu.

330   **The Belgian Congo.**
Ruth M. Slade, with an additional chapter by Marjory Taylor.
London; New York: Oxford University Press, 1961. 2nd ed. 82p.
maps.

Ruth Slade depicts the political world of the Belgian Congo: paternalism; isolation from
the rest of Africa; the Catholic missions; and the class of *évolués*, the European-educated
African élite. She describes the Belgian solution to the colonial impasse – of reforms and
the inclusion of the *évolués* in the colonial system of government. As independence
approached, the whole institutional system of the Belgians cracked and precipitously
disintegrated. The author gives a well-rounded view of politics, social conditions, and
public attitudes in the crucial years before and after independence.

331   **Belgian rule in the Congo and the aspirations of the 'évolué' class.**
Roger Anstey.   In: *Colonialism in Africa, 1870-1960*.   Edited by
Lewis H. Gann, Peter Duignan.   London: Cambridge University
Press, 1970, vol. 2, p. 194-225. map. bibliog. (Hoover Institution
Publications).

Anstey defines the development and evolution of the Zairian élite or *évolués* under
Belgian colonial rule. It is a predominantly male population, living outside of the village
and the sway of custom. He notes that their education was European; anyone with a
post-secondary education would be considered *évolué*. For the most part, they lived in
towns and cities and occupied white-collar positions. Having defined this élite group,
Anstey chronicles their political awakening in the late colonial period, which could be
termed the birth of Zairian political life. The fact that, following independence, the
évolués continued to identify with European culture and to desire association with
Belgium – and with other Western powers as well – speaks much for the political and
foreign policy orientation of the Zairian state.

332   **Class struggles and national liberation in Africa: essays on the
political economy of neocolonialism.**
Nzongola-Ntalaja.   Zyangue, Zaire; Roxbury, Massachusetts:
Omenana, 1982. 125p. bibliog.

This is a series of essays by Nzongola-Ntalaja on the theme of national liberation. The
author's intention is to develop Marxist themes of neo-colonial economic relationships,
class struggle, and freedom from economic exploitation in the Third World context. The
essays apply generally to all of Africa but more specifically to Zaire where the author
analyses the nature of the post-colonial state.

333   **Le Congo de la colonisation belge à l'indépendance.** (The Congo
from Belgian colonization to independence.)
Auguste Maurel.   Paris: L'Harmattan, 1992. 352p. (Collection Zaïre
– Histoire et Société).

A re-edition of a work originally published in 1962, this analysis of the political,
economic, and social conditions in Zaire under Belgian rule and into early independence
remains an authority for that period. The history of the political crisis leading up to
independence and the ferment of political parties, ideologies, and major political figures
is particularly well reported.

334 **Congo disaster.**
Colin Legum.   Gloucester, Massachusetts: P. Smith, 1972. 174p.
map.

The author's stated purpose is to provide the political background to the Congo crisis. He analyses Belgian colonization and describes the political structure, which they established in Zaire. The political hesitations of the Belgians are described in detail and the sudden collapse of their authority with the mass defection of the *évolués*, the European-educated African élite. This turbulent period witnessed the birth of truly Zairian politics, which is discussed in this work along with the major public figures in the new state.

335 **Congo, my country.**
Patrice Lumumba, foreword by Colin Legum, translated from French.
New York: Praeger, 1966. 195p. (Books that Matter).

In the lengthy foreword, Colin Legum traces the mercurial career of Zaire's first great national political figure, Patrice Lumumba, who led the country to independence and later perished in the ensuing political chaos and violence. The work includes a number of texts by Lumumba, written prior to independence, which set out the future course of Zairian politics and co-operation with the former Belgian colonial masters. Lumumba's written style should give some impression of the oratory that so moved Zairians to rally to his support. The work was originally published in French in 1961.

336 **Congo political parties revisited.**
Crawford Young.   In: *Footnotes to the Congo story: an Africa report anthology.*   Edited by Helen A. Kitchen.   New York: Walker, 1967, p. 77-84. (Africa Report).

Writing in the early 1960s, Young outlines the leading political formations and parties in the early years of the independent Zairian state. Behind the chaotic scene of political life, the strong administrative structure of Zaire holds the government together.

337 **Congo-Zaïre, 1874-1981: la perception du lointain.** (Congo-Zaire, 1874-1981: view from the distance.)
Bernard Piniau.   Paris: L'Harmattan, 1992. 285p. maps. bibliog.
(Racines du Présent).

The work may be of minimal value to the general user, but it offers special insights into the perception by informed Belgian public opinion, of Zairian politics and government from 1874-1981 as reported in the press. It is, in many instances, a testimony to the shortsightedness and lack of depth of understanding that surrounds the Belgian-Zairian relationship.

338 **Congo (Zaïre), démocratie néo-coloniale ou deuxième indépendance?: actes du Colloque de La Mouvance Progressiste pour la Démocratie au Zaïre, Bruxelles, 18-20 octobre 1991.** (Congo [Zaire], neo-colonialist democracy or second independence?: proceedings of the Progressive Movement for Democracy in Zaire, Brussels, 18-20 October 1981.)
Brussels: Mouvance Progressiste du Congo (Zaïre); Paris: L'Harmattan, 1992. 190p. biblio31g.

This work consists of papers presented at a meeting of the Mouvance Progressiste pour la Démocratie au Zaïre, an opposition political party. The meeting took place in Brussels because organized political opposition to the régime is not tolerated within Zaire. As one might expect, many of the papers express highly critical views of the Mobutu régime, the neo-colonial position of the Zairian economy, and the political repression that now holds sway in Kinshasa. The opposition leaders talk of renewal for Zaire under a democratically based government. The conference acquaints the reader with the names and ideas of many exiled opposition leaders. A change of régime could eventually bring many of these individuals and their views into positions of influence in Zaire.

339 **Le dinosaure: le Zaïre de Mobutu.** (The Dinosaur: the Zaire of Mobutu.)
Colette Braeckman. Paris: Fayard, 1992. 382p. map. bibliog.

Braeckman presents an up-to-date, critical study of the Mobutu régime. She analyses the economic, political, social, and international supports of a régime built on corruption, injustice, and violence. Written by a journalist, the style is lively, engaging, and suited to a general audience.

340 **Du Congo de Lumumba au Zaïre de Mobutu.** (From the Congo of Lumumba to the Zaire of Mobutu.)
Jean Kestergat. Brussels: P. Legrain, 1986. 319p. maps. bibliog.

Jean Kestergat has long studied Zaire, and he has previously published works on Zairian politics and government. In this work, he takes the reader from the Belgian days and decolonization through the turbulent years of early independence into the Mobutu régime. The style and broad coverage are aimed at a general audience.

341 **Les élections sous la Deuxième République.** (Elections under the Second Republic.)
Institut Makanda Kabobi. Kinshasa: Forcad: Institut Makanda Kabobi, 1982. 207p. (Collection Etudes. Série II, Histoire, no. 2).

Published by a branch of the ruling party, the Mouvement Populaire de la Révolution (Popular Movement of the Revolution), the work discusses the constitutional and statutory arrangements for the holding of elections in Zaire under the Second Republic. The formal theoretical organization of the political process is set forth, and many legal texts are included.

342 **Ethnic politics in Zaire.**
Crawford Young.   In: *The politics of cultural pluralism.*   Edited by
Crawford Young.   Madison, Wisconsin: University of Wisconsin
Press, 1976, p. 163-215. map. bibliog.

Zaire is a mosaic of ethnic groups. Many observers of the Zairian political scene do not
sufficiently discuss the influence of ethnic politics in the public life of the country but
Young analyses the multiple influences of ethnic divisions within the political and
administrative structure of the state.

343 **Les fleurs du Congo: suivi de commentaires.** (Flowers of the Congo:
followed by commentaries.)
Gérard Althabe.   Paris: Maspéro, 1972. 374p.

Gérard Althabe examines the troubled political history of Zaire from an ideological point
of view. He reconstructs the system of colonial and neo-colonial exploitation of Zaire
under the Belgians and the post-independence governments and talks of the development
of class structure in the newly independent nation that is reflected in the political and
administrative organization of the state. He notes the political resistance on the part of
nationalist politicians and the Zairian masses to the subjugation of their country to this
economic and political control as well as the determination of the régime to maintain the
present situation of impasse through a system of political repression.

344 **Glossaire idéologique du M.P.R.** (Ideological glossary of the M.P.R.)
Mouvement Populaire de la Révolution.   Kinshasa, Zaire: Forcad,
1986. 96p. (Collection ECIVIPO).

The MPR, or Mouvement Populaire de la Révolution (Popular Movement of the
Revolution), has monopolized the political life of Zaire under the Mobutu régime. As the
only legally recognized political party in the country for much of its existence, the MPR
extended its organization and influence throughout this great Central African land mass.
This work is not a history of the party, but a political lexicon, providing explanations for
much of the ideology, corporate bodies, and specialized vocabulary of the MPR. This
handbook is an excellent resource for users requiring detailed, precise information to
orient their investigation into the political life of Zaire.

345 **La grande mystification du Congo-Kinshasa: les crimes de
Mobutu.** (The great mystification of Congo-Kinshasa: the crimes of
Mobutu.)
Cléophas Kamitatu-Massamba.   Paris: Maspéro, 1971. 298p. (Cahiers
Libres, nos. 207-8).

The author began his participation in the political life of his country when this became
possible at the moment of independence. Offering his testimony on the politics of Zaire
as a member of the political élite of his young country, he speaks of the evolution of
Zairian government following independence and writes frankly and critically of the rôle
of Mobutu Sese Seko.

346 **Les grands textes du mobutisme.** (The great texts of Mobutism.)
Mobutu Sese Seko. Kinshasa, Zaire: Forcad: Institut Makanda
Kabobi, 1984. 109p. bibliog. (Collection Bibliothèque de l'Ecole du
Parti).

Les grands textes du mobutisme provides primary sources on the politics and political ideology of Zaire. This political anthology is gathered from the speeches and public statements of President Mobutu, explaining his policies and visions for his country. This is a highly specialized work that will be most useful to those engaged in serious research on the politics and government of Zaire.

347 **L'impact de la coutume sur l'exercice du pouvoir en Afrique
noire: le cas du Zaïre.** (The impact of custom on the exercise of
power in black Africa: the case of Zaire.)
Djelo Empenge-Osako. Ottignies-Louvain-la-Neuve, Belgium: Le
Bel Elan, 1990. 168p. bibliog. (Esprit Libre).

This takes a penetrating look at the impact of customs and traditional attitudes toward power upon the political life of Zaire, where under Mobutu the exercise of power is highly personal. The author also examines the constitutional structure, the nature of the Mobutu régime, and the workings of the Zairian political process.

348 **Lumumba speaks: the speeches and writing of Patrice Lumumba,
1958-1961.**
Patrice Lumumba, edited by Jean van Lierde, translated from the
French by Helen R. Lane, introduction by Jean-Paul Sartre. Boston:
Little, Brown & Co., 1972. 433p. map.

A collection of Patrice Lumumba's speeches and writings, originally published in French as: *La pensée politique de Patrice Lumumba* (1963). This work gathers nearly all of Lumumba's public utterances from December 1958 through January 1961, the date of his death. There is a long (45p.) preface to this collection by Jean-Paul Sartre in which Sartre interprets Lumumba's career and decolonization from an existentialist perspective.

349 **Luttes politiques au Zaïre: le processus de politisation des masses
rurales du Bas-Zaïre.** (Political struggles in Zaire: the process of
politicization of the rural masses of Bas-Zaire.)
Paul Demunter. Paris: Editions Anthropos, 1975. 333p. bibliog.

Under the Belgians the Zairians were totally excluded from government to an extent unparalleled in the rest of Africa, and the isolation enforced on the African population removed Zairians from the political winds of change sweeping the continent in the years following the Second World War. In this work, Demunter describes the process of politicization that occurred in the Bas-Zaire province at the time of independence. The province of Bas-Zaire, where the capital Kinshasa is located, has long been considered the most advanced region of Zaire and the author describes the political awakening in the rural areas of this province as large numbers of people found that they wanted a say in their own governance.

350 **Mobutu et l'argent du Zaïre: les révélations d'un diplomate ex-agent des services secrets.** (Mobutu and Zaire's money: revelations of a diplomat/ex-secret services agent.)
Emmanuel Dungia. Paris: L'Harmattan, 1992. 215p. maps.
Dungia catalogues in great detail the process of the political and economic disintegration of Zaire under the Mobutu régime. He offers insights into the personal tastes and mentality of the president, influencing the high-level decision-making of Zaire. This is a political biography of Mobutu Sese Seko and an analysis of the governing style and decisions that have led to the corruption and economic ruin of the country.

351 **Mobutu or chaos?: the United States and Zaire, 1960-1990.**
Michael G. Schatzberg. Lanham, Maryland: University Press of America; Philadelphia: Foreign Policy Research Institute, 1991. 115p. bibliog.
Michael Schatzberg, a frequent writer on Zaire, presents the political history of the country from independence to the present (1991). The turbulent period of the First Republic is traced in a very succinct first chapter and Schatzberg discusses the Mobutu régime ('The present tyranny') in a chapter on the Second Republic, 1965-90, showing the evolution and decline of the state under the presidential dictatorship. In the third chapter, the author discusses US policy toward Zaire and the linking of US interests with the corrupt Mobutu government. This is a short but cogent summation of Zairian politics and US foreign policy toward the Central African country.

352 **Mort sur le grand fleuve: du Congo au Zaïre: chronique d'une indépendance.** (Death on the great river: from the Congo to Zaire: chronicle of independence.)
Peter Scholl-Latour, translated from German to French by Jean-Claude Capèle. Paris: Presses de la Cité, 1988. 326p. map. (Collection Documents).
Translated from German to French, this study of Zairian political life places Zairian independence aspirations within the context of African nationalism and increasingly strong independence movements throughout the continent. There is a strong focus on the political biography of Patrice Lumumba, following the steps to Zairian independence and the crises which followed, leading to Lumumba's death. The figures of Moïse Tshombe and Mobutu Sese Seko also figure prominently in this work.

353 **Myths and realities of the Zairian crisis.**
Ilunga Kabongo. In: *The crisis in Zaire:myths and realities.* Edited by Nzongola-Ntalaja. Trenton, New Jersey: Africa World Press, 1986, p. 3-25. bibliog.
This work chronicles the politics of independent Zaire under the rubric of 'crisis'. The question is raised: 'Is there still a state in Zaire?' This is a highly critical account of the rôle of Mobutu Sese Seko in Zairian political life.

Politics

354 **Les origines sociales du sous-développement politique au Congo belge: 'de padroado à la loi fondamentale', 1482-1960.** (The social origins of political underdevelopment in the Belgian Congo: 'from padroado to the fundamental law', 1482-1960.)
Zala L. N'kanza. Kinshasa: Presses Universitaires du Zaïre, 1985. 411p. bibliog.
The author has taken a very abstract and theoretical approach to analysing the socio-political structure of Zaire. Beginning in the pre-colonial period, he examines the government of the peoples in the vast region that later became Zaire, looking especially at the Kongo and Portuguese forms of government, as well as the pervasive influence of the Catholic Church. He dwells upon Belgian colonization and the form of government of the colonial state and discusses the transfer of power from the Belgians to the African élite, the *évolués*. At the point of independence, the author notes the weakness of the political parties in their organizational structure and in their representation in all of the provinces of Zaire. The national institutions, which hold the state together, were those of the colonial régime: the army; the administration; and the network of Christian missions. The analysis, however, is not carried into the period of the Mobutu régime.

355 **Patrice Lumumba.**
London: Panaf Books, 1973. 215p. bibliog. (Panaf Great Lives).
A political biography of Patrice Lumumba, which places Zaire's independence leader in the social and ideological context of colonialism, and the exploitation of the Zairian masses by Belgium interests. As a member of the European-educated class of *évolués*, Lumumba and his fellow members of the African élite were trusted by the colonial power to provide a long, slow transition to independence that would protect the Belgian economic and political interests in their country. In the context of colonial Zaire, Lumumba at first accepted this subservient political rôle. Yet as he came more into contact with other African nationalists Lumumba developed the commitment to the Zairian masses to liberate them from the yoke of economic and political exploitation. He died in the struggle for that revolution.

356 **Patrice Lumumba: la crise congolaise revisitée.** (Patrice Lumumba: the Congolese crisis revisited.)
Jean-Claude Willame. Paris: Karthala, 1990. 496p. bibliog. (Les Afriques).
This well-known writer on Zaire has taken up the subject of Patrice Lumumba in this recent publication. In the 1960s, studies on Lumumba and the crisis of Zairian independence abounded. Now, with a critical distance of thirty years from many of these turbulent events, Jean-Claude Willame has revisited the political life of the Zaire of Lumumba in a well-documented and highly readable narrative. This is a work that looks within Zaire for the forces of change and takes into account the international interests and interventions of outside powers and the United Nations.

357 **Patrimonialism and political change in the Congo.**
Jean-Claude Willame. Stanford, California: Stanford University Press, 1972. 223p. bibliog.
This English language work examines the political structure of the Zairian state under the Mobutu régime. Patrimonialism, clientelism, private armies, and a stifling

centralizing state bureaucracy characterize this period in Zairian political life. Willame maintains some optimism about the future political development of Zaire, which is not present in his 1992 French language publication: *L'automne d'un despotisme* (q.v.).

358 Patrons and clients: the role of the military in Zairian politics.

David J. Gould. In: *The performance of soldiers as governors: African politics and the African military.* Edited by Isaac James Mowoe. Washington, DC: University Press of America, 1980, p. 465-511. bibliog.

In a short essay David Gould explains how the Zairian military fits into the class system and patron class political structure of the Zairian state. He analyses the corruption endemic in the military and the state administration, which accompanies the clientelism so prevalent in the political process in Zaire.

359 Political awakening in the Belgian Congo.

René Lemarchand. Berkeley, California: University of California Press, 1964. 357p. maps. bibliog.

Extensive details are provided in this work on the political and administrative life of colonial Zaire and the newly independent Zairian state. The author discusses the political issues of the period, the political and administrative personnel, and the party organization. This is not a recent publication (1964), and the reader will be disappointed if more up-to-date information is expected.

360 Political power and class-formation in Zaire: the 'Zairianization measures', 1973-1975.

Edward Kannyo. PhD thesis, Yale University, New Haven, Connecticut, 1979. 205p. bibliog. (Available from University Microfilms International, Ann Arbor, Michigan, order no. 7926254).

Kannyo's PhD dissertation discusses the emerging structure of a political and administrative class within Zaire in the post-colonial period. This social class, under the rubric of a 'national bourgeoisie', occupies all upper positions within the administrative structure of government and offers the personnel for the political life of the country. The political and economic implications are extensively analysed.

361 Political protest in the Congo: the Parti Solidaire Africain during the independence struggle.

Herbert F. Weiss. Princeton, New Jersey: Princeton University Press, 1967. 326p. bibliog.

Herbert Weiss writes on the birth of politics in Zaire from the perspective of an objective, outside observer of the political scene in Kinshasa. As Belgian authority began to loosen its grip in 1959, Zairians for the first time participated in discussions and negotiations to determine the future of their country. Weiss speaks of the beginnings, organization, and development of political parties and groups at the national and local level in the months that lead up to the first national elections. The time period is limited in scope to the late colonial and early independence period.

362 **Politics and class in Zaire: bureaucracy, business and beer in Lisala.**
Michael G. Schatzberg. New York: Africana Publishing, 1980. 228p. map. bibliog.

A re-write of the author's PhD dissertation, this work is dated and limited in scope to the Lisala region of Zaire. However, its author has become a widely published authority on African politics. His findings create the social and economic backdrop for the polity of Zaire.

363 **Politics of cultural conflict in Zaire and Uganda.**
Crawford Young. [n.p.]: [n.p.], 1973. 9p.

A longtime observer of Zaire, Crawford Young writes extensively on the politics of Zaire, the social and ethnic conditions that form the body politic, and the transition from colonial rule to independence. This short work on Zaire and Uganda examines the ethnic and territorial divisions that underlie the political life of each country. The paper was prepared for a United States State Department sponsored conference, which was never formally published, and the work may be difficult to locate.

364 **La politique en République du Zaïre: 1955-1er semestre 1981.**
(Politics in the Republic of Zaire: 1955-1st semester 1981.)
Françoise Detemmerman, Maria Verhaegen, with the collaboration of Didier Reubens, Marc Meurrens. Brussels: CEDAF, 1982. 174p.
(Bibliographies Analytiques sur l'Afrique Centrale, t. 6).

This annotated bibliography on Zairian political life is yet another issued by the Centre d'Etude et de Documentation Africaines as part of its series of topical bibliographies on Central Africa. Containing 298 entries, it is arranged by individual works, masters' theses, and dissertations. A second volume, containing periodical articles, collections, and documents has yet to be published.

365 **Principes et règles d'organisation des élections libres et démocratiques.** (Principles and rules of the organization of free and democratic elections.)
Marcel Mumba M. Shabane. Kinshasa: Centre d'Etudes pour l'Action Sociale, 1993. 72p. bibliog.

This is a succinct but thorough guide to electoral laws and regulations as well as the governmental organization and administration of elections in Zaire.

366 **Rébellions-révolution au Zaïre, 1963-1965.** (Rebellions-revolution in Zaire, 1963-1965.)
Catherine Coquery-Vidrovitch, Alain Forest, Herbert F. Weiss.
Paris: L'Harmattan, 1987. 2 vols. (Racines du Présent).

Using essays from many contributors, the authors trace the politically and militarily turbulent years that led up to the seizure of power by Mobutu Sese Seko. Although the focus (1963-65) is rather narrow, much of the background of Zairian political life is discussed.

367 **The rise and fall of Moïse Tshombe: a biography.**
Ian Colvin. London: Frewin, 1968. 262p. maps. bibliog.

Moïse Tshombe has played a major rôle in the political life of Zaire. As leader of Katanga (now Shaba) Province, his secession from Zaire in 1960 precipitated the Congo crisis. The darling of the Belgian interests, he was maintained in power with their support for two years. Exiled, he was allowed to return to Zaire, and in July 1964, Zairian President Kasavubu called upon him to form a new government for the country. He was finally expelled from power with Mobutu's military seizure of power in November, 1965. This political biography of one of Zaire's most significant public figures traces the politics and government of the early years of the country's independence.

368 **The rise and fall of Patrice Lumumba: conflict in the Congo.**
Thomas Kanza. London: R. Collings, 1978. 386p.

This is an expanded version of Kanza's 1978 work: *Conflict in the Congo* and it constitutes the political biography of the author. Between the ages of twenty-three and thirty-three, Thomas Kanza occupied positions as an official of the European Economic Community and the newly-formed independent government of Zaire. As special envoy, ambassador, and minister of foreign affairs, Kanza travelled widely and became well acquainted with the major figures in Zairian politics. As a member of Zaire's newly formed political élite, Kanza observed his country's political life and participated in many of the momentous events in Zairian politics. His insights on the people and politics are flavoured with many personal observations.

369 **Spear and scepter: army, police, and politics in tropical Africa.**
Ernest W. Lefever. Washington, DC: Brookings Institution, 1970. 251p. maps. bibliog.

Lefever's study includes the problems of state formation, stability, and politics in the whole of Sub-Saharan Africa. The author points to the 'precipitous shift of sovereignty from governments in London, Paris, and Brussels to inexperienced African régimes' (p. ix), thrusting political leadership upon those who had at most a brief apprenticeship of political responsibility. The lack of internal cohesion of the regions that were suddenly, with the stroke of a pen, formally transformed into nation states did not help the situation. Lefever devotes a chapter of his work to Zaire (p. 81-131), which he begins with a quote from Mobutu Sese Seko: 'Though there is political discontinuity in the Congo, there must be military continuity' – an altogether fitting statement from a general who seized supreme power in a military coup and has maintained his régime with the firm support of the army. The author gives the history and structure of the Zairian military and police and follows its evolution through the stormy days of early independence. Writing in 1970, Lefever concedes the positive aspects of the political stability brought to Zaire by the strong-armed Mobutu régime but cautions that in terms of broad participation in the political process, the country had not moved very far under Mobutu.

370 **State formation and absolutism in comparative perspective: seventeenth-century France and Mobutu Sese Seko's Zaire.**
Thomas M. Callaghy.   PhD thesis, University of California, Berkeley, California, 1979. 713p. maps. bibliog. (Available from University Microfilms International, Ann Arbor, Michigan, order no. 8014627).

This work accomplishes a comparative study in state formation on the model of absolutism in the France of Louis XIV and the Zaire of Mobutu Sese Seko. In the words of the author, the process of state formation is a search for sovereignty, the idea of a final and absolute political authority. It is a process of political and economic struggle, which has both internal and external dimensions. The state is the ruling organization seeking to consolidate and expand its power over the national territory. Callaghy comes to the conclusion that Mobutu Sese Seko is the new prince, in the terms of Machiavelli, the first presidential monarch. The author wonders if, under current conditions, an African absolutist state can outlast its creator?

371 **Troisième République du Zaïre: perestroika, démocrature, ou catastroika?** (Third republic of Zaire: perestroika, demo-dictatorship, or catastroika?)
Lobho Lwa Djugudjugu.   Kinshasa, Zaire: Bibliothèque du Scribe, 1991. 219p. bibliog.

Writing at the beginning of the political and governmental reorganization that accompanied the inauguration of the Third Republic, Lobho Lwa Djugudjugu asks whether Zaire is heading towards a period of reform and renewal or will continue the downward slope of dictatorship and chaos. Mobutu Sese Seko has made an opening to the political opposition, institutionalizing in principle a multiparty system. The author reveals that this move toward political pluralism is a means of formalizing the multiplicity of opinions issuing forth from the state mandated party, the MPR. Nonetheless, there is some hope that increased participation by larger numbers of Zairians will transform the politics of the country.

372 **Troisième République du Zaïre: le round décisif.** (Third Republic of Zaire: the decisive round.)
Ntombolo Mutuala.   Brussels: Editions du Souverain, 1991. 126p. bibliog.

In 1990 President Mobutu ended the political monopoly of the ruling party (Mouvement Populaire de la République) and declared a multiparty régime. These and other political and constitutional changes occasioned the formation of the Third Republic of Zaire. The author has a strong academic background, but this comprehensive work on the political life of the new republic is written in a lively, engaging style, intended for a general public.

373 **Uncertain mandate: politics of the U.N. Congo operation.**
Ernest W. Lefever.   Baltimore, Maryland: Johns Hopkins University Press, 1967. 254p. map. bibliog.

Considers the political aspects of the 'Congo crisis', involving the UK, France, the US, and the UN in Zaire's domestic governmental crisis. This is a detailed account of foreign intervention in the political life of the newly independent state.

374 **A view from Zaire.**
Patrick M. Boyle. *World Politics*, vol. 40 no. 2 (Jan. 1988),
p. 269-87. bibliog.

Drawing upon the works of three pivotal writers on Zaire (M. G. Schatzberg, T. M.
Callaghy, and C. Young), the author reviews the principal reasons for the dismal
failure of the Zairian state. The Mobutu régime, enjoying institutional longevity, has
not increased bureaucratic efficiency or political development. The endemic
corruption and mismanagement of the country, with its accompanying clientelism,
patrimonialism, social immobility and stratification of society, have brought about an
institutionalization of the state that has prevented both economic prosperity and the
development of civil society. Boyle allows that Zaire remains an accurate – albeit
disturbing – model of politics within Sub-Saharan Africa.

375 **Voices of Zaire: rhetoric or reality?**
Edited by Jeffrey M. Elliot, Mervyn M. Dymally. Washington, DC:
Washington Institute Press, 1990. 175p.

Voices of Zaire is composed of a series of interviews with prominent Zairians, including
an academic, government officials, opposition figures, government political leaders, and
the President of Zaire himself, Mobutu Sese Seko. The questions in these interviews
centre upon the public life and politics of Zaire. The mix of pro- and anti-government
opinion provides a broad perspective of politics in Zaire today.

376 **Zaire and the African revolution.**
Lawrence Baraebibai Ekpebu. Ibadan: Ibadan University Press,
1989. 283p. maps. bibliog.

This work traces the political awakening of Zairians under Belgian colonial rule and
details Zairian political life, issues, and personnel up to the present (1989). The work
provides up-to-date information on Zairian politics.

377 **Zaïre, années 90.** (Zaire in the 90s.)
Jean-Claude Willame. Brussels: CEDAF: ASDOC, 1991. vol. 1,
318p. (Cahiers du CEDAF = ASDOC Studies, no. 5/6 1991).

In 1990 Mobutu Sese Seko opened a new political era in Zaire by proclaiming the Third
Republic and extending his hand to the opposition through the inauguration of a
multiparty system. This work, assembled from such sources as the press, political party
documents, speeches, and public statements by Jean-Claude Willame, a well-known
authority on Zaire, constitutes a new look at the Zairian political scene in the light of the
reforms. At the writing of this book, the outcome of the reforms is not entirely clear, but
the evolution of the change is meticulously traced.

378 **Zaire: continuity and political change in an oppressive state.**
Winsome J. Leslie. Boulder, Colorado: Westview Press, 1993. 204p.
maps. bibliog. (Westview Profiles. Nations of Contemporary Africa).

The formation of the Zairian polity is discussed from a long-term historical perspective,
beginning with the early kingdoms, external penetration, and colonization. Much is given
on the social and economic underpinnings of Zairian society, which form the basis for
the political life of Zaire. There is a long chapter entitled: 'Zaire in the international

arena', which summarizes the foreign relations of the country. The analysis is very timely (1992), and the narrative style makes it highly readable.

379   **Zaïre: le pouvoir à la portée du peuple.** (Zaire: power within the reach of the people.)
Cléophas Kamitatu-Massamba.   Paris: L'Harmattan, 1977. 203p. map.

The author participated in the heady events of Zairian independence as a political associate of Patrice Lumumba and a minister in various governments from 1960 to 1965. The Mobutu seizure of power in 1965 forced him out of power, into prison for five years, and finally into exile. He judges the political leadership of Mobutu Sese Seko with a very critical eye: the decline of the economy; the financial ruin of the state; the propping up of the state by foreign powers and institutions; and the likely threat to the national unity of the country. Yet the author looks hopefully to the future – to social, political and economic reforms and a break with the past system of government. Despite his sufferings and exile, Cléophas Kamitatu-Massamba has not lost his optimistic faith in the Zairian people to take control of their own destiny.

380   **Zaïre: quel changement pour quelles structures?: misère de l'opposition et faillite de l'Etat: (la mémoire historique d'un peuple).** (Zaire: what change for what structures?: misery of the opposition and collapse of the State: [the historic memory of a people].)
C. K. Lumuna Sando.   Brussels: Editions AFRICA, 1980. 154p. bibliog.

The author writes about the looming political crisis in Zaire, posing the frightening question: Is the national union of the peoples of Zaire possible? He reviews the political climate within the country of monopartism, an ideology of alienation, de-participation in the political process, and the lack of an effective and organized opposition movement. He also points to some signs of hope for the future, but essentially his prognosis of 'le mal zaïrois' (the Zairian sickness) is highly pessimistic.

381   **Zaire since independence.**
John B. Wright.   London: Institute for the Study of Conflict, 1983. 18p. map. bibliog. (Conflict Studies, no. 153).

This very brief overview of the political development and economic conditions of Zaire following independence offers a quick, easy-to-read summary of the major events and players of the period.

382   **Zaire: the unending crisis.**
Crawford Young.   *Foreign Affairs*, vol. 57, no. 1 (Fall 1978), p. 169-85.

Crawford Young, a widely published authority on political matters, writes regularly for the respected *Foreign Affairs*. He chronicles some of the outward events marking the decline of Zaire and analyses the underlying processes of national disintegration. The upper level political process is increasingly centralized in Kinshasa and appears to an ever greater extent divorced from the reality of the country it pretends to govern;

decisions made in Kinshasa are rarely carried out at the national, regional, or local level. Crawford speaks of the pervasive corruption that affects all levels of government, the extraordinarily high proportion of the gross domestic product absorbed to pay the costs of government, and the mass pauperization of the population as the economy continues to decline. Yet Mobutu remains the essential figure that no one can do without. He maintains a modicum of stability required for the extraction and exportation of the country's mineral wealth. In domestic politics, the régime has such a stranglehold on the political process that the resulting deadlock has produced no alternatives to the current government. Young, writing at the midpoint of the Mobutu régime, successfully contrasts the economic and political successes of the early years with the looming political crisis of the future.

Du Congo au Zaïre, 1960-1980: essai de bilan.
See item no. 3.

Zaire.
See item no. 10.

Zaïre-Afrique.
See item no. 11.

Zaire, what destiny?
See item no. 14.

Challenge of the Congo.
See item no. 130.

Congo: background of conflict.
See item no. 131.

The Congo since independence, January 1960-December, 1961.
See item no. 133.

Crisis in the Congo: a United Nations force in action.
See item no. 135.

Lumumba: the last fifty days.
See item no. 139.

Un avenir pour le Zaïre.
See item no. 143.

The rise and decline of the Zairian state.
See item no. 146.

The state-society struggle: Zaire in comparative perspective.
See item no. 147.

Zaire: stalemate and compromise.
See item no. 148.

Zaire: the roots of the continuing crisis.
See item no. 149.

The Church-State conflict in Zaire, 1969-1974.
See item no. 249.

Cross and sword: the political role of Christian missions in the Belgian Congo, 1908-1960.
See item no. 252.

L'Eglise du Christ au Zaïre: formation et adaptation d'un protestantisme en situation de dictature.
See item no. 255.

L'église zaïroise au service de quelle nation?
See item no. 258.

Mission and state in the Congo: a study of the relations between Protestant missions and the Congo Independent State authorities with special reference to the Equator District, 1985-1903.
See item no. 272.

The political role of Christian missions in the Belgian Congo, 1908-1960.
See item no. 276.

Bureaucratic corruption and underdevelopment in the Third World: the case of Zaire.
See item no. 398.

City politics: a study of Leopoldville, 1962-1963.
See item no. 403.

The political economy of Third World intervention: mines, money, and U.S. policy in the Congo crisis.
See item no. 431.

The situation in Zaire: hearing before the Subcommittee on African Affairs of the Committee on Foreign Relations, United States Senate, One Hundred Second Congress, first session, November 6, 1991.
See item no. 437.

Zaire under Mobutu: consistencies and contradictions of U.S. policy.
See item no. 448.

The Zairian crisis and American foreign policy.
See item no. 449.

The political economy of African debt: the case of Zaire.
See item no. 463.

Zaire, Rwanda, Burundi: country profile, annual survey of political and economic background.
See item no. 475.

Zaire, Rwanda, Burundi: country report, analyses of economic and political trends.
See item no. 476.

The dialectics of oppression in Zaire.
See item no. 554.

Info-Zaïre: feuillet d'information produit par la Table de Concertation sur les Droits Humains au Zaïre.
See item no. 556.

Military violence against civilians: the case of the Congolese and Zairean military in the Pedicle, 1890-1988.
See item no. 557.

Zaire, repression as policy: a human rights report.
See item no. 561.

Constitution and Legal System

383 **La conclusion des traités en droit constitutionnel zaïrois: étude de droit international et de droit interne.** (Conclusion of treaties in Zairian constitutional law: study of international law and internal law.) Lunda-Bululu.   Brussels: Bruyland: Editions de l'Université de Bruxelles, 1984. 456p. bibliog. (Collection de Droit International, no. 12).

This work is a formal treatise on the legal and constitutional basis of treaty making between Zaire and other countries. The author begins with a review of the international legal framework for treaty negotiation and ratification. Then he proceeds to the constitutional treaty making powers of the Zairian government, starting with the fundamental law of 1960, the constitutions of 1964 and 1967, and the constitutional revisions of 1974 and 1978. Much of the Zairian constitutional framework is reviewed up to the 1984 publication of this work, and many constitutional texts are cited.

384 **Constitution de la République Démocratique du Congo.** (Constitution of the Democratic Republic of the Congo.) Kinshasa: Imprimerie de la République Démocratique du Congo, 1964. 172p.

Presented here is the complete text of the 1964 constitution of the Democratic Republic of the Congo (Zaire) in French. There is no commentary.

385 **Constitution de la République du Zaïre: telle que modifiée par la loi no 90-008 du 25 novembre 1990.** (Constitution of the Republique of Zaire: such as it was modified by law no. 90-008 of November 25, 1990.)
Journal Officiel de la République du Zaïre, Numéro spécial (Nov. 1990). 55p.

This is a relatively recent, updated version of the Zairian national constitution, the text of which is contained in its entirety, and without commentary in this official government publication.

386 **Dette de clarification: propositions pour parachever la révision de la constitution du Zaïre.** (Debt of clarification: propositions to complete the revision of the constitution of Zaire.)
Djelo Empenge-Osako. Louvain-la-Neuve, Belgium: Bel Elan, 1990. 90p. bibliog. (Esprit Libre).

The author of this work is a law professor and former high official of the Mobutu régime. When he discusses the revision of the constitution and the harmonization of the relationship between the governing party, the MPR, and the state, he speaks as a member in good standing of the Zairian political establishment. The concerns expressed in this work are to provide a firmer legal and constitutional structure, which reflects the organization of the state and the political life of the régime.

387 **Les droits de la défense devant les juridictions répressives de Kinshasa.** (The rights of defense before the repressive jurisdictions of Kinshasa.)
Linganga Mongwende Nzengo. Pijnacker, Netherlands: Dutch Efficiency Bureau, 1982. 337p. bibliog.

This publication of a Dutch doctoral thesis (University of Amsterdam, 1982) constitutes a highly specialized study of the legal defenses of defendants before the Zairian courts of Kinshasa. The author discusses the framework of human rights – the Universal Declaration of Human Rights – as a background for this analysis of the Zairian penal code. The work is so specialized and abstract as to be of little use to a general public, but it does define general rights of defendants (such as the right to remain silent) in the Zairian legal system. The author makes comparisons with other legal systems and points out the need for reforms.

388 **Les droits des citoyens zaïrois.** (The rights of Zairian citizens.)
Pierre de Quirini. Kinshasa-Gombe: CEPAS, 1980. 79p.

Outlines the legal system supporting civil rights in Zaire, including a small section on the civil rights of foreigners in Zaire. The study quotes frequently from the official legal documents, such as the constitution and the penal code. The analysis is highly theoretical and abstract in its coverage of civil rights and does not attempt to assess the general human rights situation or the degree to which these legal civil rights protections are actually enforced by the Zairian government.

Constitution and Legal System

389 **Les institutions dans la constitution congolaise.** (The institutions in
the Congolese constitution.)
Victor Promontorio.   Leopoldville: Concordia, 1965. 206p.

The author has drawn together various articles of the 1964 constitution in sections, with
commentary, to define the rôle of the Chief Executive, the parliament, the forms of local
government, and the judiciary. The entire text of the 1964 constitution is included at the
end of the work.

390 **Les institutions politiques du Congo indépendant au 30 juin 1960.**
(The political institutions of the independent Congo on June 30, 1960.)
François Perin.   Leopoldville: Institut Politique Congolais, 1960.
151p.

Published in 1960, this work presents the constitutional and legal framework of the
newly independent Zairian state, outlining the administrative structure, the attribution of
powers, and the rights of citizens. In the annexes of the work are the basic constitutional
texts of the new state, negotiated between the Zairian political class and the departing
Belgians, including the electoral law and the fundamental law, which represents the first
Zairian constitution.

391 **Lois en vigueur dans l'Etat indépendant du Congo.** (Laws in force
in the Congo Free State.)
Octave Louwers.   Brussels: P. Weissenbruch, 1905. 759p. bibliog.

Published in 1905, when Zaire was known as the Congo Free State, a personal
possession of the Belgian King Leopold II, this work brings together the laws and
statutes that governed the country, such as: the penal code; the civil code; judicial
proceedings; and treaties with other countries. The official texts are all given without
commentary but with explanatory footnotes. This compendium would be useful for a
study of the legal history of Zaire.

392 **Le nouveau droit constitutionnel zaïrois.** (The new Zairian
constitutional law.)
Gérard Balanda.   Paris: Nouvelles Editions Africaines, 1972. 352p.
bibliog.

Gérard Balanda notes in his introduction that Zaire is on its third constitution. Since the
writing of this book (published in 1972), there have been numerous other constitutional
changes and an extensive revision in 1991 with the establishment of the Third Republic.
The author contends that the nature of the state in the newly independent African
countries is constantly changing and evolving, necessitating these constitutional
revisions. The administrative structure of the state is discussed as a prelude to
constitutional law. Then the work proceeds to outline the constitutional history of Zaire
and the attribution of powers within the constitution to the appropriate offices and
institutions. Included are the texts of articles of the constitution and other fundamental
laws or statutes of the state.

393   **Précis de droit international privé congolais.** (Summary of
Congolese international private law.)
Jacques de Burlet.   Kinshasa: Université Lovanium; Brussels:
F. Larcier, 1971. 370p. bibliog.

This is a very specialized work on private law (laws governing interpersonal and family relations). In focusing on the concept of international private law, as it applies to Zaire, and comparing it to Zairian private law, the work may be of primary interest to legal researchers and lawyers, but will also be of use to a more general public who may wish to know a foreigner's rights in business dealings, family law, nationality law, and laws governing civil rights and public safety.

394   **La République du Zaïre.** (Republic of Zaire.)
Jacques Vanderlinden.   Paris: Berger-Lévrault, 1975. 77p. map.
bibliog. (Encyclopédie Politique et Constitutionnelle. Série Afrique).

This short work reviews the history and structure of constitutional government in Zaire. Considering the political life of the newly independent state, the author recounts the failure of classical parliamentary government and the consequent concentration of constitutional powers in the office of the State President and the ruling party, the MPR, within the legal framework of the state. Included in the work are the text of the 1974 constitution of the Republic of Zaire and various other statutes outlining the constitutional and political structure of Zaire.

The policy of national integration in Zaire.
See item no. 294.

Les élections sous la Deuxième République.
See item no. 341.

Principes et règles d'organisation des élections libres et démocratiques.
See item no. 365.

Administration and Local Government

395 **L'administration publique du Zaïre: l'impact du milieu socio-politique sur sa structure et son fonctionnement.** (The public administration of Zaire: the impact of the socio-political environment upon its structure and functioning.)
Mpinga Kasenda.   Paris: Pedone, 1973. 316p. bibliog. (Série Afrique Noire, no. 3).

Mpinga Kasenda offers a very comprehensive review of the administrative structure of the Zaire of the Second Republic. He speaks very briefly about the administrative traditions inherited from the Belgians but delves more deeply into the administrative organization, offices, and reporting structure. The political interplay between the ruling élites and the administrative structure is a main focus of the work. The author is also very concerned about the adaptation of the administration to the task of nation building and economic development, and he evaluates the effectiveness of the government structure in achieving these goals.

396 **L'administration zaïroise.** (The Zairian administration.)
Serge A. Vieux.   Paris: Berger-Lévrault, 1974. 96p. bibliog. (Encyclopédie Administrative).

This brief but comprehensive work looks at the structure of the Zairian state and is a useful and quick-reference tool for the administrative and political organization of government and political life in Zaire. The user must be cautioned, however, that the description of the state structure is highly abstract, showing how the national institutions are theoretically designed to function within the state. In Zaire, the reality often does not conform with the theory.

397   **Belgian administration in the Congo.**
       Georges Brausch.   London; New York: Oxford University Press,
       1961. 92p. bibliog.
An in-depth account of the structure and organization of Belgian government in Zaire
which also covers the changes in government administration as independence
approached. Starting with the clichés about the high standards of living, health, and
housing in the Belgian colony, the author delves into the detail of Belgian policy and the
underlying political attitudes in Zaire as well as in Belgium.

398   **Bureaucratic corruption and underdevelopment in the Third
       World: the case of Zaire.**
       David J. Gould.   New York: Pergamon Press, 1980. 183p. bibliog.
       (Pergamon Policy Studies on International Development).
Zaire is potentially one of the richest states in Africa, with abundant mineral wealth,
fertile soil, and enormous water resources. However, the country has seen its economic
infrastructure decline, its masses increasingly separated from participation in political
life, and a level of per capita income among the lowest in the Third World. Gould
identifies and analyses the chief cause of this precipitous national decline, the corrupt
structure of the bureaucracy. He discusses the development of the state bureaucratic
structure in Zaire from early colonial times and follows its evolution to the present. In
1980 at the publication of this work, Zaire was in virtual receivership, indebted to the
outside and unable to provide the necessities to its own people. Only continued foreign
assistance, propping up the régime, has spared the country from a total collapse of the
state structure.

399   **Les chefferies au Congo Belge: contribution à l'étude de la
       législation et de la sociologie coloniales.** (Chieftaincies in the Belgian
       Congo: contribution to the study of colonial legislation and sociology.)
       Jacques Sourdillat.   Paris: Domat-Montchrestien, 1940. 440p.
       bibliog.
This early work (1940) outlines the local and national administrative structure set up by
the Belgians to rule their vast equatorial colonial empire. The author enters into great
detail on the statutes and regulations governing the lives of communities and individuals,
demonstrating the type of comprehensive control over the population that the Belgians
hoped to achieve. He outlines the relationship between the colonial administrative
structure and customary law, with a degree of local authority exercised by communities,
maintained in place by the colonial administrators. This study represents a fascinating
first-hand look at the functioning of local government during the colonial period and
would be very useful for the reader who wants to have an historical perspective on the
colonial experience in government and administration.

400   **City politics: a study of Leopoldville, 1962-1963.**
       Jean S. La Fontaine.   Cambridge, England: Cambridge University
       Press, 1970. 246p. maps. bibliog. (African Studies Series, no. 1).
This work purports to study the political life of Kinshasa in the early years of
independence, a period which the author characterizes as full of political instability and
struggles in the city and throughout Zaire. However, the author goes far beyond his
stated purpose to talk about the history, development, and city planning of the Zairian

111

capital, discussing the social, religious, and urban environment that underlies the political life of this vibrant city. The reader should be cautioned that today (thirty years after the 1962-63 scope of the study), Kinshasa is a very different city, swollen with the excess population of the impoverished countryside and increasingly sunk in the chaos that is engulfing the entire country.

401 **La consolidation du management public au Zaïre.** (The consolidation of public management in Zaire.)
Ibula Mwana Katanga.   Kinshasa: Presses Universitaires du Zaïre, 1987. 333p. bibliog.

The author discusses the administrative structure of the Zairian state. He details the recent history of the bureaucracy and proposes areas where reform is possible in order to increase the efficiency and effectiveness of the administration in carrying out the economic and social development programmes of the political leaders. The work examines the relationship between the administration and the governing political party, the Mouvement Populaire de la Révolution, and the need for accountability within the bureaucracy. Published in 1987, this study has not detailed the widely reported more recent disintegration of the administrative structure at the local level.

402 **Development administration at the local level: the case of Zaire.**
Richard Vengroff.   Syracuse, New York: Syracuse University, Maxwell School of Citizenship and Public Affairs, 1983. 89p. bibliog. (Foreign and Comparative Studies. African Series, no. 40).

The author states in his preface that he wishes to examine some of the problems of development administration in Zaire from an empirical perspective. He has gathered information from a survey of government administrators – civil servants – and has presented his conclusions in this work. Although this study is written from a narrow perspective of the impact of administration upon economic development, the user can gain a more comprehensive view of Zairian public administration as well as a perspective on the difficulties of economic development in this Central African nation. Given the endemic corruption of the civil service in Zaire, the reader may wish to be highly critical of information gathered from Zaire's 'public servants'.

403 **Impératif du développement et réforme de l'administration locale au Zaïre.** (Development imperative and reform of the local administration in Zaire.)
Muyere Oyong.   Kinshasa: Presses Universitaires du Zaïre, 1986. 124p. bibliog.

Professor at the University of Kinshasa, Muyere Oyong sets a goal of outlining possible reforms in state administration and local government to alleviate the inadaptation of government to local reality. He follows the development of the administration during the colonial period, the sudden changes brought about by independence, and the tight central control resumed under the Mobutu régime. The author suggests that decentralization or some form of self-government with autonomous local control of the bureaucracy would be a major step toward correcting the problem of inadaptation by letting local people take a greater decision-making rôle in economic planning and the provision of state services. Although the focus of this work is administrative reform, it also does an excellent job of reviewing the history and structure of local government.

404 **Politics in the Congo: decolonization and independence.**
Crawford Young.   Princeton, New Jersey: Princeton University Press,
1965. 659p. maps. bibliog.

Crawford Young is a frequently cited authority on Zaire. Although his *Politics in the Congo* is dated, it is rich in detail about the administrative/governmental structure of the colonial régime, the transition to independence, and the organization of the newly independent state. The Zaire ruled by the Belgians was the most densely governed and administered of the larger African colonies. With over 10,000 Belgians in the government and army, the foreigners regulated almost every detail of Zairian public life, right down to the local level. The Africanization of the administration and army, which followed independence, was among the most thoroughgoing and rapid within Africa, bringing in a totally untested administrative and political personnel. The task of the new government was to re-build the administrative structure as well as the political structure from the bottom up in order to preserve the unity of the new state. Young mentions that trends in Zaire reflect those in the rest of Africa; nationalists had to make the transition from attempting to destroy government (the colonial régime) to building government when they took control. Parliamentary and judicial traditions inherited from the colonizers quickly had to be adapted to local conditions, and authoritarian rule was increasingly used to preserve the unity of fledgling states. In Zaire, as elsewhere, the new régime presided over an increasingly unequal distribution of the national wealth. Young's analysis of Zaire is a detailed narrative, which helps the reader to conceptualize the structure of government, politics, and the wrenching changes of independence.

405 **Les provinces du Congo: structure et fonctionnement.** (The provinces of the Congo: structure and functioning.)
Jean-Claude Willame, under the direction of Benoît Verhaegen.
Leopoldville: Université Lovanium, 1964-65. 5 vols. maps. bibliog.
(Cahiers Economiques et Sociaux. Collection d'Etudes Politiques, no. 1-5).

This dated but comprehensive work covers the political and administrative structure of local government in each of the Zairian provinces. The study includes information on the political personnel of each province as well as economic, population, and legal information on the provinces.

406 **Les réformes administratives au Zaïre, 1972-1973.** (The administrative reforms in Zaire, 1972-1973.)
Mpinga Kasenda, David J. Gould.   Kinshasa: Presses Universitaires du Zaïre, 1975. 339p.

Brought together in this work are the texts of statutes, administrative documents, and speeches by government officials, which represent the efforts of the Mobutu régime to re-form and re-shape the state structure of Zaire. These materials for the most part date from the early 1970s, a time when the Zairian government made a major effort to re-establish and regularize the power of the central administration over the national territory. The user should be cautioned once again that these documents represent the theoretical, not the actual, basis of government in Zaire. Moreover, these structures have since been superseded by later changes with the inauguration of the Third Republic.

407 **The rulers of Belgian Africa, 1884-1914.**
Lewis H. Gann, Peter Duignan. Princeton, New Jersey: Princeton
University Press, 1979. 265p. maps. bibliog.

The authors offer a history of Belgian involvement in the colonization and government
of Zaire, which is very rich in details about the structure of government and
administration in Zaire under Belgian rule.

408 **Le statut de la fonction publique: le décret-loi du 20 mars 1965 et
ses mesures d'exécution.** (The civil service statute: decree-law of
March 20, 1965, and measures of its enforcement.)
Serge A. Vieux. Kinshasa: Office National de la Recherche et du
Développement, 1970. 628p. bibliog.

This work includes the legal statutes and decrees concerning the civil service and the
state administration of the young Zairian state. It is a very detailed and comprehensive
account of the regulations surrounding hiring, conditions of employment, involuntary
separation, duties, and remuneration. The work is intended for official state use within
the government.

Zaïre-Afrique.
See item no. 11.

The state-society struggle: Zaire in comparative perspective.
See item no. 147.

**L'appareil gouvernemental du Zaïre (1960-1987): des restructurations
pour quelles finalités?**
See item no. 327.

The Belgian Congo.
See item no. 330.

Ethnic politics in Zaire.
See item no. 342.

Political awakening in the Belgian Congo.
See item no. 359.

Foreign Relations

409 **America and the first Congo crisis, 1960-1963.**
Michael Wayne Williams. PhD thesis, University of California,
Irvine, California, 1991. 266p. bibliog. (Available from University
Microfilms International, Ann Arbor Michigan, order no. 9233701).
Recounts the history of the US-Zairian bilateral relationship in the early years of Zairian
independence, from 1960 to 1963. A recent work, this study has the advantage of
historical perspective and takes into consideration the considerable literature on the
subject, including many primary sources in government archives, which may not have
been available to earlier researchers. It contains a detailed account of the major events
and figures of this period.

410 **America's tyrant: the CIA and Mobutu of Zaire: how the United
States put Mobutu in power, protected him from his enemies, and
helped him become one of the richest men in the world, and lived
to regret it.**
Sean Kelly. Washington, DC: American University Press, 1993.
273p. bibliog.
Kelly tells the story of a very personal, longlasting relationship between US foreign
policy and Mobutu Sese Seko. In repeated Rose Garden ceremonies, the President of
Zaire is anointed with the balm of superpower support by a succession of American
Presidents, from Kennedy to Bush. In an overarching desire to bring stability – pro-US
stability – to the crumbling Zairian state, American foreign policy has inextricably
embraced this autocratic leader. The work recounts this long relationship from its
inception up to 1993. At the end of this account, one wonders who owns whom. Is
Mobutu 'America's tyrant', or has the US sold itself entirely to the illusion of controlling
a situation beyond its power to control?

411 **American foreign policy in the Congo, 1960-1964.**
Steve Weissman. Ithaca, New York; London: Cornell University
Press, 1974. 325p. bibliog.

Weissman gives a complete account of American/Zairian foreign relations from the
Eisenhower to the Johnson administrations. He begins with an inventory of American
and European interests in the former Belgian colony, and then relives in detail the
development of Western and African foreign policies in the events surrounding Zairian
independence and the country's early years of statehood. Throughout this narrative,
Zaire is treated as a passive entity acted upon by the foreign policies of other nations,
rather than a state capable of conceiving and initiating its own policies. Conditions
prevailing in Zaire are described in great detail, giving a vivid impression of the political
and social state of the country at that time. The author minutely examines the various
motives of American foreign policies, the different domestic groups that exercised
pressure upon this policy, and gives a thorough critique of American foreign policy
toward Zaire and the assumptions upon which it was built.

412 **American policy in the Congo.**
George W. Ball.   In: *Footnotes to the Congo story: an Africa report
anthology.*   Edited by Helen Kitchen.   New York: Walker, 1967,
p. 61-68.

This essay by a chief American foreign policy-maker is based on an address by the
Under Secretary of State. As the title indicates, the essay enunciates in a few pages the
official US policy toward Zaire and sums up the political situation in the turbulent former
Belgian colony. Although dated, the chapter reveals the motivating forces behind US
policy toward Zaire during the period of the country's crisis-filled early independence.
Ball's statement offers an illuminating background to the 1991 policy formulations
presented to the US Senate Subcommittee on African Affairs by then Assistant Secretary
of State for African Affairs, Herman Cohen. See also: *The situation in Zaire* (q.v.).

413 **Aussenwirtschaftliche Abhängigkeitsfaktoren.** (Factors of foreign
economic dependency.)
Dagmar Simon.   In: *Internationale Abhängigkeit und nationale
Entwicklung seit der Unabhängigkeit: am Beispiel Zaire.*
(International dependency and national development since
independence: the example of Zaire.)   Edited by Dagmar Simon.
Frankfurt am Main: P. Lang, 1987, p. 234-82. bibliog. (Berliner
Studien zur Politik in Afrika, Bd. 8).

Dagmar Simon systematically reviews Zaire's relationship with all non-African
industrial powers as well as the European Union. In a succinct analysis, the author
resumes the major factors and events in each bilateral relationship. The work offers a fast
and comprehensive summation of Zaire's foreign relations for those readers understanding German.

414 **Belgique-Zaïre: le grand affrontement.** (Belgium-Zaire: the great confrontation.)
Gauthier de Villers.   Brussels: CEDAF, 1990. 171p. bibliog. (Cahiers du CEDAF).

The author chronicles in great detail the bilateral relationship between Zaire and its former colonial master, Belgium. The foreign relations between the two countries are vastly complicated by the continuing deep involvement of both parties in the political life of the other country. Great attention is paid to the political personalities of the policy-makers and the direct involvement of Mobutu Sese Seko in the direction of Zairian diplomacy. From a more optimistic period of 'normalization', the bilateral relations between the two countries have deteriorated through misunderstandings and mutual antagonisms to the point of crisis in the relationship.

415 **Bureaucratic influence in the U.S.-Zairian special relationship.**
Peter J. Schraeder.   *Transafrica Forum*, vol. 9, no. 3 (Fall 1992), p. 31-56.

Born out of the American fear of strategic Soviet advances in the heart of Africa, the US-Zairian special relationship continues to this day. This bilateral relationship, however, is not without its shifts and starts. The initial American embrace of Zairian President Mobutu grows cold during the Carter Administration when Zaire's lamentable human rights record alienates US public opinion. Reforged for strategic reasons under the Reagan Administration, this relationship survives to the present day because of a lack of viable alternatives to the increasingly odious Mobutu régime.

416 **CIA covert action in Zaire and Angola: patterns and consequences.**
Steve Weissman.   *Political Science Quarterly*, vol. 94, no. 2 (Summer 1974), p. 263-86.

Steve Weissman has intricately researched and detailed the strong arm of American foreign policy, that is, covert action by the CIA. Weissman traces the pattern of manipulation and influence-wielding exercised by American foreign policy-makers in the service of national foreign policy objectives. In this narrative, the strategic interests of Cold War bipolarization take the lead over the economic interests of US concerns in the setting of foreign policy objectives. Weissman places American actions into the context of a worldwide foreign policy practice, characteristic of the United States' diplomatic stand in the Cold War environment.

417 **Conflict and intervention in Africa: Nigeria, Angola, Zaire.**
Herbert Ekwe-Ekwe.   Basingstoke, England: Macmillan, 1990. 195p. bibliog.

In terms of civil conflict and foreign intervention, Zaire's case is unfortunately not unique in Africa. The author studies the genesis of civil strife in three countries: Nigeria, Angola, and Zaire. In the chapter on Zaire (p. 112-30), Herbert Ekwe-Ekwe chronicles the political, geographical, and economic situation of the country, and he analyses the interests and intentions of foreign powers toward Zaire, proceeding through the list of the country's crises and internal disruptions. Mobutu is generally held up as the great ally of the foreign powers, which in turn have done their utmost to maintain him in power.

418 **Conflit belgo-zaïrois: fondements historiques, politiques, économiques et culturels.** (Belgian-Zairian conflict: historical, political, economic and cultural foundations.)
Paris: Présence Africaine, 1990. 206p. map. bibliog. (Collection Regard des Africains sur leur Continent).

'Foreign relations' is an egregious malapropism in depicting the relationship between Zaire and Belgium during the colonial period. The experience of colonization is so intimate and so penetrating that to trace the colonial relations of the two countries is to tell much of the history of that period for both. In the details of the colonial relationship, much of the social, economic and political history of Zaire emerges from the cliché of 'model colony', so often used to characterize the Belgian Congo. Consisting of essays by various authors, this compilation carries the study of Zaire into the post-colonial period, to establish the place of Zaire within Africa and the world during the early reign of Mobutu.

419 **The Congo.**
Evan Luard. In: *A history of the United Nations.* Evan Luard.
New York: St. Martin's Press, 1989, vol. 2, p. 217-316.

Luard provides a highly detailed account of the UN rôle in the crises surrounding the emergence of Zaire as a state and so doing illuminates the diplomatic history of the country as it explodes onto the world scene. The time period covered in Zairian foreign relations is less than two years, but it is the crucial and formative period in the foreign relations of the former Belgian Congo.

420 **The Congo betrayal: the UN-US and Lumumba.**
D. K. Orwa. Nairobi: Kenya Literature Bureau, 1985. 241p. bibliog.

The Congo betrayal is the story of Zaire from early colonial times through independence in the context of conflicted international politics and competing big power interests. Zaire is depicted as an area of weak political power, both as a colony and as a newly emergent state, which is acted upon and manipulated by the rival political and economic interests of foreign powers. The focus of the work is on the period preceding and following independence, with emphasis on the emergence of Lumumba and US policy toward Zaire. The author's treatment of foreign policy intrusion into Zaire is objective, but the perspective is clearly 'third world', with an implicit critique of a world political system that favours big power interests and relegates weaker developing countries to a colonial or neo-colonial subservience.

421 **The Congo cables: the cold war in Africa – from Eisenhower to Kennedy.**
Madeleine G. Kalb. New York: Macmillan, 1982. 466p. maps. bibliog.

This book concentrates upon the events surrounding Zairian independence as a key moment in the Cold War competition between the US and the Soviet Union. The author has carefully researched the behind-the-scenes manoeuvring, drawing upon recently declassified US government documents in a detailed analysis of US policy toward Zaire during the Eisenhower and Kennedy administrations. There emerges an unflattering portrait of ruthless American policy-makers within the foreign policy establishment and the CIA, who would stop at nothing – even political assassination – to achieve their foreign policy objectives of countering Soviet influence, stabilizing the newly emerging states of Africa, and drawing them into the US sphere of influence. This study has not lost its timeliness in an era when the rôle of covert operations by the CIA and other government agencies is still hotly debated as an arm of US foreign policy. The work is widely cited in other sources, indicating its importance as the most influential and definitive study on the subject.

422 **The Congo emerges from diplomatic quarantine.**
Victor D. du Bois.   In: *Footnotes to the Congo Story: an Africa report anthology.*   Edited by Helen Kitchen.   New York: Walker, 1967, p. 129-43.

Zaire is by far the largest and most populous French-speaking country in Africa. When it joined the fourteen other former French colonies in Africa in the Organisation Commune Africaine et Malgache in 1965, this event marked an end to the diplomatic and moral isolation that marred the early years of the emergent state. This chapter describes the political personalities and the foreign policy manoeuvring that were present in this foreign policy opening and examines the emerging francophonic tendencies of the new African governing élite.

423 **Foreign policy making in Africa: an analysis of foreign policy decision-making in Tanzania, Zambia, Zaire and Ivory Coast.**
Aggrey Joel Otieno.   PhD thesis, Northern Arizona University, Flagstaff, Arizona, 1990. 259p. bibliog. (Available from University Microfilms International, Ann Arbor, Michigan, order no. 9112833).

The foreign policy decision-making process of four African countries (Tanzania, Zambia, Zaire, and Côte d'Ivoire) is examined in this PhD dissertation. The author uses abstract decision-making models in government to analyse foreign policy and scrutinizes the two most important foreign policy issues to face African countries: relations with the International Monetary Fund and South Africa. The exclusion of superpower rivalry and other important foreign policy issues marks the study as less than comprehensive. Nevertheless, the work as a whole serves as a general background to the foreign policy decision-making process in the four countries. Information specific to Zaire is found in separate sections on Zaire within several chapters. In all four countries, decision-making is dominated by a head-of-state, who holds predominant influence within the ruling political party and the administrative structure of government, and the analysis of the decision-making structure extends into the realm of internal politics and government.

424 **The foreign policy of the Republic of Zaire.**
Edward [Edouard] Bustin.   *The Annals of the American Academy of Political and Social Science*, vol. 489 (Jan. 1987), p. 63-75.

Bustin traces the course of Zairian foreign policy from the inception of an independent state in 1960 up to 1987. He details and analyses all of the major events of this troubled period, pointing out the chief theme of the country's foreign policy: dependency. The author touches on some of the major domestic factors, economic and political, behind this dependency on foreign support. Within the narrow margins of dependency, the Mobutu régime has shown considerable skills in playing foreign interests off against one another, limiting some of the worst consequences of the country's lack of a firm power base. In a few pages, Bustin gives a quite comprehensive outline of Zairian foreign policy.

425 **French policy toward Zaire: with emphasis on the Giscard d'Estaing presidency.**
Theodore Trefon. PhD thesis, Boston University, Boston, Massachusetts, 1988. 369p. bibliog. (Available from University Microfilms International, Ann Arbor, Michigan, order no. 8813651).
This PhD dissertation traces the history of French/Zairian relations from the French perspective, starting in colonial times and continuing into the Mitterrand era, with a special focus upon the Giscard d'Estaing government as a period of maximum French economic, political, and military penetration of Zaire. Primary emphasis is placed on the motivations, means, and style of French foreign policy, but there is also discussion of the Zairian rôle in this bilateral relationship. The study characterizes French foreign policy as neo-colonial, serving constant French economic and political interests, irrespective of the ideological complexion of the government ruling in Paris. The French have consistently supported the Mobutu régime, and this has had results that are inherently detrimental to the economic and political development of Zaire. The author examines the political economy of Zaire under Mobutu, which serves as a backdrop for this bilateral relationship.

426 **La géopolitique internationale du Zaïre.** (International geopolitics of Zaire.)
Yezi Pyana-Fumu. Lubumbashi, Zaire: Aux Editions Africa, 1979. 96p. bibliog. (Collection Savoir et Connaître).
In the tradition of cartesianism, this work begins with a definition of abstractions, such as geopolitics, nationalism, national ideology, historical and social community, and then applies these concepts to the situation of Zaire. The emphasis of the work is on Zaire, its definition as a political entity, and its conceptual relationship with the rest of Africa and the world. Within this geopolitical perspective, foreign relations is defined as the interplay of various power relationships in a constantly changing and competitive mix. The work is almost totally consumed with the abstract and does not analyse concrete situations in any detail. This effort to understand politics and foreign relations from a European rationalist point of view is quite comprehensive and presents a perspective that is usually not available in English-language studies.

427 **Israel's diplomatic offensive in Africa: the case of Zaire.**
Noah Dropkin. *Transafrica Forum*, vol. 9, no. 1 (1992), p. 15-26. bibliog.
In 1982 Zaire renewed its formal diplomatic relations with Israel, following the Israeli-Egyptian peace treaty. Noah Dropkin examines some of the ulterior motives of Zaire's President Mobutu for re-establishing this bilateral relationship. Faced with increasing criticism of his political and economic leadership of Zaire from Washington and other Western capitals, Mobutu sought additional economic and military support from a small but highly capable partner in an effort to shore up his rule over an increasingly troubled land. Although limited to the Israeli-Zairian bilateral relationship, the article reveals the inner motivations and modalities of Zairian foreign policy.

428 **Military intervention and the myth of collective security: the case of Zaire.**
Michael G. Schatzberg. *Journal of Modern African Studies*, vol. 27, no. 2 (1989), p. 315-40.

More than most other African states, Zaire has been subjected to repeated foreign military interventions. The crisis of independence and the rebellions in Shaba set off a multilateral armed involvement that bolstered national unity and preserved the fledgling state. Foreign powers participating in these interventions have declared their primary interests to be: stability; national unity; and friendliness to the West. Both in their interventions and in their foreign policy, these powers (the US, France, Belgium, and the UN) have supported a strong national leader – at first Tshombe, then Mobutu. Yet both of these leaders have lacked the stature and the internal political support to rule effectively in the example of other, more stable African states. Zaire remains hobbled with an increasingly unpopular régime, kept in place by the foreign interests that have sponsored past interventions. Schatzberg gives a brief, cogent analysis of this sorry state of affairs in Zaire.

429 **Our man in Kinshasa: U.S. relations with Mobutu, 1970-1983: patron-client relations in the international sphere.**
Elise Forbes Pachter. PhD thesis, Johns Hopkins University, Baltimore, Maryland, 1987. 452p. bibliog. (Available from University Microfilms International, Ann Arbor, Michigan, order no. 8716678).

The author describes the mechanics of US foreign policy decision-making in the American relationship with Zaire. She offers a sharp critique of the US policy-making process and the failed American foreign policy, tied to the corrupt client régime of Zairian President Mobutu. As the title indicates, the work closely details the central rôle of President Mobutu in the formulation of Zairian foreign policy. A relationship of Zairian dependency on the US is outlined in which the client (Mobutu) often acts independently of American foreign policy interests. The study includes an extensive analysis of the US economic and strategic interests in Zaire as well as Zaire's rôle in international economic and diplomatic relations.

430 **La pénétration américaine au Congo.** (American penetration of the Congo.)
Luc Mosheje. Brussels: Editions 'Remarques Congolaises', 1964. 64p. (Collection 'Etudes Congolaises', no 10).

Luc Mosheje depicts the events surrounding the independence of Zaire from the point of view of the power interests of the US, Belgium, and other European colonial powers, continuously vying with one another for political and particularly economic influence over a troubled land undergoing a wrenching transition to self rule. The process of power politics, which Mosheje describes, is nearly Manichaean in the use of foreign policy for the service of economic self interests. In this interplay of influence and raw will to control, the author recounts the underlying political reasons for the lamentable failure of the Belgians to prepare the Zairians for independence as well as the starts and shifts of American foreign policy in its will to dominate the mineral-rich heart of Africa. The study is dated (1961) and in French, but it provides a unique analysis of the events of Zairian independence.

431 **The political economy of Third World intervention: mines, money, and U.S. policy in the Congo crisis.**
David N. Gibbs. Chicago; London: University of Chicago Press, 1991. 322p. bibliog. (American Politics and Political Economy).

Examines multilateral foreign relations with Zaire from the perspective of foreign intervention in the Central African country. The author establishes a number of political science models for the patterns of this intervention. The study is significant as a specialized political science analysis, but it also serves a more general public. In looking at foreign intervention, the work outlines foreign policy interests in Zaire from colonial times through 1970, and it traces the major events in foreign policy as well as the internal politics of the country. The motives and actions of foreign policy are discussed in great detail. The focus rests more on the policy of foreign powers than that of Zaire, which is treated as a passive partner, the recipient of the policy initiatives of others. Nonetheless, the work teaches a great deal about the pattern of Zairian foreign relations.

432 **La politique africaine de la Belgique.** (The African policy of Belgium.)
Belgium. Ministère des Affaires Etrangères, du Commerce Extérieur et de la Coopération au Développement. Brussels: Ministère des Affaires Etrangères, du Commerce Extérieur et de la Coopération au Développement, 1983. (various pagings). maps.

The opening pages of this work follow the evolution of the Zairian-Belgian relationship in diplomatic and economic terms. From a nearly exclusive concentration on its former Central African colonies, Belgium has diversified its diplomatic and economic relations in Africa, lessening but not neglecting its ties with Zaire. An official Belgian government publication, the work furnishes exact figures for the commercial and foreign assistance relationship with Zaire. The study is slightly dated and in French, but it greatly illuminates Zairian foreign relations from the Belgian perspective.

433 **Le regroupement régional dans la politique étrangère du Zaïre: évolution et problèmes.** (Regional grouping in the foreign policy of Zaire: evolution and problems.)
Mamba wa Ngindu. Kinshasa-Gombe: Presse de l'Institut de Recherche Scientifique, 1980. 263p. bibliog.

The author explores the complex web of political and economic interests that both unite and divide Central Africa. In this context, the work describes the relationship of Zaire to its Central African neighbours (Rwanda, Burundi, Cameroon, Chad, Gabon, Congo [Brazzaville], and the Central African Republic). The prospect of Pan-Africanism as economic and political co-operation or integration is presented as a positive development for the eight countries of Central Africa, which share the French language as well as economic and monetary ties to France. The author also depicts the obstacles to regional co-operation: the differences between the 'haves' and the 'have nots' of the area; the fear of Zairian hegemony; and the divergent interests of outside powers. Yet the benefits of regional co-operation can be realized if leaders and their peoples have the vision to see beyond their narrow national and local interests.

434 **Les relations entre les Etats-Unis et le Zaïre.** (Relations between the United States and Zaire.)
Romain Yakemtchouk. Brussels: Institut Royal des Relations Internationales, 1986. 127p. bibliog. (Studia Diplomatica, vol. 29 [1986], no. 1).

In a short but highly detailed work, Yakemtchouk describes the bilateral relations between the United States and Zaire. The study is comprehensive in scope, tracing US-Zairian ties from the inception of the Congo Free State in the 1880s up until the Reagan Administration, with greater weight placed on the period from Zairian independence to the present. Emphasis is given to the diplomatic relationship between the two countries, but there is considerable analysis of the economic relationship. The author frequently quotes official US pronouncements on its relationship with Zaire, outlining American positions, and includes twenty-two pertinent diplomatic documents.

435 **The relationship between the OAU and the UN: a case study of the Congo crisis, 1960-1964.**
Tunde Adeniran. *Nigerian Journal of International Affairs*, vol. 14, no. 1 (1988), p. 112-23.

The author examines the Congo crisis from the perspective of the relationship between two major international organizations: the United Nations and the Organization of African Unity. The events of early Zairian independence sow mistrust of the motives and intentions of the UN among African states, but they also lay the foundation for a future co-operation between the UN and the community of emerging African states.

436 **Rôle géostratégique du Zaïre dans l'aire conflictuelle d'Afrique Australe.** (Geostrategic rôle of Zaire in the area of conflict of Southern Africa.)
Laurent Monnier. *Genève-Afrique*, vol. 26, no. 2 (1988), p. 83-96.

The article provides a brief biographical sketch of Mobutu Sese Seko as a prelude to a discussion of his leadership of Zaire. The author's area of focus is the multiple theatres of conflict in Southern Africa, and the delicate balancing act of Zairian foreign policy in relationship to these conflicts. From a political and economic point of view, the weakness and decline of Zaire creates a need for dependency on the part of the tottering Mobutu régime. The destabilizing conflict across the border in Angola, recalling earlier ethnic and regional conflicts within Zaire itself, creates, in the mind of Zairian policy-makers, a need for a strong American tie. The art of the Mobutu foreign policy has been to balance various foreign interests; on the issue of Southern Africa, Zaire's foreign policy has been closely linked to the US while on the surface avoiding close public identification with American foreign policy.

437   **The situation in Zaire: hearing before the Subcommittee on
      African Affairs of the Committee on Foreign Relations, United
      States Senate, One Hundred Second Congress, first session,
      November 6, 1991.**
      United States. Congress. Senate. Committee on Foreign Relations.
      Subcommittee on African Affairs.   Washington, DC: US GPO, 1992.
      38p.

This hearing before the Subcommittee on African Affairs of the Committee on Foreign
Relations, United States Senate, contains statements by four experts on various aspects
of US-Zairian relations and general conditions in Zaire. The statements are followed by a
question-and-answer session with the Senators, which offers unique insights into the
opinions and motives of the people actively involved in formulating American foreign
policy. The first to testify before the Committee is Assistant Secretary of State for
African Affairs, Herman J. Cohen, who sums up some basic US objectives in Zaire:
national stability; political democracy and economic prosperity. Cohen characterizes
Zaire's President Mobutu as a 'leader who was able to unite his country following the
1960s civil war but who had failed in later years to make necessary economic and
political reforms.' US officials have repeatedly expressed to President Mobutu the need
for improved human rights, democratic institutions, and stabilizing economic
development in Zaire. Cohen stressed that in the future US policy toward all of Africa
would seek to establish links between the democratization process and US foreign
assistance. This hearing is published as a US government document and should be
readily available through many American depositary libraries or US Information Agency
centres in other countries.

438   **U.S. foreign policy: a study of CIA and external intervention in
      Central Africa.**
      Amulya Kumar Tripathy.   Delhi: Discovery, 1989. 243p. bibliog.

In spite of its title, this work by an Indian author deals only peripherally with the CIA. It
focuses instead on general US-Zairian relations. Zairian politics and foreign policy are
chronicled in great detail from the advent of Zairian independence to the present. The
perspective of the study is geopolitical, emphasizing the strategic location and resources
of the Zairian state as well as the world-wide competition for influence between the US
and the USSR. The bilateral relationship between the US and Zaire is characterized as
one of 'mutual dependence'. Zaire, as an unstable emerging state, has sought the
economic, political, and at times the military support of Western powers and has relied
heavily upon US aid for the bolstering of its shaky and dictatorial régime. The US, in
turn, has committed itself to the stability of the Mobutu régime, and American foreign
policy shows a high degree of dependency upon the régime's continuing survival,
despite reservations about its economic policies, its corruption, and its human rights
record.

439   U.S. foreign policy toward Zaire.
      Peter J. Schraeder.   In: *United States foreign policy toward Africa:
      incrementalism, crisis, and change.*   Edited by Peter J. Schraeder.
      Cambridge, England; New York: Cambridge University Press, 1993,
      p. 51-113. bibliog. (Cambridge Studies in International Relations,
      no. 31).

In the third chapter of his work, Peter Schraeder traces US-Zairian relations from independence to the present from the American point of view. He depicts US policy-makers as hobbled by ideological constraints, which shape the formulation of US policy. Under the colonial régime, the US took great pains not to offend its Belgian ally, while implementing a Eurocentric policy toward the colonial Zaire. From the back burner of American concerns, Zaire jumped to the forefront of US attention during the crisis that surrounded the country's independence. Since that time, US policy has been largely moulded by fears of Soviet incursion into Central Africa as well as a justified apprehension of chaos in the unstable new state. These outlooks have cemented the US 'special relationship' with Zaire and Mobutu Sese Seko. Although increasingly disillusioned with the Mobutu régime, Washington has continued to nurture this relationship, a prisoner of its own foreign policy assumptions.

440   The United Nations, the superpowers and the Congo crisis.
      Chidi Onwumere.   *Nigerian Journal of International Affairs*, vol. 13,
      no. 2 (1987), p. 51-82.

Onwumere reviews the Congo crisis, delving deeply into the details of the UN intervention in Zaire and the diplomatic stand of other countries during the multiple birth pains of the new state. The analysis is largely carried out from the perspective of the UN and foreign powers and does not adequately represent the facts and details of Zairian diplomatic reactions to the events.

441   United States policy toward Zaire.
      Nzongola-Ntalaja.   In: *African crisis areas and U.S. foreign policy.*
      Edited by Gerald J. Bender, James S. Coleman, Richard L. Sklar.
      Berkeley, California: University of California Press, 1985, p. 225-38.
      bibliog.

This brief essay reviews some of the elements and events in the US-Zairian bilateral relationship. The author analyses the political and strategic motivations behind US support for Mobutu.

442   Zaire.
      Michael G. Schatzberg.   In: *The political economy of African foreign
      policy: comparative analysis.*   Edited by Timothy M. Shaw, Olajide
      Aluko.   New York: St. Martin's Press, 1984, p. 283-318. bibliog.

In a remarkably cogent and incisive essay, Schatzberg reviews the economic, political and social underpinnings of Zairian foreign policy. A national bourgeoisie has emerged in Zaire to replace the personnel of the colonial state. Zaire is seen as part of a vast, interconnected international economic system. The Mobutu régime, recognizing the dependent nature of the Zairian state and its economy, has skilfully balanced the interests of competing foreign powers, remarkably catholic in its willingness to accept assistance from a wide variety of countries. Within this system of multiple dependencies, Zaire has carved out a position of autonomy, which preserves the class interests of the national bourgeoisie, the stability of the state, and the survival, to date, of the régime. Beyond the realm of foreign policy, this essay gives a well-balanced, comprehensive view of Zaire. Writing before 1984 however, Schatzberg's optimistic analysis of Zaire does not reflect a decade of unmitigated economic decline, increasing social unrest, and governmental instability.

443 **Zaire and Israel: an American connection.**
Najib J. Hakim, Richard P. Stevens. *Journal of Palestine Studies*,
vol. 12, no. 3 (Spring 1983), p. 41-53.

The authors outline a Zairian-Israeli bilateral relationship largely characterized by arms, diamonds and political influence. From the very inception of the Mobutu régime, Zaire maintained a close diplomatic relationship with Israel although she was compelled to sever formal ties following the 1973 Middle Eastern War. In Mobutu's words, Zaire was forced to choose between a 'friendly country' (Israel) and a 'brother country' (Egypt). Despite this break, Zaire retained some degree of military and economic co-operation with Israel. As relations with the US soured under withering Congressional criticism of Zairian human rights violations, Mobutu sought in the early 1980s to renew formal diplomatic ties with Israel. Israeli support for Zaire's military was deemed of great importance for the decaying Mobutu régime, and the government of Zaire hoped that Israel, with its strong Washington lobby, would be an effective advocate for restored US support for the Central African nation. Israel, for its part, saw in Zaire a friendly leading African nation that would break the continent's diplomatic quarantine of the Jewish state and facilitate the restoration of relations with other nations in the region. The trade in diamonds and other precious natural resources played a secondary but significant rôle in this relationship. Beyond the narrow confines of the Israeli-Zairian relationship, the authors show the pattern that Zairian foreign policy has followed under Mobutu Sese Seko.

444 **Zaire and Southern Africa.**
Thomas M. Callaghy.   In: *Southern Africa in the 1980s.*   Edited by
Olajide Aluko, Timothy M. Shaw.   London; Boston: Allen & Unwin,
1985, p. 61-86. bibliog.

It has been noted that for many years an unwritten *'entente cordiale'* existed between Zaire and South Africa. From Zaire's refusal to vote for the expulsion of South Africa from the UN in 1975 and the extensive overt and covert financial ties between the two states, it is clear that a special relationship existed between the two. The author analyses this relationship from the point of view of both of the parties. Despite the multiple levels of co-operation between the two parties, Zaire's diplomatic rhetoric and explicit foreign policy reflected the anti-South African attitudes of other independent African states.

445 **Le Zaïre, la Belgique et les Etats-Unis d'Amérique: une guerre,
une alliance, 1850-1989.** (Zaire, Belgium and the United States of
America: a war, an alliance, 1850-1989.)
Pilipili Kagabo.   Brussels: CAUA, 1989. 118p.

The author has assembled various essays on topics surrounding Zaire's foreign relations. Some of these are so specialized as to be of little use to the general reader. For those who can take the time and read the language (French), some interesting points of view become apparent. The author describes a troubled world, which has affected Zaire greatly, much to its detriment. Yet amidst this political turbulence, several long-term policies and a community of interests emerge. Zaire is portrayed as part of the 'American commonwealth', sharing common interests and political objectives with the US superpower. Relations with Belgium are also extensively discussed. The view shared by the author looks beyond the events of the day to discover the long term trends and the underlying factors that propel foreign policy.

446 Zaire: Mobutu and beyond.
Madeleine G. Kalb. *Washington Quarterly*, vol. 5, issue 3 (Summer 1983), p. 143-48.

This short, succinct article details an important turning point in the evolution of US foreign relations. In early 1981, the US underwent a change of governments as Jimmy Carter exited the White House and Ronald Reagan entered. The Carter administration, viewing Zaire through the prism of human rights, was justifiably appalled by the violations of international political and civil norms by the Mobutu régime. The Reagan government, by way of contrast, saw Mobutu as an stalwart ally, a bulwark against communism and a vital link in the chain that supplied the United States with strategic natural resources. This difference of views illuminates the shift in American foreign policy in the early 1980s and does much to dispel the opinion that unchanging political and economic interests produce an unbroken continuity of foreign policy.

447 Zaïre: une politique étrangère conviviale. (Zaire: an agreeable foreign policy.)
Mobutu Sese Seko. *Politique Internationale*, vol. 33 (Fall 1986), p. 353-60.

In an interview granted to *Politique Internationale* in 1986, Zairian President Mobutu Sese Seko outlines in glowing tones the foreign policy of his country. Mobutu expresses the ideal that authentic African values will lead the states of Africa to renew and rejuvenate the world community of nations. Specific questions are asked about Zairian relations with South Africa and Libya, and the President reiterates Zaire's policy. The smoothness of Mobutu's delivery and his optimistic tone do not reflect the distressing economic and political state of Zaire. The interest of this interview lies in gauging the official gloss of Zairian foreign policy, as expressed by the one person who formulates that policy.

448 Zaire under Mobutu: consistencies and contradictions of U.S. policy.
Michael G. Schatzberg. In: *Friendly tyrants: an American dilemma.* Edited by Daniel Pipes, Adam Garfinkle. New York: St. Martin's Press, 1991, p. 421-47.

Michael Schatzberg is a much-cited author in this bibliography. In this short essay, he sums up many of his observations on the US-Zairian bilateral relationship, concluding that, as long as the present régime remains, Zaire's 'eternal' crisis will continue. The options for US foreign policy to effect significant improvement in Zaire are not appealing. Only Zairians are capable of solving their own problems. The US may apply pressure for change, but if the régime resists, Schatzberg concludes that the best path for American policy makers is total disengagement.

449 **The Zairian crisis and American foreign policy.**
Crawford Young. In: *African crisis areas and U.S. foreign policy.*
Edited by Gerald J. Bender, James S. Coleman, Richard L. Sklar.
Berkeley, California: University of California Press, 1985, p. 209-24.
map. bibliog.

Young reviews in a brief essay the relationship between the US and the Zaire of the Mobutu régime, recounting stages of the crisis of the Zairian government.

Britain and the Congo in the nineteenth century.
See item no. 103.

Britain and the Congo Question, 1885-1913.
See item no. 111.

The rise and decline of the Zairian state.
See item no. 146.

Agony of the Congo.
See item no. 326.

Mobutu or chaos?: the United States and Zaire, 1960-1990.
See item no. 352.

Uncertain mandate: politics of the U.N. Congo operation.
See item no. 373.

Zaire: continuity and political change in an oppressive state.
See item no. 378.

La conclusion des traités en droit constitutionnel zaïrois: étude de droit international et de droit interne.
See item no. 383.

The Economy and Economic Development

450 Assistance to Zaire.
United States. Congress. House. Committee on Foreign Affairs.
Subcommittee on Africa. In: *Economic and military assistance
programs in Africa.* Washington, DC: US Government Printing
Office, 1979, p. 351-441.

This chapter consists entirely of statements made on 5 March, 1979 before the
Subcommittee regarding American economic assistance to Zaire. These statements
reveal the level of corruption and the seriousness of the economic situation in Zaire at
that time, as well as a high level of anguish shared by the US government and the people
testifying. Witnesses include Richard Moose, then Secretary of State for African Affairs,
Dr. Crawford Young and Dr. David Gould, both professors who have written about
Zaire, and Dr. Guy Gran, a private economics consultant.

451 The Congolese economy on the eve of independence.
Fédération des Entreprises Congolaises. Brussels, Fédération des
Entreprises Congolaises, 1960. 84p.

Following a brief history of Zaire's economy from about 1900 to 1950, this work
discusses its expansion from 1950 to 1960, and considers the development of various
sectors of the economy, including mining, agriculture, manufacturing, energy, transport,
and commerce.

452 The crisis in Zaire: myths and realities.
Edited by Nzongola-Ntalaja. Trenton, New Jersey: Africa World
Press, 1986. 327p. bibliog.

Previously presented at a conference sponsored by Howard University in Washington,
DC, this collection of papers exemplifies current research on Zaire in the humanities and
social sciences. Specifically, these essays offer, through a wide variety of viewpoints, a
comprehensive analysis of the economic and social crisis facing a country which, despite
its vast resources, has failed miserably on the path to economic growth and development

since independence. Worth noting is a revealing section on how Zairians cope with low wages and survive unemployment.

453 **L'économie de la République du Zaïre, 1960-1er semestre 1980.**
(The economy of the Republic of Zaire, 1960-first semester 1980.)
Daniel Van der Steen, Anne-Françoise Roget, with Danièle Sinechal,
Marc Meurrens. Brussels: CEDAF, 1980-85. 2 vols. (Bibliographies
Analytiques sur l'Afrique Centrale, vols. 5, 7).

As the title indicates, this work is an annotated bibliography of materials on the Zairian economy, covering the years 1960-80. Part one (tome five), containing 590 entries, lists individual works, government documents, and collections of different materials on a specific subject. Part two (tome seven), with 885 entries, lists masters' theses, dissertations, and periodical articles, which form the bulk of this volume. Works cited are grouped by type of material and are mostly in French.

454 **The effects of trade and exchange rate policies on agriculture in Zaire.**
Tshikala B. Tshibaka. Washington, DC: International Food Policy
Research Institute, 1986. 65p. bibliog. (Research Report [International
Food Policy Research Institute], no. 56).

Analyses how certain trade, exchange rate and other price policies have negatively affected Zaire's agricultural sector and overall economy since they were adopted in 1960.

455 **Evading male control: women in the second economy in Zaire.**
Janet MacGaffey. In: *Patriarchy and class: African women in the home and workforce.* Edited by Sharon B. Stichter, Jane L. Parpart.
Boulder, Colorado; London: Westview Press, 1988, p. 161-76.
(African Modernization and Development Series).

Traces the history of how the economic position of Zairian women and their opportunities to generate income have fluctuated with the economic and political changes that took place from the colonial period through the 1980s. The author discusses how the second, or 'underground', economy expanded greatly during the widening economic crisis of the past two decades, supplying women with the chance to do much more than merely assist their families in survival.

456 **Evolution et transformation des structures de l'économie zaïroise, 1970-1984.** (Evolution and transformation of the structure of the
Zairian economy, 1970-1984.)
Gamela Nginu Diamuan Gana, Tomasikila Kioni-Kiabantu, Maphana
ma Nguma. Kinshasa: Presses de l'Université de Kinshasa, 1987.
227p. maps. bibliog.

This book, a collaborative effort by three economists from the University of Kinshasa, focuses on the measures taken by the Zairian government to restructure the economy from 1970-84. During these years, Zaire came to be faced with the problems of servicing a heavy debt, reduced capacity to import goods, and a dramatic increase in the unemployed and underemployed, problems to which the authors suggest there will probably be no real solution unless the Mobutu government shows a true voluntary will to reverse certain negative tendencies. The book contains numerous statistical tables and figures, interpreted clearly and succinctly by the text.

457   **Food production in a land-surplus, labor-scarce economy: the Zairian basin.**
Tshikala B. Tshibaka.   Washington, DC: International Food Policy Research Institute, 1989. 70p. map. bibliog. (Research Report [International Food Policy Research Institute], vol. 74).

Describes the state of the small-farm sector in the Zairian Basin, an important agro-ecological region in a tropical rain forest zone. Although land is readily available, food production is lower than it could be. The mode of farming, poor roads and infrastructure, and few resources allocated to agricultural production, especially labour, all limit the volume of food produced, causing shortages and other hardships.

458   **Foreign Economic Trends and Their Implications for the United States.**
Washington, DC: US Department of Commerce, Industry and Trade Administration, 1969- . annual.

Each issue of this serial publication is devoted to a particular country, and one about Zaire is available. It summarizes the current state of and dominant trends in the Zairian economy, and analyses economic relations with the United States.

459   **From the Congo Free State to Zaire: how Belgium privatized the economy: a history of Belgian stock companies in Congo-Zaire from 1885-1974.**
Jacques Depelchin.   Dakar: Codesria, 1992. 235p. bibliog. (Codesria Book Series).

This work is divided generally into two parts, although, as the author states, 'its chapters might be read each on its own'. The first part is an analysis of selected sources that have traditionally been used by scholars, historians and researchers to formulate positions on the political and economic history of Zaire, as well as the positions themselves. The second part, which forms the bulk of the work, is mainly a history of specific joint Belgian stock companies operating in the Congo from 1885-1974, and how their operations and investment strategies affected the Zairian economy.

460   **The Great Depression and the making of the colonial economic system in the Belgian Congo.**
Bogumil Jewsiewicki.   *African Economic History*, no. 4 (Fall 1977), p. 153-76.

An analysis of the state of the Zairian economy during the Great Depression, and how during this time period the colonial economic system, with its political, ideological, and social impact, fully developed and remains dominant in Africa today.

461 **Indicateur économique et fiscal, République du Zaïre.** (Economic and fiscal indicators, Republic of Zaire.)
Agence Zaïroise d'Edition et d'Expansion, 5th ed. 1984/85. 106p.

This periodical issue contains statistical information on the Zairian economy, and some condensed legal texts which discuss expenditures of tax dollars. More than half of it consists of a directory of Zairian business firms, complete with addresses and telephone numbers.

462 **Peripheral capitalism, the state and crisis: the determinants of public policy in Zaire, 1965-1980.**
Sang Ngeen Sang-Mpam.   PhD thesis, University of Chicago, Chicago, Illinois, 1984. 451p. bibliog.

A detailed economic study which revolves around the following thesis: Zaire's political crisis, its economic deprivation, and the characteristics of its state are the result of policies associated with class and linked with a capitalist production mode. This is a rather technical study that would be of interest largely to those with a strong economics background.

463 **The political economy of African debt: the case of Zaire.**
Thomas M. Callaghy.   In: *Africa in economic crisis.*   Edited by John Ravenhill.   New York: Columbia University Press, 1986, p. 307-46.

An analysis of the complex, ever-changing and often competing sets of interests, both internal and external, that exist within the Zairian political sphere and greatly influence Zaire's debt crisis.

464 **1er plan quinquennal de développement économique et social, 1986-1990.** (First five-year economic and social development plan, 1986-1990.)
Département du Plan.   Kinshasa: République du Zaïre, Département du Plan, 1986. 316p. map.

Zaire's First Five-Year Development Plan is divided into three parts: a discussion of the macro-economic and institutional framework of the Plan, a presentation of the Plan's objectives and investment strategies concerning Zaire's economic, social, and administrative sectors, and plans for development programmes within nine regions.

465 **Productivity and factor proportions in less developed countries: the case of industrial firms in the Congo.**
J. Gouverneur.   Oxford: Clarendon Press, 1971. 171p. map. bibliog.

A revision of the author's thesis, this is a rather technical micro-economic study using data gathered for eight Belgian companies established in Zaire prior to the Second World War. It deals primarily with problems associated with long-run changes within industrial firms, operating in developing countries, in the following areas: techniques; productivity; and factor proportions.

466   **The real economy of Zaire: the contribution of smuggling & other unofficial activities to national wealth.**
Janet MacGaffey, with Vwakyanakazi Mukohya.   London: James Currey; Philadelphia: University of Pennsylvania Press, 1991. 175p. maps. bibliog.

This study documents and analyses Zaire's second, or 'underground' economy. The first part consists of an overview of issues associated with a second economy, and a general discussion of the second economy of Zaire. The second part contains four regional studies; three deal with cross-border and rural-urban trade, and the fourth is on women's trade and how earnings from illicit trade documented in the other studies are used to enhance spending power in Kinshasa households. A concluding chapter assesses the positive and negative effects of Zaire's second economy, and how it has transformed the country's society.

467   **Répertoire de développement, Zaïre 1985.** (Directory of development, Zaire 1985.)
Waltraud Fleischle-Jaudas, under the direction of Didier de Failly.
Kinshasa: Centre d'Etudes Pour l'Action Sociale, 1985. 428p.

The primary goal of the Centre d'Etudes Pour l'Action Sociale, which has existed since 1965, is to aid development in Zaire. Since its formation, it has continuously gathered information on institutions, organizations, and activities associated with development, and the public has readily consulted the Centre for such information. As a result, it was thought that a reference tool such as this would be worth publishing. Arranged by type of institution or firm, it contains names, addresses, and phone numbers; references are accompanied by a summary of the principal activities of each institution or firm.

468   **Rural society and the Belgian colonial economy.**
Bogumil Jewsiewicki.   In: *History of Central Africa*, vol. 2.   Edited by David Birmingham, Phyllis M. Martin.   New York: Longman, 1983. p. 95-125.

Examines the rôle and transformation of the Congolese peasantry within the Belgian colonial production system that was imposed upon it.

469   **The social and economic development of Zaire since independence: an historical outline.**
Jean Philippe Peemans.   *African Affairs*, vol. 74, no. 295 (April 1975), p. 148-79.

Discusses the main features of economic development in Zaire from 1960-75, and predicts the country's future economic problems. The author also considers the links between Zaire's economy and its political situation.

470 **State against development: the experience of post-1965 Zaire.**
Mondonga M. Mokoli. Westport, Connecticut: Greenwood Press,
1992. 147p. maps. bibliog. (Contributions in Afro-American and
African Studies, no. 150).

Evaluates the effect of state-sponsored economic and agricultural policies on the Zairian
people in post-1965 Zaire. The author shows how these policies have been driven by
politics and have therefore failed to foster socio-economic development within the
country.

471 **Structures économiques du Congo Belge et du Ruanda-Urundi.**
(Economic structures of the Belgian Congo and Ruanda-Urundi.)
Jacques Lefebvre. Brussels: Editions du Treurenberg, 1955. 142p.

A general overview of post-Second World War colonial economic conditions, systems,
and institutions in Belgian Africa, with accompanying maps and statistics.

472 **The World Bank & structural transformation in developing
countries: the case of Zaire.**
Winsome J. Leslie. Boulder, Colorado: Lynne Rienner, 1987. 208p.
map. bibliog.

The rôle of the World Bank in the development process has been and continues to be the
subject of heated debate. This study examines the nature, effectiveness, and limits of
World Bank policies and activities in its attempts to manage Zaire's economic and debt
crisis of the 1980s.

473 **Zaire.**
Mumpasi Lututala, Mafuku Kintambu, Matingu Mvudi. In: *The
impact of structural adjustment on the population of Africa: the
implications for education, health, & employment.* Edited by
Aderanti Adepoju. London: James Currey; Portsmouth, New
Hampshire: Heinemann, 1993, p. 130-43.

After outlining the major trends in the Zairian economy from 1970 to 1990, the authors
describe the vigorous structural adjustment measures taken to correct the
macro-economic imbalances which emerged after 1975, and how they impacted
negatively on Zaire's health, education and employment sectors.

474 **Zaire, current economic situation and constraints.**
World Bank. Eastern Africa Regional Office. Washington, DC: East
Africa Regional Office, World Bank, 1980. 191p. map. bibliog.

This report analyses the causes, effects, and implications of the major economic crisis in
Zaire that began in 1975 and continued to the first half of 1979, caused principally by a
fall in the price of copper and a subsequent deterioration in Zaire's trade terms.

475   **Zaire, Rwanda, Burundi: country profile, annual survey of
       political and economic background.** *The Economist.*
       London: Economist Intelligence Unit, 1986- . annual.
A specialized publication of *The Economist*, this is an excellent source of current
background information pertinent to business and economic research. Text and statistical
information is provided on the following topics: politics; population and society;
currency; the economy; national accounts; employment; wages and prices; agriculture
and forestry; mining; energy; manufacturing; transport and communications; finance;
foreign trade; external payments and debt; and exchange, trade and investment
regulations.

476   **Zaire, Rwanda, Burundi: country report, analyses of economic
       and political trends.** *The Economist.*
       London: Economist Intelligence Unit, 1986- . quarterly. (Profile,
       no. 58).
Carefully monitors, analyses, and predicts economic and political trends, in a coherent
and readable style. Charts, graphs, and statistics that provide various information about
the economy supplement the text.

477   **Zaire: the political economy of underdevelopment.**
       Edited by Guy Gran, with the assistance of Galen Hull.   New York:
       Praeger, 1979. 331p. map. bibliog. (Praeger Special Studies).
This collection of essays analyses how Zaire has struggled and failed to develop
politically and economically within the modern world since independence. It examines
how the development system, fuelled by money and advice from Western institutions
(such as the World Bank, the Agency for International Development, and others),
together with the activities of multinational business enterprises and Third World
governments, has severly hampered fundamental change and improvement in the lives of
the Zairian people.

478   **Zaire to the 1990s: will retrenchment work?**
       Gregory Kronsten.   London: Economist Intelligence Unit, 1986. 97p.
       map. (Special Report [Economist Intelligence Unit, Great Britain],
       no. 227).
Kronsten examines the bold and sometimes drastic measures that were taken by Zaire's
government after 1983 to restore the health of the country's economy, and assesses the
possibilities of achieving positive results to 1990.

Du Congo au Zaïre, 1960-1980: essai de bilan.
See item no. 3.

Zaire.
See item no. 10.

Zaïre-Afrique.
See item no. 11.

Zaire, what destiny?
See item no. 14.

Decline or recovery in Zaire?
See item no. 145.

The rise and decline of the Zairian state.
See item no. 146.

Eglise et développement: rapport du 3e séminaire national, Kinshasa, 15-22 novembre 1981.
See item no. 257.

Class relations in a dependent economy: businessmen and businesswomen in Kisangani, Zaire.
See item no. 285.

God and man in Zaire.
See item no. 289.

The role of women in rural Zaire and Upper Volta: improving methods of skill acquisition.
See item no. 295.

L'automne d'un despotisme: pouvoir, argent et obéissance dans le Zaïre des années quatre-vingt.
See item no. 329.

Le Congo de la colonisation belge à l'indépendance.
See item no. 333.

Mobutu et l'argent du Zaïre: les révélations d'un diplomate ex-agent des services secrets.
See item no. 351.

Zaire since independence.
See item no. 381.

Development administration at the local level: the case of Zaire.
See item no. 401.

Aussenwirtschaftliche Abhangigkeitsfaktoren.
See item no. 413.

The political economy of Third World intervention: mines, money, and U.S. policy in the Congo crisis.
See item no. 431.

A case study in exploring time series: inflation and the growth of the money supply in Zaire, 1965-1982.
See item no. 479.

Investment and investment policy in a small open economy: the Zairean case, 1965-75.
See item no. 483.

The problems and management of development finance in African countries: proceedings of the symposium.
See item no. 484.

Rapport Annuel.
See item no. 485.

The role of the state into the capital accumulation process: the case of the Congo during the colonial period (1885-1960).
See item no. 487.

U.S. loans to Zaire: hearing before the Subcommittee on International Finance of the Committee on Banking, Housing, and Urban Affairs, United States Senate, Ninety-sixth Congress, first session . . . May 24, 1979.
See item no. 488.

Zaire is in turmoil after the currency collapse.
See item no. 490.

Marketing in Zaire.
See item no. 494.

The agricultural development of Zaire.
See item no. 515.

Le transfert de technologie dans les pays en développement: le secteur agro-alimentaire au Zaïre.
See item no. 530.

Land-locked countries of Africa.
See item no. 536.

Paths of authority: roads, the State and the market in eastern Zaire.
See item no. 537.

Bulletin Trimestriel des Statistiques Générales.
See item no. 564.

L'Economie du Zaïre au [ ] : Quelques Indicateurs Conjoncturels.
See item no. 566.

Profils de l'économie du Zaïre: années 1955-1987.
See item no. 569.

Ecole, éducation et développement au Zaïre: actes du 2e Séminaire Régional de l'Académie des Professeurs pour la Paix Mondiale, Afrique Centrale, Kinshasa, Zaïre, 8 septembre 1983.
See item no. 599.

The Economy and Economic Development

Recherche scientifique et développement: 1980 répertoire des institutions francophones.
See item no. 625.

Finance and Banking

479 **A case study in exploring time series: inflation and the growth of the money supply in Zaire, 1965-1982.**
Nlandu Mamingi, Marc Wuyts. The Hague, Netherlands: Institute of Social Studies, 1986. 38p. bibliog. (Occasional Paper [Institute of Social Studies (Netherlands)], no. 104).
Using a case study of inflation in Zaire, this paper analyses problems specific to time series. It explores quarterly data from 1965-82 related to the evolution of Zaire's consumer price index and money supply, and considers the link between inflation and the money supply. This study is on the technical side and would mostly be of interest to those with an economics background.

480 **The choice of an exchange rate régime for developing countries: with special reference to Zaire.**
Bolaluete Mbwebembo. Geneva: Université de Genève, Institut Universitaire de Hautes Etudes Internationales, 1984. 249p. (Thèse, Graduate Institute of International Studies [Geneva, Switzerland], no. 386).
This thesis focuses on Zaire as an example of a developing country that must consider certain factors when choosing an appropriate exchange rate régime in a world where major currencies are typically floating.

481 **Foreign trade and exchange control regulations in the Republic of Zaire.**
Banque de Zaïre. Brussels: Belgolaise, 1987. [138p.].
A manual which presents, in summary form, various provisions regulating Zaire's foreign exchange control and trade. All information contained in this publication consists entirely of extracts of regulations and other texts issued by the Banque du Zaïre.

482 **The funding of the permanent crisis: a study of IMF intervention in Zaire.**
Anthony Wood. In: *International Monetary Fund policies in the Third World: case studies of Turkey, Zaire, and Peru.* Norwich, England: University of East Anglia, School of Development Studies, 1981, p. 1-34. (Development Studies Occasional Paper, no. 8).
The relationship between Zaire and the international banking community has guided Zaire steadily deeper into debt, and led to continued Western support of the corrupt and unpopular Mobutu government. This paper examines the reasons why. Wood's documentation reveals how unsavoury some of the international and domestic machinations have been concerning foreign aid to and financial negotiations with Zaire.

483 **Investment and investment policy in a small open economy: the Zairean case, 1965-75.**
Kamoto Ka Yanape Lungunga. PhD thesis, University of Pittsburgh, 1979. 172p. bibliog. (Available from University Microfilms, Ann Arbor, Michigan, order no. 80-28037).
A study of investment policy and its impact on Zaire's economy from 1965-75. The period covered was selected because it is the only time during which Zaire experienced, as an independent country, economic and social conditions favourable to development, thus allowing the author to avoid biases in his analysis.

484 **The problems and management of development finance in African countries: proceedings of the symposium.**
Association of African Central Banks and the African Development Bank, joint sponsors, organized by the African Centre for Monetary Studies in collaboration with the Banque du Zaïre in Kinshasa, Zaire. Dakar: The Centre, 1987. 362p. bibliog.
Held on 4-6 November, 1987, this symposium was organized so that central and development bankers and others involved in development finance would have a forum in which to share ideas and experiences. The papers presented here discuss present and future trends in development finance, and ways African countries could improve, from both domestic and external sources, and through implementation of monetary and fiscal policies, and availability of finance. While Zaire is not often referred to specifically, a number of conference participants were from Zaire, and all issues considered are relevant.

485 **Rapport Annuel.** (Annual Report.)
Banque du Zaïre. Kinshasa: Banque du Zaïre, 1970/71- . annual.
Contains information on the organization, administration, and activities of the Banque du Zaïre as well as an analysis of economic activity in the country, including development, investments and credit, production, prices, salaries, and public finance and employment. Information on other financial institutions in Zaire is included as well.

486 **The ritual dance of the debt game.**
Thomas M. Callaghy. *Africa Report*, Sept.-Oct. 1984, p. 22-26.
Callaghy outlines the political and financial reasons why, by the early 1980s, Mobutu and his associates came to be dependent on aid from Western banks and governments, the IMF, and the World Bank, and how they continuously manipulated these institutions into rescheduling debt payments and loaning money in amounts too great for the country to finance. By 1983, Mobutu had instituted some economic reforms which brought praise from the US and others, but, as the author demonstrates, there was little reason for such optimism.

487 **The role of the state into the capital accumulation process: the case of the Congo during the colonial period (1885-1960).**
Jean-Philippe Peemans. Dakar: United Nations, African Institute for Economic Development and Planning, 1974. 64p. bibliog.
This monograph analyses the rôle of the state in establishing structural relations between foreign capital and indigenous labour in Zaire during the colonial period. The study is divided into two main parts; the first considers the interdependence between foreign capital and the colonial state; the second studies certain aspects of the rôle of the state in developing a process of capital accumulation.

488 **U.S. loans to Zaire: hearing before the Subcommittee on International Finance of the Committee on Banking, Housing, and Urban Affairs, United States Senate, Ninety-sixth Congress, first session . . . May 24, 1979.**
United States. Congress. Senate. Committee on Banking, Housing, and Urban Affairs. Subcommittee on International Finance. Washington, DC: US Government Printing Office, 1979. 68p. map.
This document consists of the statements made by six individuals at a hearing before the Subcommittee on International Finance on May 24, 1979. Its purpose was to review American loans to Zaire. The participants debate the desirability and wisdom of extending more credit to Zaire to continue funding construction of the Inga-Shaba power transmission line, in the light of Zaire's monumental political, economic, and structural problems.

489 **Vicissitudes óf the Zairian exchequer since 1960.**
Rwanyindo Ruzirabwoba. In: *Zaire, what destiny?* Edited by Kankwenda Mbaya. Dakar: CODESRIA, 1993, p. 264-87. (Codesria Book Series).
Specific problems that have haunted Zaire's public finances since independence are examined in this chapter, which includes specific recommendations for change and reform.

490   **Zaire is in turmoil after the currency collapse.**
      Kenneth B. Noble.   *New York Times (Late New York Edition),*
      December 12, 1993. p. 3.

This informative and well-written article describes how the introduction of a new
currency by the Zairian government precipitated another grave crisis which has further
eroded the economy and threatens to recreate the level of violence and turmoil that
followed independence in 1960.

Trade

491   Black mother: Africa, the years of trial.
Basil Davidson.   London: Longman, 1970. 269p. maps. bibliog.
Praised and recommended by distinguished scholars, this book discusses the enduring
alliances and commercial ties, based largely on the slave trade, that linked Africa and
Europe from the 15th to the 19th centuries. One section in particular is concerned with
the Kongo Kingdom, one of the regions renowned during the slave trade era and affected
profoundly by the coming of the Europeans.

**492   Food supply and the state: the history and social organization of
the rice trade in Kisangani, Zaire.**
Diane Russell.   PhD thesis, Boston University, Boston,
Massachusetts, 1991. 384p. maps. bibliog. (Available from University
Microfilms, Ann Arbor, Michigan, order no. 9110833).
Zaire's third largest staple food crop is rice, for which the demand in its cities can
supposedly not be met by what is produced nationally; imports have made up the
difference between production and consumption since the 1960s. Focusing on the rice
trade in Haut Zaïre, the largest area of rice cultivation in the country, this study examines
how rice production has suffered dramatically because of the parasitic nature of the
Zairian state. Using ethnography and historical research, the author has also shown how
trade in this most important food crop has changed since colonial times.

493   Long-distance trade-routes in Central Africa.
Jan Vansina.   *Journal of African History*, vol. 3, no. 3 (1962),
p. 375-90.
A description of the long-distance trade that was established in the 15th century and
existed until about 1900, when the administrative and economic organization of the
European colonies caused its demise.

494 **Marketing in Zaire.**
Prepared by the Office of Africa, with assistance from the
Economic/Commercial Staff at the US Embassy in Kinshasa.
Washington, DC: US Dept. of Commerce, International Trade
Administration, 1991. 61p. Available from the Superintendent of
Documents, US GPO, (Overseas Business Reports, OBR 91-04).

The aim of this guide is to present information important for firms interested in
marketing exports to Zaire, although it is equally useful for anyone who wishes to find
out more on Zairian commerce and economic conditions in general. Included are
sections on the trade outlook for Zaire, the state of the Zairian economy, transportation,
utilities, trade regulations and documentation, banking, selling and investing in Zaire,
taxes, and guidance for business travellers. Issues of this title are regularly superseded by
new ones; this is the most current issue.

495 **Mboma and the lower Zaire: a socioeconomic study of a Kongo
trading community, c. 1785-1885.**
Norm Schrag.   PhD thesis, Indiana University, Bloomington, Indiana,
1985. 194p. maps. bibliog. (Available from University Microfilms,
Ann Arbor, Michigan, order no. 8617811).

The author of this thesis has reconstructed a history of Mboma, which became the most
important slave port on the lower Zaire by the end of the 18th century and the capital of
the Congo Free State soon after the Belgian colonial conquest in 1885. Mboma had a
highly organized export trade in slaves, which was effectively suppressed in the 1860s.
In its place, trade developed in commodities that included peanuts, palm oil, ivory, gum
copal, and rubber, but Mboma lost its commercial independence in the 1870s as the
result of famine, a toll war with foreign traders, and its political independence with the
European takeover.

496 **Pre-colonial African trade: essays on trade in central and eastern
Africa before 1900.**
Edited by Richard Gray, David Birmingham.   London; New York:
Oxford University Press, 1970. 308p. maps.

Nine of the thirteen chapters of this book were previously presented as papers at
seminars held at the School of Oriental and African Studies, University of London,
and the University of California at Los Angeles. Together they discuss numerous
aspects of and provide detailed information on trade in such staples as salt, pottery,
and iron in the central and eastern African regions, including former kingdoms and
territories that were part of what is now Zaire.

497 **Sub-Saharan agriculture: synthesis and trade prospects.**
Shamsher Singh.   Washington, DC: World Bank, 1983. 157p. bibliog.
(World Bank Staff Working Papers, no. 608).

Agricultural commodities account for high percentages of export earnings in many
Sub-Saharan African countries, including Zaire, making agricultural production the most
important cause of economic growth in this area of the world. This paper is divided into
three parts: part one summarizes the state of agriculture in Sub-Saharan Africa, and
discusses the constraints that hinder its development; part two is a summary of the price,

trade, and consumption outlook for major Sub-Saharan agricultural commodities; and part three presents brief projections for individual commodities.

The fall of the Congo Arabs.
See item no. 104.

River of wealth, river of sorrow: the central Zaire basin in the era of the slave and ivory trade, 1500-1891.
See item no. 109.

Tippu Tip and the East African slave trade.
See item no. 110.

Red rubber: the story of the rubber slave trade flourishing on the Congo in the year of grace 1906.
See item no. 120.

The real economy of Zaire: the contribution of smuggling & other unofficial activities to national wealth.
See item no. 466.

Foreign trade and exchange control regulations in the Republic of Zaire.
See item no. 481.

Industry and Trade Directory of the Democratic Republic of the Congo.
See item no. 502.

Trypanotolerant cattle and livestock in west and central Africa: the international supply and demand for breeding stock.
See item no. 532.

Annuaire des statistiques du commerce extérieur.
See item no. 563.

Commerce extérieur.
See item no. 565.

Statistique du Commerce Extérieur du Congo Belge.
See item no. 570.

Late beads in the African trade.
See item no. 681.

Mining and Other Industries

498   Diamond fever grips Zaire.

Francois Misser.   *African Business*, no. 183, (Dec. 1993), p. 10-11.

A brief report on the spread of diamond production throughout Zaire, possible smuggling and other illicit activity by the Mobutu government concerning both Zairian and Angolan diamonds, and predictions for the future of the diamond sector in Zaire.

499   The diamond invention.

Edward Jay Epstein.   London: Hutchinson, 1982. 270p.

This work had its origins in a meeting the author obtained with a diamond broker in 1978, as part of an effort to produce a report on diamond mining for the German magazine *Geo*. Intrigued by the possibility that the value of diamonds is artificially maintained, Epstein investigated the diamond cartel and reports his findings in this book, which outlines how the DeBeers company has successfully controlled and manipulated the diamond market worldwide. Several chapters contain information on DeBeers' activities concerning the mining and marketing of the substantial reserves of Zaire's chiefly industrial-grade diamonds.

500   Forminière in the Kasai, 1906-1939.

Richard Derkson.   *African Economic History*, no. 12 (1983), p. 49-65.

Like the large and important Union Minière du Haut-Katanga, the Société Internationale Forestière et Minière, or Forminière, was created by King Leopold of Belgium in 1906 and marked the beginning of long-term exploitation of mineral resources in Zaire. This article focuses on the Forminière's important differences from UMHK, including its capital structure, labour policies, and workforce, and how these differences impacted on the peoples of the Kasai.

501 **The gold mines of Kilo-Moto in northeastern Zaire: 1905-1960.**
Bakonzi Agayo. PhD thesis, University of Wisconsin-Madison,
Madison, Wisconsin, 1982. 943p. maps. bibliog. (Available from
University Microfilms, Ann Arbor, Michigan, order no. 82-08283).

Based extensively on the archives of a major corporation, this thesis is a complete
history of the Kilo-Moto gold mining industry, the second largest mining industry of
colonial Zaire.

502 **Industry and Trade Directory of the Democratic Republic of the
Congo.**
Kinshasa: SADIAPAC-Congo, 1969- . 2nd ed. annual.

The first English translation of this directory provides a profile of industry and trade in
Zaire at a time when its economy was steadily expanding and evolving. More than half
of it consists of an extensive list of commercial and industrial enterprises in existence at
the time of publication. It appears that no further editions have been published.

503 **Mineral industries of Africa.**
United States. Bureau of Mines. Washington, DC: US Dept. of the
Interior, 1984. 153p. maps. bibliog. (Mineral Perspectives).

A ready reference tool that presents a summary review, in text, tables, and maps, of the
mineral industries of fifty-two African countries, including Zaire. This is an updated and
revised edition of the Bureau's 1976 work with the same title.

504 **Mineral resources, the State and industrialization in Zaire.**
Kankwenda Mbaya, translated from the French by Ayi Kwei Armah.
In: *Zaire, what destiny?* Edited by Kankwenda Mbaya. Dakar,
Senegal: CODESRIA, 1993, p. 319-56. (Codesria Book Series).

This chapter begins with an assessment of the political economy of mineral resources
and the state of mining production in Zaire. The remainder considers two major
questions: what has been the effect of Zaire's attempts to control its mining sector, since
independence, on the country's financial position; how has the industrialization process
been impacted by these attempts?

505 **Minerals Yearbook.**
United States. Department of the Interior. Bureau of Mines.
Washington, DC: US Government Printing Office, 1932- . annual.

An annual review of the mineral industries of the United States and other countries of the
world. Volume three is presented as five area reports, one of which concerns Africa and
contains a chapter on Zaire. It offers a current review of Zaire's mineral industry and the
importance of minerals to its economy. Data on mineral production and trade is included.

506 **Mining in the Belgian Congo.**
Jean-Luc Vellut. In: *History of Central Africa*, vol. 2. Edited by
David Birmingham, Phyllis M. Martin. New York: Longman, 1983.
p. 126-62.

A history of the mining industry in the Belgian Congo and how its rise and development
affected the country's economy and society.

507 **Monograph.**
Union Minière du Haut-Katanga. Brussels: Louis Cuypers,
[1938]- . irreg.

This journal focuses on the activities and achievements of the Union Minière du
Haut-Katanga, one of the largest mining and metallurgical companies to result from
European colonization of Africa. It was also issued in French with the title:
Monographie.

508 **The nationalization of Zaire's copper: from Union Minière to
GECAMINES.**
Wolf Radmann. *Africa Today*, vol. 25, no. 4 (Oct.-Dec. 1978),
p. 25-47.

A review of the history of the Union Minière du Haut-Katanga and its expropriation by
the Mobutu government, including details of the transfer of its assets to a new company,
the Société Générale Congolaise de Minerais, and the Africanization of its personnel.

509 **Union Minière du Haut-Katanga, 1906-1956.**
Union Minière du Haut-Katanga. Brussels: Louis Cuypers, 1956.
281p. maps.

A detailed history of the Union Minière du Haut Katanga, from its very beginnings to
1956. This work was published to commemorate the fiftieth anniversary of the
company's formation.

510 **Union Minière du Haut-Katanga, 1906-1956: évolution des
techniques et des activités sociales.** (Union Minière du
Haut-Katanga, 1906-1956: evolution of techniques and social
activities.)
Union Minière du Haut-Katanga. Brussels: Louis Cuypers, 1957.
355p. maps.

Published on the fiftieth anniversary of its founding, this work records activities of the
Union Miniere du Haut-Katanga, including its research, expansion of it mining activities,
changes in and improvement of its mining techniques, and the structure and evolution of
both its African and European personnel.

511 **Zaire.**
United Nations Industrial Development Organization. Regional and
Country Studies Branch. Vienna: Regional and Country Studies
Branch, United Nations Industrial Development Organization, 1986.
50p. (Industrial Development Review Series).
Provides an overview and brief analysis of Zaire's industrial sector.

512 **Zaire's rich mines are abandoned to scavengers.**
Kenneth B. Noble. *New York Times (Late New York Edition)*,
February 21, 1994, p. A3.
Discusses the political and economic causes of the disintegration of operations at the
state-owned Gécamines company, once the industrial jewel of Zaire. The resulting chaos,
misery, and political tensions have the potential to affect neighbouring African countries
as well.

Pêche maritime au Congo: possibilités de développement.
See item no. 73.

**Development and growth of the fishing industry in Mweru-Luapula,
1920-1964.**
See item no. 521.

Railways and the copper mines of Katanga.
See item no. 539.

**Black mineworkers in central Africa: industrial strategies and the
evolution of an African proletariat in the Copperbelt, 1911-41.**
See item no. 544.

**Bringing the workers back in: worker protest and popular intervention in
Katanga, 1931-1941.**
See item no. 545.

**Disputing the machines: scientific management and the transformation of
the work routine at the Union Minière du Haut-Katanga, 1918-1930.**
See item no. 546.

**Good lawyers but poor workers: recruited Angolan labour in the copper
mines of Katanga, 1917-1921.**
See item no. 547.

**A working class in the making: Belgian colonial labor policy, private
enterprise, and the African mineworker, 1907-1951.**
See item no. 552.

Agriculture

513 African agrarian systems.
International African Seminar, 2nd, Leopoldville, 1960, edited with an
introduction by Daniel Biebuyck.   London: Oxford University Press,
1963. 407p. maps. bibliog.

In addition to the excellent general introduction by Daniel Biebuyck, there are six other
studies on land tenure in the Belgian Congo contained in the proceedings of this
conference. The Zairian peoples covered include the Kongo, Lunda, Zande, and Kuba.
All of these contributions are written in French with lengthy English summaries.

514 Agricultural change in the Belgian Congo, 1945-1960.
V. Drachoussoff.   Stanford, California: Food Research Institute,
Stanford University, 1965. p. 137-200.

This is the best English-language study of agricultural change in the Belgian Congo
during the colonial period. It is a reprint from the Food Research Institute Studies, vol. 5,
no. 2, 1965.

515 The agricultural development of Zaire.
David Shapiro, Eric Tollens.   Aldershot, England; Brookfield,
Vermont: Avebury, 1992. 201p. maps. bibliog.

This is one of the few and most recent books published in English on the subject of
Zairian agriculture and development and is an outgrowth of the 1990 USAID agricultural
sector assessment of Zaire. The description and analysis of agriculture in the economy of
Zaire includes a discussion of agricultural production as well as economic and
institutional factors affecting agriculture. For the period 1982-89, the agricultural sector
makes the largest contribution to Zaire's economy, averaging thirty per cent of Zaire's
total gross domestic product. The promotion of agricultural development is the subject of
the second half of the book.

516 **Agriculture in the Congo basin: tradition and change in African rural economies.**
Marvin P. Miracle. Madison, Wisconsin: University of Wisconsin Press, 1967. 355p. maps. bibliog.

In this in-depth survey of traditional agriculture in the Congo basin, the author thoroughly analyses production techniques (for example, twelve variations of long-fallow systems such as 'cut, plant, burn' are included) followed by technological change. Chapter twelve on technological changes by tribe or area provides a brief convenient summary of each tribe/area covered. An interesting appendix consists of a table of crop and livestock introductions to the Congo basin from 1830 to 1960, as taken from the writings of European travellers, administrators, and missionaries.

517 **Aménagement du territoire: schéma national, utilisation de l'espace.** (Administration of the territory: national scheme, use of space.)
Zaire. Bureau d'Etudes, d'Aménagements et d'Urbanisme. Zaire: BEAU, 1990. 11p. maps.

This is the most recent source from Zaire on the agricultural use of land. The brief text covers the forest sector and animal production and twelve black-and-white maps of vegetable production and one colour map of soils are included.

518 **Atlas de l'agriculture des régions du Bandundu, du Bas-Zaïre et de Kinshasa.** (Agricultural atlas of the regions of Bandundu, Bas-Zaïre and Kinshasa.)
Maria Uyttebroeck, Bart Leirs, Frans Goossens, Bart Minten. Heverlee, Belgium: Katholieke Universiteit Leuven, Centre de Recherche en Economie Agricole des Pays de Développement, Faculté des Sciences Agronomiques, 1991. 127p. maps. (Projet 'Commercialisation des Produits Agricoles', Publication, no. 28).

Three regions of Zaire are covered in this atlas, for which no text accompanies the 127 maps of physical characteristics, household composition, annual production of each important crop, quantities of the crop bought and sold, revenue, use on the farm (in calories and grammes of proteins), and prices.

519 **Bibliographie analytique pour l'agronomie tropicale: Zaïre, Rwanda, Burundi.** (Analytical bibliography on tropical agronomy: Zaire, Rwanda, Burundi.)
B. de Halleux, A. B. Ergo, W. de Haes, A. G. Bal. Tervuren, Belgium: Centre d'Informatique Appliquée au Développement et à l'Agriculture Tropicale, 1972-73. 2 vols.

In this early computer-produced bibliography on all aspects of colonial-era agriculture in Zaire, Rwanda and Burundi, the citations are taken from French language periodicals and books in Belgian libraries. Although not the easiest of publications to use because of all the encoded data, the user will however easily determine the detailed geographical location and subject(s) of the citation.

520 **Bibliography of the soils of the tropics: Vol. 1: Tropics in general and Africa.**
Arnold C. Orvedal.   Washington, DC: US Agency for International
Development, Technical Assistance Bureau, Office of Agriculture,
1975. 228p. (Agriculture Technology for Developing Countries).
The soils of Zaire, Rwanda and Burundi are covered in a single chapter on pages
195-208 of this comprehensive bibliography. The earliest of the approximately 225
sources on Zaire dates from 1932. Publications are primarily in French, but also include
English-language materials.

521 **Development and growth of the fishing industry in Mweru-Luapula, 1920-1964.**
Mwelwa Chambika Musambachime.   PhD thesis, University of
Wisconsin-Madison, 1981. (various pagination). maps. bibliog.
(Available from University Microfilms International, Ann Arbor,
Michigan, order no. 82-05547).
In this historical study of the fishing industry on the border between Katanga and
Northern Rhodesia, the author explores the influence of the fishing industry on the
Katangan mining industry.

522 **Farming systems in Africa: the Great Lakes highlands of Zaire, Rwanda, and Burundi.**
William I. Jones, Roberto Egli.   Washington, DC: World Bank, 1984.
107p. maps. (World Bank Technical Paper, no. 27).
In this scientific study of agricultural farming systems in Eastern Zaire, Rwanda, and
Burundi, Zaire's Maniema slope of the Great Lakes is described. Recommendations are
made on agricultural innovations, soil conservation, as well as the possible
diversification in export crops.

523 **Index des documents microfichés par l'équipe CIPEA/CRDI au Zaïre.** (Index of documents microfiched by the ILCA/IDRC team in
Zaire.)
International Livestock Centre for Africa.   Addis Ababa: Centre
International pour L'Elevage en Afrique, 1982. 24p.
Of the 136 monographs, theses, and journal articles on Zairian animal production that
were microfilmed by the ILCA and the IDRC, 130 are in French and 6 are in English. All
are available at ILCA in Addis Ababa, and many are also available in the the US and UK
in the periodicals in which they were originally published.

524 **Land tenure and agricultural development in Zaire, 1895-1961.**
Robert W. Harms.   Madison, Wisconsin: University of Wisconsin,
Land Tenure Center, 1974. 26p. map. bibliog. (LTC, no. 99).
In this brief historical survey of land tenure and agricultural change in Zaire before
independence, Harms first surveys the Kuba, Nyanga, Zande, and Mongo land tenure
systems before analysing the rôle of the state in determining rural development and land
tenure.

152

525   **Man and Biosphere in Zaire.**
       Brooke Grundfest Schoepf.   In: *The politics of agriculture in tropical Africa*.   Beverly Hills, California: Sage Publications, 1984, p. 269-90. bibliog. (Sage Series on African Modernization and Development).

This is a critical look at Unesco's Man and Biosphere (MAB) Programme in Zaire. The author criticizes the efforts of the MAB Lufira Valley programme in southeastern Shaba, where the Lemba people predominate. Instead of improving the management of their ecosystem, this programme has the potential of worsening social inequality, for small cultivators cannot compete against the national and international commercial enterprises sanctioned by MAB.

526   **Répertoire des recherches agronomiques en cours, au sein de la Communauté économique des pays des grands lacs (C.E.P.G.L.): Burundi, Rwanda, Zaïre.** (Directory of agronomic research in progress, in the heart of the Economic Community of the Great Lakes Countries [E.C.G.L.C.]: Burundi, Rwanda, Zaire.)
       Institut de Recherche Agronomique et Zootechnique.   Gitega, Burundi: IRAZ, 1988. 322p.

This recent directory lists each institution, subject category (given in French only), and researcher working on agricultural research in Zaire, Rwanda and Burundi. Some 265 Zairian research stations and 247 researchers working in Zaire are included.

527   **Shifting cultivation in Africa.**
       Pierre de Schlippe.   London: Routledge & Kegan Paul, 1956. 304p. maps. bibliog.

Although this classic study on the Zande system of agriculture is based on research on the Zande in southern Sudan, it also applies to Zaire's Zande located in the northern part of Haut-Zaïre.

528   **Situation actuelle de l'agriculture zaïroise.** (Current situation of Zairian agriculture.)
       Compiled by Mubenga Mukendi, Georges Condé.   Kinshasa: Division de Stratégie et de Planification Agricole, 1987. 554p. maps. bibliog.

Although the authors mention that this work is not to be taken as an agricultural encyclopaedia of Zaire, it represents a thorough investigation of the recent state of Zairian agriculture. It addresses the agricultural sector, systems of agricultural exploitation, animal and plant production, the politics of agriculture, water and forests, the agricultural infrastructure, agricultural mechanization, rural hydraulics, and alimentary needs in Zaire.

529 **Techniques agricoles améliorées pour le Kwango-Kwilu =
Mutindu ya kutomisa kisalu ya bilanga sambu na Kwango-Kwilu.**
(Improved agricultural techniques for Kwango-Kwilu.)
Louise Fresco.   Kinshasa: Projet PNUD/FAO, 1984. 145p. 2 maps.

This manual of traditional agricultural methods in Kwango-Kwilu (Bandundu region of
Zaire) is written in simple French and Kikongo. It also describes how to improve soil
fertility and the yields of some two dozen fruits and vegetables.

530 **Le transfert de technologie dans les pays en développement: le
secteur agro-alimentaire au Zaïre.** (The transfer of technology in
developing countries: the agro-food sector in Zaire.)
Tshimanga Bakadiababu.   Louvain-la-Neuve, Belgium: Université
Catholique de Louvain, 1985. 343p. bibliog.

Little has been written about technology transfer in Zaire. The first part of this doctoral
dissertation describes the theoretical foundations of technology transfer whilst the second
part is a detailed study of technology transfer in the Zairian agro-food industry.

531 **Trends and prospects for cassava in Zaire.**
Tshikala Tshibaka, Kamanda Lumpungu.   Washington, DC:
International Food Policy Research Institute, 1989. 45p. bibliog.
(Working Paper on Cassava, no. 4).

This is an excellent recent examination of the production, utilization, and trade prospects
of cassava (also known as tapioca, yuca, or manioc), the most important food crop in the
Zaire basin.

532 **Trypanotolerant cattle and livestock in west and central Africa:
the international supply and demand for breeding stock.**
A. P. M. Shaw, C. H. Hoste.   Rome: FAO of the United Nations,
1987. 2 vols. maps. bibliog. (FAO Animal Production and Health
Paper, no. 67/1).

The data in this regional publication on cattle production dates from 1984. Volume one
is a regional overview (economic context, past trade experiences, future trade prospects)
and volume two contains individual country studies, including one on Zaire (p. 299-315).

533 **Trypanotolerant livestock in west and central Africa.**
International Livestock Centre for Africa, Food and Agriculture
Organization of the United Nations, United Nations Environment
Programme.   Addis Ababa: ILCA, 1979-92. 3 vols. maps. bibliog.
(ILCA Monograph, no. 2).

This regional and country study of trypanotolerant cattle, sheep and goats analyses their
classification, distribution, description, performance, and productivity. Although the first
two volumes were published in 1979 and contain data from 1977, volume three is an
update which contains data from 1983-84. Zaire is covered in individual chapters in both
volumes two and three.

Zaire.
See item no. 10.

Zaire, what destiny?
See item no. 14.

Food crisis and agrarian change in the Eastern Highlands of Zaire.
See item no. 286.

Food production in a land-surplus, labor-scarce economy: the Zairian basin.
See item no. 457.

Food supply and the state: the history and social organization of the rice trade in Kisangani, Zaire.
See item no. 492.

Sub-Saharan agriculture: synthesis and trade prospects.
See item no. 497.

Labor in the rural household economy of the Zairian Basin.
See item no. 548.

Transport

534 **Atlas général de la République du Zaïre: notice de la carte des transports de surface.** (General atlas of the Republic of Zaire: explanatory note for the map of surface communications.)
André Lederer.   Brussels: Académie Royale des Sciences d'Outre-Mer, 1976. 20p. map. bibliog.

This map of surface transport is accompanied by twenty pages of factual information on Zaire's railways, roads, and waterways. It is a sequel to other such maps previously published by the Academy, and is the first to appear since the Democratic Republic of the Congo changed its name to Zaire. Also included is a list of new appellations that came into use after the previous maps were issued. The text is in French, Dutch, and English.

535 **L'exploitation des transports au Congo pendant la décennie, 1959-1969.** (Use of transport in the Congo during the decade, 1959-1969.)
André Lederer.   Brussels: Académie Royale des Sciences d'Outre-Mer, 1970. 147p. map. bibliog.

The author examines the use of methods of transport in Zaire by region and type from 1959-69, and describes the condition of transport equipment and routes, citing what improvements are desired and possible.

536 **Land-locked countries of Africa.**
Edited by Zdenek Cervenka.   Uppsala, Sweden: Scandinavian Institute of African Studies, 1973. 369p. maps. bibliog.

Although Zaire is not land-locked, this is nearly the case. The problems discussed in this book that truly land-locked African countries face involving transport, administration, and economics are therefore also relevant to Zaire.

537 **Paths of authority: roads, the State and the market in eastern Zaire.**
James Fairhead. *European Journal of Development Research*, vol. 4, no. 2 (Dec. 1992), p. 17-35.
Examines the relationship between roadbuilding, market integration, social change and rural development in the Zairian context.

538 **Le rail au Congo belge, 1890-1920. Tome 1.** (Railroads in the Belgian Congo. Volume 1.)
Brussels: G. Blanchart & Cie, 1993. 400p. maps, bibliog.
A lavishly illustrated history of the Zairian railway system. The text, which includes historical background information about Zaire itself, is highlighted by many maps, archival photographs, and extracts from travellers' accounts, reports, and other works. A second volume in preparation will cover the years 1920-60.

539 **Railways and the copper mines of Katanga.**
S. E. Katzenellenbogen. Oxford: Clarendon Press, 1973. 165p. map. bibliog.
A detailed history of the construction of the Benguela Railway through Zaire and Angola, which was inspired by the desire to exploit the Katanga copper mines and the focal point of a myriad of conflicting political, economic, and financial interests.

540 **Second Zaire Round-Table on Transport and Transit.**
Second Zaire Round-Table on Transport and Transit. Addis Ababa: Economic Commission for Africa, 1986. 2 vols.
The first volume provides a general overview and description of the transport network in Zaire. Volume two contains information on eight public corporations responsible for a number of modes of transport within Zaire, and descriptions of projects with which they are involved: the National Transport Authority; the Zaire Shipping Company; the Inland Waterways Authority; Maritime Navigation; Civil Aviation; Maritime Freight Co-ordination; the National Railway Company; and the Highway Authority.

541 **Transports et structures de développement au Congo: étude du progrès économique de 1900 à1970.** (Transport and structures of development in the Congo: a study of economic progress from 1900 to 1970.)
André Huybrechts. Paris: Mouton, 1970. 418p. maps. bibliog.
(Recherches Africaines, no. 12).
Originally presented as the author's thesis, this is a study of the rôle of transport in the development of the Zairian economy from 1900-70. Following a summary of the history of transport in Zaire from 1878-1970, it discusses the structure, politics, price, and expansion of transport, plus its links with development.

Transport

Lifeline for a nation: Zaire River.
See item no. 40.

Histoire de la navigation au Congo.
See item no. 48.

Labour, the Labour Movement and Trade Unions

542 **Beyond the bend in the river: African labor in Eastern Zaire, 1865-1940.**
David Northrup.   Athens, Ohio: Ohio University Center for International Studies, 1988. 264p. maps. bibliog. (Monographs in International Studies. Africa Series, no. 52).

Described by the author as a possible 'biography of the Zairian working class from its infancy to its adolescence', this work takes a broad approach toward labour history and policy in eastern Zaire during the three-quarters of a century that followed its penetration. It examines how mobilization of all forms of labour, including slavery, porterage, mining, cashcrop farming and military service, whether public or private, for wages or not, shaped both African and European attitudes toward employment, and affected the supply of and demand for labour.

543 **The black man's burden: African colonial labor on the Congo and Ubangi rivers, 1880-1900.**
William J. Samarin.   Boulder, Colorado: Westview, 1989. 276p. maps. bibliog.

Unlike most recent books written about the history of African labour, which deal with the topic after colonization was firmly established, this one starts somewhat earlier. Samarin examines the beginnings of labour in Central Africa, when French and Belgian colonizers created an indigenous work force in the region through which the Congo and Ubangi rivers flow. Chapters discuss such topics as the suppression of slavery, how the missions contributed to the development of the work force, how particular ethnic groups were exploited, and the investigations into the serious abuses of the African labour force.

544 **Black mineworkers in central Africa: industrial strategies and the evolution of an African proletariat in the Copperbelt, 1911-41.**
Charles Perrings.   London: Heinemann, 1979. 302p. bibliog.
Based on the author's thesis, this work analyses the proletarianization of black workers in the copper mines of Zaire and Zambia during the first three decades of large-scale capitalist mining operations in this particular region.

545 **Bringing the workers back in: worker protest and popular intervention in Katanga, 1931-1941.**
John Higginson.   *Canadian Journal of African Studies*, vol. 22, no. 2 (1988), p. 199-223.
Analyses the experiences of African mineworkers in Katanga in order to attempt to explain how workers' consciousness is linked to a particular strategy of protest. Examined here is the worker protest that erupted in the 1930's and culminated in a general strike in 1941. The author concludes that it is impossible to consider the place of the migrant worker and of the rural world in the mineworkers' consciousness without making allowances for the constraints imposed on industrial production by colonial domination.

546 **Disputing the machines: scientific management and the transformation of the work routine at the Union Minière du Haut-Katanga, 1918-1930.**
John Higginson.   *African Economic History*, issue 17 (1988), p. 1-21.
During the period covered in this article, the Union Minière du Haut-Katanga was forced to 'stabilize' its operations by diversifying, increasing output, and disciplining workers with cost-cutting measures, because of conditions which arose from the global recession of 1922. The author examines how this stabilization of the work routine unintentionally increased the social awareness of the African workers, resulting in various forms of unrest.

547 **Good lawyers but poor workers: recruited Angolan labour in the copper mines of Katanga, 1917-1921.**
Charles Perrings.   *Journal of African History*, vol. 18, no. 2 (1977), p. 237-59.
Documents an episode in the history of industrial labour management of the Zairian copper mining industry, when 3,479 Angolans were recruited for work in the mines of the Union Minière du Haut Katanga between 1917 and 1921. During that period, 536 workers died on company premises, and 778 deserted. The article analyses the significance of recruitment as an industrial strategy at the time, how it was an instrument of control, and the implications this had for the workers.

548 **Labor in the rural household economy of the Zairian Basin.**
Tshikala B. Tshibaka. Washington, DC: International Food Policy
Research Institute, 1992. 64p. map. bibliog. (Research Report
[International Food Policy Research Institute], no. 90).

This study was conducted in the Zairian Basin, one of the least-studied areas of the
developing world. It examines various aspects of labour in the rural household economy:
labour use and allocation; labour productivity; and how to increase productivity of labour
devoted to agriculture. This report is a follow-up study based on the survey that led to
the publication of the author's *Food production in a land-surplus, labor scarce
economy: the Zairian Basin* (q.v.); both fill a gap in the knowledge of the rural
household economy and provide useful information to those who make agricultural
policy.

549 **Reinventing the past and circumscribing the future: authenticité
and the negative image of women's work in Zaire.**
Francille Rusan Wilson. In: *Women and work in Africa.* Edited by
Edna G. Bay. Boulder, Colorado: Westview Press, 1982, p. 153-70.
(Westview Special Studies on Africa).

The first part of this chapter traces the changes in the labour system and resulting decline
in the status of Zairian women under colonial rule. The second part discusses how the
political ideology of *authenticité* (authenticity) has been adopted as government policy
by Mobutu and used to maintain control of the masses, shift attention away from Zaire's
pressing economic and social problems, and further erode women's status. *Authenticité*
has been used to continue the promotion of negative Belgian characterizations of women
and women's work, to limit women's entrance into the work force, and to suppress
women's organizations.

550 **Revue du Travail.** (Labour Review.)
Kinshasa: Editions LULE, 1989- . quarterly.

Aimed in particular at both workers and heads of public and private enterprises, this
periodical contains articles discussing pertinent labour issues of the day. It also includes
the full text of recently issued documents relating to the worker's domain, such as laws
and ordinances, plus the text of judgements rendered by the *Cours et Tribunaux* (Courts
and Tribunals) during litigation involving individual workers.

551 **Le syndicalisme et ses incidences socio-politiques en Afrique: le
cas de l'UNTZa.** (Trade-unionism and its socio-political occurences
in Africa: the case of the UNTZa.)
Gassana Muhirwa. Kinshasa: Presses Universitaires du Zaïre, 1982.
213 p. bibliog.

A history of trade unions in Zaire, particularly the Union Nationale des Travailleurs du
Zaïre (National Union of Zairian Workers), formed in 1967 by the merger of all existing
trade unions at that time, and presently Zaire's only trade union. The author analyses the
impact of trade unions on Zairian society and politics. Unfortunately, and according to
prediction, the UNTZa has become an instrument used to defend the interests of the
government more than the Zairian worker.

552   **A working class in the making: Belgian colonial labor policy,
      private enterprise, and the African mineworker, 1907-1951.**
      John Higginson.   Madison, Wisconsin: University of Wisconsin
      Press, 1989. 307p. bibliog.

This history of the Union Minière du Haut-Katanga mineworkers analyses the changes
that occurred in their way of life before and after the Depression and the Second World
War. It explains why, between 1907 and 1949, the Belgian colonial government and
private industry failed in their attempts to proletarianize the miners without creating a
working class which was capable of demanding rights and pursuing interests that
conflicted with those of the UMHK and the state.

553   **Zaire.**
      Zaire (United States. Embassy [Zaire]) (American Embassy,
      Kinshasa).   Washington, DC: US Dept. of Labor, Bureau of
      International Labor Affairs, [1987]- . annual. (Foreign Labor Trends,
      FLT).

Each issue lists key labour indicators and provides a summary of the current labour scene
in Zaire.

The story of a Congo victim.
See item no. 300.

**Productivity and factor proportions in less developed countries: the case of
industrial firms in the Congo.**
See item no. 465.

Human Rights

554   **The dialectics of oppression in Zaire.**
Michael G. Schatzberg.   Bloomington, Indiana: Indiana University
Press, 1988. 193p. map. bibliog.

Schatzberg is a frequent writer on Zaire and personally researched this book within the
country. Although the information that he gathered is specific to one area of Zaire — the
Lisala region – Schatzberg speaks in general of the repressive, authoritarian nature of the
state in Zaire. It seizes property, spies on its citizens, and persecutes them in the courts
and all for the security and continued rule of Mobutu Sese Seko. The author successfully
conveys the social atmosphere of this repressive régime, where the exercise of power is
arbitrary and more often than not ignores the legal and administrative structure of the
state.

555   **Human rights violations in Zaire: an Amnesty International
report.**
Amnesty International.   London: Amnesty International Publications,
1980. 22p. map.

This short publication by Amnesty International chronicles the violations of human
rights in Zaire at the time of writing. The political and legal framework of this
persecution is covered and a number of areas under the direct responsibility of the
Zairian government are impugned: prison conditions, political imprisonment, and
unlawful executions.

556 **Info-Zaïre: feuillet d'information produit par la Table de Concertation sur les Droits Humains au Zaïre.** (Info-Zaire: information bulletin produced by the Table of Concern on Human Rights in Zaire.)
Table de Concertation sur les Droits Humains au Zaïre.   Montreal: Table de Concertation sur les Droits Humains au Zaïre, 1992- . weekly.

This serial publication provides very current, up-to-date information on the human rights situation in Zaire. There are also many articles on the politics and government of Zaire and the Zairian President, Mobutu Sese Seko.

557 **Military violence against civilians: the case of the Congolese and Zairean military in the Pedicle, 1890-1988.**
Mwelwa Chambika Musambachime.   In: *African nationalism and revolution.*   Edited by Gregory Maddox.   New York; London: Garland, 1993, p. 109-30. bibliog. (Colonialism and Nationalism in Africa, vol. 4).

In this twenty-two page chapter the author details the policy of force and intimidation instigated by the Zairian armed forces against the civilian population of the southern arm of the province of Shaba. Violence and repression in today's Zaire have become the primary control feature in the political life of the country. Seen in the tradition of Belgian colonialism, armed force and coercion have always been a prominent feature in the effort of an autocratic government to enforce its will upon the people in the absence of consensual government.

558 **Religious persecutions in Zaire.**
Boston, Massachusetts: Afrika Baraza, 1982. 23p. bibliog. (Document [Afrika Baraza], no. 2).

This brief work reviews the political life of Zaire since independence, weighing in heavily against the political repression of the Mobutu régime. The major focus of the work concerns the history of relations between the government and the Roman Catholic Church. The Mobutu régime has used its ideology of African 'authenticity' to exert control over institutions which resist its authoritarian control, and the Roman Catholic Church has been a major target of this repression. This work chronicles the major dates in the church/state struggle and details individual acts of repression against the Church.

559 **Tribune des libertés: bulletin hebdomadaire destiné aux membres de Ligue des Droits de l'Homme (Zaïre).** (Tribune of liberties: weekly bulletin for the members of League of Human Rights [Zaire].)
Kinshasa: Ligue des Droits de l'Homme (Zaïre), 1992- . weekly.

Up-to-date information is provided in this weekly serial on the human rights situation in Zaire. There are short articles on individual instances of human rights violations as well as more comprehensive articles on the general civil rights environment in Zaire.

560 **Zaïre, dossier sur l'emprisonnement politique et commentaires des autorités.** (Zaire, file on political imprisonment and commentaries by officials.)
Amnesty International. Paris: Editions Francophones d'Amnesty International, 1983. 91p.

This assessment of human rights violations in Zaire by one of the leading independent human rights organizations is an unmitigated criticism of the Zairian human rights record. Amnesty chronicles specific cases of biased judicial proceedings in repressing dissidents and also extrajudicial violence and executions. Considerable attention is paid to official government policy, some of it describing the political organization which sustains repression in Zaire. The general picture of the Mobutu régime painted by Amnesty International is that of a government operating outside of any strict legal framework, and above the law. Amnesty International also outlines specific measures for the Zairian government that could be taken to improve the human rights situation in Zaire, such as the end of extrajudicial detention and the notification of the condition and charges of individuals held by security forces.

561 **Zaire, repression as policy: a human rights report.**
Makau wa Mutua, Peter Rosenblum. New York: Lawyers Committee for Human Rights, 1990. 232p. map. bibliog.

In countries where political repression of the opposition is a matter of public policy at the national level, the account of human rights violations becomes a red-letter page in political life. This is an investigation of repressive policies and the individuals who suffered from these policies.

562 **Zaire, violence against democracy.**
Amnesty International. New York: Amnesty International, 1993. 25p.

This work is a brief recent assessment by Amnesty International of violations of human rights in Zaire. It includes ethnic persecution, unlawful detention, unlawful security force killings, the repression of reporters and opposition party members, and the inhumane conditions in Zairian prisons. Amnesty characterizes this period as the worst human rights crisis in Zaire since the end of the civil war in the 1960s and directly blames the Mobutu régime for this situation.

Les droits des citoyens zaïrois.
See item no. 388.

Statistics

563 **Annuaire des statistiques du commerce extérieur.** (Annual of statistics of foreign trade.)
Zaire. Direction de la Statistique et des Etudes Economiques.
Kinshasa: Direction de la Statistique et des Etudes Economiques, 1964. 372p.

This publication of yearly statistics (1964) for foreign trade is a continuation of the 1962 publication entitled *Commerce extérieur*. A useful compilation of foreign commerce information, it was apparently not continued as a separate publication so for later Zairian foreign trade statistics, the researcher should consult the *Bulletin Trimestriel des Statistiques Générales* (q.v.).

564 **Bulletin Trimestriel des Statistiques Générales.** (Quarterly Bulletin of General Statistics.)
Institut National de la Statistique. Kinshasa-Gombe: Institut National de la Statistique, 1965- . quarterly.

With four volumes each year, this serial offers general statistics on the economic activity and population for Zaire. Beginning in 1965, possibly as a continuation of the *Bulletin des Statistiques Générales*, this government publication does not appear on a regular basis, indicating the irregularity of the functioning of the Zairian government.

565 **Commerce extérieur.** (Foreign trade.)
Zaire. Direction de la Statistique et des Etudes Economiques.
Leopoldville: Imprimerie de la République Démocratique du Congo, 1962. 270p.

This is a publication of the annual statistics of the foreign trade of Zaire for 1962.

566 **L'Economie du Zaïre au [. . .]: Quelques Indicateurs Conjoncturels.** (The Economy of Zaire for [. . .]: Some Conjunctural Indicators.)
Institut National de la Statistique.   Kinshasa: République du Zaïre, Mouvement Populaire de la Révolution, Département du Plan, Institut National de la Statistique, 1988- . quarterly.

Started as the quarterly statistical report on the economy, with a later synthesis of the yearly figures, this government publication presents detailed statistical information on the economic activity of Zaire. Unfortunately, it does not seem to have appeared with any regularity.

567 **Indice Officiel des Prix à la Consommation des Ménages à Kinshasa.** (Official Index of Prices on Household Consumption in Kinshasa.)
Institut National de la Statistique.   Kinshasa: République du Zaïre, Mouvement Populaire de la Révolution, Département du Plan, Institut National de la Statistique, 1987- . monthly.

This government serial is in principle a monthly publication, but in fact it is produced on a very irregular basis and may even have ceased publication after 1991. It appears to be a continuation of *Notes sur les Prix à la Consommation Familiale, Ville de Kinshasa* (q.v.) and contains mainly statistics on household consumption in the Zairian capital, Kinshasa. This publication would be very useful for a socio-economic study of the people of Kinshasa.

568 **Notes sur les Prix à la Consommation Familiale, Ville de Kinshasa.** (Notes on the Prices of Family Consumption, City of Kinshasa.)
Institut National de la Statistique.   Kinshasa/Gombe: République du Zaïre, Mouvement Populaire de la Révolution, Département du Plan, Institut National de la Statistique, 1979-81. monthly.

Although it appeared irregularly and is now no longer published, this government serial was, in fact, supposed to appear monthly. It mainly includes statistics on household consumption in Kinshasa, the Zairian capital and home to nearly one quarter of the population of the country. It was apparently published only between 1979 and 1981 but it was continued later under the name: *Indice Officiel des Prix à la Consommation des Ménages à Kinshasa* (q.v.).

569 **Profils de l'économie du Zaïre: années 1955-1987.** (Profiles of the economy of Zaire: years 1955-1987.)
Charles Léonard.   Kinshasa: République du Zaïre, Département de l'Economie Nationale et de l'Industrie, 1987. 243p. bibliog.

In this relatively recent government publication Léonard provides comprehensive statistics on the economic performance of Zaire.

570 **Statistique du Commerce Extérieur du Congo Belge.** (Statistics of the foreign trade of the Belgian Congo.)
Belgium. Office Colonial.   Brussels: Goemaere, 1918-39. annual.

This yearly publication of statistics on Zairian foreign trade by the Belgian colonial régime covers approximately the years 1918 to 1939.

571 **Le Zaïre en chiffres.** (Zaire in figures.)
Institut National de la Statistique.   Kinshasa: République du Zaïre, Mouvement Populaire de la Révolution, Département du Plan, Institut National de la Statistique, 1988. 36p.

Figures for climatology, rainfall, various categories of national population, city and province population, health, education, employment, agriculture, industries, transportation, and public finances are included in this short statistical compilation. It is a brief but well-organized government publication, which could give the scholar or casual user a quick overall view of Zaire from a statistical perspective.

Rapports sur les pays ACP, Zaïre.
See item no. 7.

EDOZA: étude démographique de l'ouest du Zaïre, 1975-1976.
See item no. 157.

Recensement pilote, août 1982: rapport.
See item no. 161.

Recensement scientifique de la population, 1er juillet, 1984: résultats provisoires.
See item no. 162.

Recueil des rapports et totaux: calculés à partir des résultats officiels du Recensement de la population de la R.D.C. en 1970.
See item no. 163.

Résultats officiels du recensement général de la population de la République démocratique du Congo: proclamés par arrêté no. 1236 du 31 juillet 1970 du Ministère d'Etat Chargé de l'Intérieur.
See item no. 165.

Environment, Ecology and Urban Studies

572 **Aspects de la conservation de la nature au Zaïre.** (Aspects of the conservation of nature in Zaire.)
Kabala Matuka. Kinshasa: Editions Lokole, 1976. 312p. maps. bibliog. (Série Scientifique).

This comprehensive view of the conservation of nature in Zaire includes topics such as environmental degradation, the differing concepts of ecological reservations and national parks, problems concerning fauna, tourism in Zaire, and ecological education. Each of the seven national parks is discussed and its salient features are emphasized. The texts of relevant laws are printed in their entirety.

573 **Atlas climatique du bassin congolais.** (Climatic atlas of the Congo basin.)
Franz Bultot. Brussels: Institut National pour l'Etude Agronomique du Congo, 1971-77. 4 vols. maps. bibliog.

Bultot's comprehensive atlas of the Congo River watershed covers all aspects of Zaire's climate, such as sunshine, precipitation, the temperature of air and soils, humidity, atmospheric pressure, wind, and cloudiness. Volume four was published under the title: *Atlas climatique du bassin zaïrois.*

574 **Biodiversity in Sub-Saharan Africa and its islands: conservation, management, and sustainable use.**
Simon N. Stuart, Richard J. Adams, Martin D. Jenkins. Gland, Switzerland: IUCN, 1990. 242p. maps. bibliog. (Occasional Papers of the IUCN Species Survival Commission, no. 6).

In pages 224-29 Zaire's biodiversity is covered, treating such topics as critical sites, critical species, threats, conservation measures, and conservation activities.

575 **The conservation atlas of tropical forests: Africa.**
Edited by Jeffrey A. Sayer, Caroline S. Harcourt, N. Mark Collins.
New York; London: World Conservation Union and Simon &
Schuster, 1992. 288p. maps. bibliog.

Zaire is covered on pages 270-82 of this excellent source on forest conservation in
Africa which contains maps (scale 1:4,000,000) that indicate rain forest, conservation
areas and non-forest areas. The forests are used for firewood, food, and the production of
export products (timber and palm oil) and although Zairian conservation efforts are
considerable they are not without their problems. The first section of the book, covering
general issues such as biological diversity, forest people, and the timber trade, is also
pertinent for the study of Zaire.

576 **La conservation des écosystèmes forestiers du Zaïre.** (The
conservation of forest ecosystems in Zaire.)
Charles Doumenge. Gland, Switzerland: UICN, 1990. 242p. maps.
bibliog.

This recent comprehensive study of forest conservation in Zaire includes forest
resources, ecology, the legislative situation, and forest exploitation. The second half of
the book contains detailed appendices on current protected areas (each of Zaire's
national parks, hunting domains, ecological reservations, and forest reserves),
supplementary priority sites not yet protected, and supplementary sites of local interest.

577 **Conservation of west and central African rainforests =**
Conservation de la forêt dense en Afrique centrale et de l'ouest.
Edited by Kevin Cleaver, Mohan Munasinghe, Mary Dyson, Nicolas
Egli, Axel Penker, François Wencélius. Washington, DC: World
Bank, 1992. 353p. bibliog. (World Bank Environmental Paper, no. 1).

The 1990 papers from the Conference on Conservation of West and Central African
Rainforests contain two papers specifically on Zaire as well as many others of interest to
the study of Zaire. Of primary interest are: 'Investissement en biodiversité et en
protection des zones forestières du Zaïre' (Investment in biodiversity and in the
protection of the forest zones of Zaire), by Mankoto ma Mbaelele and Armand Rioust de
Largentaye (p. 32-35) and 'Kutafuta Maisha: searching for life on Zaire's Ituri forest
frontier', by Richard B. Peterson (p. 193-201), which is an assessment of immigration
into the Ituri forest.

578 **Construire la ville africaine: chroniques du citadin promoteur.** (To
construct the African city: reports of self-made residences.)
Patrick Canel, Philippe Delis, Christian Girard. Paris: ACCT;
Karthala, 1990. 197p. bibliog. (Collection Economie et
Développement. Etudes et Manuels).

Because of a failure of urban planning efforts in the large urban centres of Africa, the
population must use 'self-help' housing to create permanent housing structures. Douala
in Cameroon and Kinshasa in Zaire are the subject of case studies on housing
construction.

579   **Histoire des villes du Zaïre: notions et perspectives fondamentales.**
       (History of cities in Zaire: notions and fundamental perspectives.)
       Léon de Saint Moulin.   *Etudes d'Histoire Africaine*, no. 6 (1974),
       p. 137-67. 2 maps. bibliog.
The history of cities in Zaire is covered from their origin up until 1970 and concludes
with a view toward 1980. Numerous useful appendices giving the creation dates of cities
and other administrative units are included.

580   **Island Africa: the evolution of Africa's rare animals and plants.**
       Jonathan Kingdon.   London: Collins, 1990. 287p. maps.
Here the 'islands' refer to land-locked centres of endemism, communities that are
distinct from the surrounding 'seas' of forest, savannah and desert. By examining the
climatic and evolutionary changes, the author is able to identify the rare plants and
animals in Africa. The chapter on the Zaire basin is the primary interest for this
bibliography, and there is also material on Zaire in the chapter on the equatorial
highlands. In the appendices, typical endemic species, conservation strategies, and a list
of reserves and national parks are all pertinent to Zaire. This book was also published in
1989 by Princeton University Press.

581   **Kinshasa, la ville et la cité.** (Kinshasa, the city [of the rich] and the
       city [of the poor].)
       Marc Pain.   Paris: ORSTOM, 1984. 267p. maps. bibliog. (Collection
       Mémoires, no. 105) (Etudes Urbaines).
The urban development of Kinshasa, Zaire's capital, and the second largest city in
Africa, is the subject of this book in which the author traces Kinshasa's evolution from
important colonial outpost to modern city in crisis. The ecological, social, economic, and
moral crises have caused two cities to emerge: *'la ville'* (the European city of the rich)
and *'la cité'* (the Black city of the poor).

582   **Kinshasa, 1881-1981: 100 ans après Stanley: problèmes et avenir
       d'une ville.** (Kinshasa, 1881-1981: 100 years after Stanley: problems
       and future of a city.)
       Mbumba Ngimbi.   Kinshasa: Centre de Recherches Pédagogiques,
       1982. 123p. maps. bibliog.
On the occasion of the centenary of the nation's capital the author describes the major
problems and needs of Kinshasa's population including lodging, public health,
transportation, and education. The chapter on demographic growth thoroughly analyses
the causes for these problems and suggests measures to stop the rural exodus. An
excellent bibliography is included. A similar work is Sakombi Inongo's *Regards sur
Kinshasa* (q.v.).

583 **Kinshasa: problems of land management, infrastructure, and food supply.**
Kankonde Mbuyi. In: *African cities in crisis.* Boulder, Colorado: Westview Press, 1989, p. 148-75. (African Modernization and Development Series).

In managing Kinshasa's explosive growth, problems include a lack of urban planning management, a lack of resources available to local authorities, and a lack of data on the cost of urban services. This translation from the French is an excellent recent introduction to the study of urban policy in Zaire.

584 **Kinshasa, ville en suspens : dynamique de la croissance et problèmes d'urbanisme: étude socio-politique.** (Kinshasa, city on hold: dynamics of growth and urban problems: socio-political approach.)
René de Maximy. Paris: ORSTOM, 1984. 476p. 2 fiche. maps. bibliog. (Travaux et Documents de l'ORSTOM, no. 176).

For the reader seriously interested in an in-depth study of Kinshasa, its urban development and future, this study is essential. An excellent detailed bibliography is included.

585 **Kisangani, 1876-1976: histoire d'une ville. Tome 1: la population.**
(Kisangani, 1876-1976: history of a city. Volume 1: population.)
L. de Saint Moulin et al, edited by Benoît Verhaegen. Kinshasa: Presses Universitaires du Zaïre, 1975- . 287p. maps. bibliog.

This interdisciplinary monograph on one of Zaire's largest cities, Kisangani (formerly Stanleyville), consists of articles by leading demographers and geographers on the Lokele, Komo, Bambole, Wagenia, and the Islamic community. Only volume one appears to have been published.

586 **Lubumbashi, un écosystème urbain tropical.** (Lubumbashi, a tropical urban ecosystem.)
Michel Leblanc, François Malaisse. Lubumbashi: Centre International de Semiologie, Université Nationale du Zaïre, 1978. 166p. maps. bibliog.

This work is an analysis of city planning in Lubumbashi, using an ecological approach.

587 **Phase 1 environmental profile of the Republic of Zaire.**
Library of Congress Science and Technology Division, prepared by Peter Hazlewood. Washington, DC: Library of Congress, Science and Technology Division, 1980. 53p. 6 maps. bibliog.

This is the only United States environmental report on Zaire. Although at the national level Zaire's renewable natural resource base is not seriously threatened, the major population centres are experiencing environmental problems due to the use of fuelwood, which results in the clearing of forests and causes water and soil problems. Chapters include discussions of water, soils, forests, wildlife and natural parks whilst the last section of the study briefly discusses environmental problems and impacts.

588 **La promotion des communautés rurales au Zaïre: réalisations, méthodologie, réflexions: projets de promotion sociale dans les régions de Bandundu et Bas-Zaïre.** (The promotion of rural communities in Zaire: realizations, methodology, reflections: projects of social promotion in the regions of Bandundu and Bas-Zaire.) Paris: Agence de Coopération Culturelle et Technique; Kinshasa: Bureau d'Etudes d'Aménagements et d'Urbanisme, 1985. 414p. maps. bibliog.

The purpose of this joint project between the ACCT and Zaire is to define a new rural development methodology for use with Zairian officials and other members of the ACCT. For these two projects, the three goals for villagers involved the revival of activities for craftsmen, the amelioration of health through projects such as building a potable water system and a medical dispensary, and the use of appropriate technology in agricultural activities.

589 **Regards sur Kinshasa: témoignages.** (A look at Kinshasa: testimony.) Sakombi Inongo, preface by Bolikango Akpolokaka. Kinshasa: Editions Réunies, 1981. 94p. bibliog.

This is the other book which coincides with Kinshasa's centenary (Mbumba Ngimbi's *Kinshasa, 1881-1981* [q.v.]). The author, a staunch supporter of President Mobutu, begins with a history of the city, and concentrates on social problems and possible solutions in 'democratic' Kinshasa.

590 **Urbanisation et aménagement en Afrique noire.** (Urbanization and management in Black Africa.) Lelo Nzuzi. Paris: SEDES, 1989. 237p. maps. bibliog.

In this study of the history and development of Black African urbanization, Lelo Nzuzi chooses Lubumbashi as a 'laboratory city' for its industrial and mineralogical beginnings, its colonial urban politics and its population boom since independence.

591 **Les villes secondaires: diagnostic et propositions, gestion urbaine, économie urbaine, équipements.** (The secondary cities: diagnostics and proposals, urban administration, urban economy, infrastructure.) Zaire. Bureau d'Etudes d'Aménagements et d'Urbanisme. Zaire: BEAU, 1991. 24p. maps. bibliog.

This brief but recent study of the secondary cities of Zaire covers their population, administration, economy, and infrastructure but excludes discussion of Kinshasa. Future projects and the urban development plans are outlined.

African wetlands and shallow water bodies.
See item no. 45.

The inland waters of tropical Africa: an introduction to tropical limnology.
See item no. 49.

Behavior and ecology of primates in the Lomako Forest, Zaire.
See item no. 56.

Primates of the world: distribution, abundance, and conservation.
See item no. 75.

The dietary repertory of the Ngandu people of the tropical rain forest: an ecological and anthropological study of the subsistence activities and food procurement technology of a slash-and-burn agriculturist in the Zaire River basin.
See item no. 181.

The ecological basis of hunter-gatherer subsistence in African rain forests: the Mbuti of eastern Zaire.
See item no. 183.

Directory of institutions and individuals active in environmentally-sound and appropriate technologies.
See item no. 624.

Education

592 **L'auto-perception des enseignants au Zaïre: contribution à la socio-psychologie professionnelle des enseignants dans les pays en développement.** (Self perception of teachers in Zaire: contribution to the professional socio-psychology of teachers in developing countries.)
Lumeka-lua-Yansenga, with help from Samuel Roller, Mbulamoko Nzenge. Kinshasa: Editions et Culture Africaines, 1985. 336p. map. bibliog.

Reviews the education of the educators in Zaire. Great attention is paid to the intellectual orientation of teachers in order to equip them and to adapt the curriculum to suit conditions in a developing country, such as Zaire. The author analyses the various categories of teachers and teaching in Zaire by academic level, supplying a social and psychological profile of the profession.

593 **Belgian educational policy.**
David G. Scanlon. In: *Traditions of African education.* Edited by David G. Scanlon. New York: Columbia University, Teachers College, Bureau of Publications, 1964, p. 141-84. (Classics in Education, no. 16).

In the chapter entitled: 'Belgian educational policy', the author presents the history and development of education in colonial Zaire, with considerable space devoted to the types of schools and the methodology of education under the Belgian régime. Although this work is not up-to-date, it provides a useful background for the educational sociology and inherited pedagogical structure of Zaire.

594 **Colonisation et enseignement: cas du Zaïre avant 1960.**
(Colonization and education: case of Zaire before 1960.)
Kita Kyankenge Masandi.   Bukavu, Zaire: Editions du CERUKI,
1982. 287p. bibliog.

The colonial régime in Zaire was often referred to as a 'trinity' – an alliance of the State, the great capitalist interests, and the Church. In the early colonial period, the Church was assigned the rôle of educating the Zairians and this is a task that the Catholic Church in Zaire maintains to the present. Two systems of education subsequently developed in Zaire: state and religious, and this work reviews the development of both systems of education before 1960 and discusses the political and ideological influences of education in a colonial régime.

595 **The Congo.**
Jean-Claude Willame.   In: *Students and politics in developing nations*.   Compiled by Donald K. Emmerson.   New York; Washington, DC; London: Praeger, 1968, p. 37-63. bibliog.

In this short but comprehensive essay, Willame covers the history of Zairian education from the founding of the first Belgian schools up to the date of publication. A good deal of attention is devoted to the atmosphere of Zairian higher education and student political activity.

596 **Congo-Leopoldville.**
Richard Dodson.   In: *Church, state, and education in Africa*.   Edited by David G. Scanlon.   New York: Columbia University, Teachers College, Teachers College Press, 1966, p. 59-108. bibliog.

In the chapter on education in Zaire Richard Dodson describes educational policy in the colonial period. The evolution of educational policy is traced from the early strong support for Catholic mission education to the increasing distance taken from sectarian education by state educational policy. The study includes the state's educational system and the education fostered by the three major religious groupings: Catholic; Protestant; and Kimbanguism. The work is dated but still highly relevant for the colonial period.

597 **The Congo Republic (Leopoldville).**
Ruth C. Sloan.   In: *The educated African*.   Edited by Helen A. Kitchen.   New York: Praeger, 1962, p. 191-206. map.

This essay is quite dated, but it manages to summarize education in Zaire. The time covered is chiefly the colonial period and the educational system established by the Belgians. The author also writes about the post-independence crash programmes in education initiated by the new Zairian state.

598 **Digging up the past: an approach to fundamental education and community development: (case of Zaire).**
Fu-Kiau K. Kia Bunseki. PhD thesis, Union for Experimenting Colleges and Universities, Yellow Springs, Ohio, 1986. 240p. maps. bibliog. (Available from University Microfilms International, Ann Arbor, Michigan, order no. 8702976).

Consists of a very specialized study of the system of education in the traditional Bantu-Kongo schools of initiation, as they existed in the precolonial and colonial past. The author offers this traditional school as a model of education adapted to the linguistic, ethical, and practical needs of the country. He discusses the values and organization of traditional education as an antidote to a European-based system, which is noted for its inadaptation to the conditions and needs of Zaire. This work may be considered a reform manifesto as well as an historical study.

599 **Ecole, éducation et développement au Zaïre: actes du 2e Séminaire Régional de l'Académie des Professeurs pour la Paix Mondiale, Afrique Centrale, Kinshasa, Zaïre, 8 septembre 1983.** (School, education and development in Zaire: proceedings of the 2nd Regional Seminar of the Professors World Peace Academy, Central Africa, Kinshasa, Zaire, 8 September 1983.)
Professors World Peace Academy. Séminaire Régional (2nd : 1983 : Kinshasa, Zaire). Kinshasa: PWPA, 1985. 81p.

These conference proceedings include papers presented on various topics by professors representing the Zairian educational establishment. The topics focus upon how to adapt national education to the development needs of Zaire. A discussion and debate follows the papers.

600 **Ecoles du Zaïre: attentes des parents, problèmes et aspirations des élèves.** (Schools of Zaire: expectations of parents, problems and aspirations of the students.)
Lieselotte Wohlgenannt. Bandundu, Zaire: CEEBA, 1979. 159p. map. bibliog. (CEEBA Publications. Série 2, vol. 56).

Following independence Zaire made a vigorous effort to provide primary and secondary education to large numbers of its citizens. At the writing of this work, there were four million pupils enrolled in primary and secondary schools, one of the highest figures for Africa in absolute terms. The author discusses the history of Zairian education, beginning in colonial times and continuing to the present (1979), including both the state and religious schools. Various aspects of education are analysed: the expectations of parents and students; the education of young women; the adaptation of education to employment; and the social impact of scholarization.

601 **Educating the bureaucracy in a new polity: a case study of l'Ecole Nationale de Droit et d'Administration, Kinshasa, Congo.**
Tamar Golan.   New York: Columbia University, Teachers College, Teachers College Press, 1968. 78p. bibliog. (Publications of the Center for Education in Africa, Institute of International Studies).
Tamar Golan writes about a single institution of higher education, the Ecole Nationale de Droit et d'Administration (National School of Law and Administration) – or ENDA – located in Kinshasa. However, this élite school, preparing students for careers in public administration, government, the legal profession, and political life, has a major impact upon national life and upon education throughout Zaire. The author provides the history of the school since its founding in 1961, discusses its curriculum, administration, faculty, and the recruitment and composition of the student body. ENDA in many ways looks to France's Ecole Nationale d'Administration as a model since British and American educational examples are considered largely irrelevant to Zaire's needs. The school has a national vocation to train an élite group of students for participation in public life, and the author endeavours to show how the school strives to fulfil that vocation.

602 **Education and elites: the making of the new elites and the formal education system in the Congo (K).**
William M. Rideout.   PhD thesis, Stanford University, Stanford, California, 1971. 553p. bibliog. (Available from University Microfilms International, Ann Arbor, Michigan, order no. 7211648).
Somewhat dated, this 1971 PhD dissertation focuses on the education of the élites in Zaire, from the colonial period to the present.

603 **Education and occupational attainment from generation to generation: the case of Zaire.**
Mwenene Mukweso, George J. Papagiannis, Sande Milton.
Comparative Education Review, vol. 28, no. 1 (Feb. 1984), p. 52-68. bibliog.
This article studies the educational and occupational attainment of Zairian students in the process of national development. There is a brief overview of the paternalistic, vocationally-oriented education of the colonial era and an account of the changes in education since independence.

604 **Education and university students in a new nation: the case of the Republic of Zaire.**
Payanzo Ntsomo.   PhD thesis, Northwestern University, Evanston, Illinois, 1974. 350p. bibliog. (Available from University Microfilms International, Ann Arbor, Michigan, order no. 7428714).
The chief focus of this dissertation is the system of higher education in Zaire, from the founding of the first universities in the 1950s. The author follows the development of higher education, through to the university 'nationalization' or reorganization of 1971, paying considerable attention to the social and political profile of Zairian students, as well as to student organizations and movements. A lengthy chapter of over fifty pages is devoted to a general description of the Zairian educational system at the primary and secondary levels.

605 **L'éducation en République du Zaïre, 1960-1979.** (Education in the
Republic of Zaire, 1960-1979.)
Thérèse Verheust.   Brussels: Centre d'Etude et de Documentation
Africaines, 1980. 285p. (Bibliographies Analytiques sur l'Afrique
Centrale, no. 4).
An annotated bibliography on education in Zaire, arranged by the following material
types: individual works; periodical articles; masters' theses; government documents; and
collections of different materials on a specific topic.

606 **Educational developments in the Congo (Leopoldville)**
Betty George.   Washington, DC: US Dept. of Health, Education and
Welfare, Office of Education, 1966. 196p. map. (Bulletin, 1966,
no. 1).
This US government document is a highly dated work (1966), but it does offer a truly
comprehensive look at Zairian education. The author begins with an examination of the
history of education in Zaire, enumerates the great changes brought about by
independence, and discusses the organization, administration, and structure of all levels
of education in Zaire. Individual institutions of higher education are listed with
commentary on each.

607 **Eglise et éducation: histoire de l'enseignement protestant au Zaïre,
1878-1978.** (Church and education: history of Protestant education in
Zaire, 1878-1978.)
J. Kimpianga Mahaniah.   Kinshasa: Centre de Vulgarisation
Agricole, 1981. 127p. bibliog.
The author, a trained historian, documents the history of Protestant education in his
country, Zaire. The Belgian authorities encouraged the Catholic missions in their
educational endeavours but in various ways discouraged evangelization by foreign
Protestant missionaries. Nonetheless, a large Protestant population (6,500,000 at the time
of writing) has grown up in Zaire, and Protestant organizations have made considerable
efforts to serve the educational needs of their flock. J. Kimpianga Mahaniah offers a
short introductory history of Protestantism in Zaire, reviews the Belgian colonial
educational policy, and chronicles the history of Protestant education in the country from
its inception to the present, noting how it has changed and transformed throughout the
various stages of Zairian national development.

608 **L'enseignement en République du Zaïre.** (Education in the Republic
of Zaire.)
Thérèse Verheust.   *Cahiers du CEDAF*, no. 1 (1974), p. 1-47.
bibliog.
This study focuses primarily on higher education in Zaire, citing the history of the
universities and higher education institutes of the Central African country. Much
attention is devoted to the administrative structure of Unaza, the umbrella organization
encompassing all of Zairian higher education. There is a listing of the institutes, their
location and the fields of study that they offer and the work includes a large section of
statistics on enrolment in higher education.

609 **L'enseignement universitaire au Zaïre: de Lovanium à l'Unaza,
1958-1978.** (University education in Zaire: from Lovanium to Unaza,
1958-1978.)
Benoît Verhaegen.   Paris: L'Harmattan; Brussels: CEDAF;
Kisangani, Zaire: CRIDE, 1978. 199p. bibliog.

The author, Benoît Verhaegen, is of Belgian nationality, but he has spent many years
teaching at the University of Lovanium (Catholic) and at the Université Nationale du
Zaïre (National University of Zaire, known as Unaza). This work brings together his
thoughts and writings throughout his academic career on the state of higher education in
Zaire and the need to adapt and reform the system to better suit the needs of the country.
The university in Zaire, as in most other African countries, draws heavily upon European
models of administration and curriculum, and it suffers from an inadaptation to the
requirements of higher education in a developing country. Verhaegen terms the Zairian
university paternalistic and authoritarian, a caricature of the Belgian system, and
expresses the hope that future generations of university students will be able to reform
the system of higher education in Zaire.

610 **The politics of education in Zaire.**
Patrick Michael Boyle.   PhD thesis, Princeton University, Princeton,
New Jersey, 1991. 393p. bibliog. (Available from University
Microfilms International, Ann Arbor, Michigan, order no. 9112281).

This recent PhD dissertation considers four decades of political and social change in the
Zairian education sector, beginning with the colonial system of education under the
Belgians, and it chronicles the sudden changes and evolution of the system following
independence. The author observes the current decline of national education in favour of
private education. Although the aspects of education relating to political and social
change are emphasized, the work gives a very comprehensive view of Zairian education
at all levels.

611 **Pour une société nouvelle, l'enseignement national: textes et
discours, 1960-1970.** (For a new society, national education: texts and
speeches, 1960-1970.)
Martin Ekwa.   Kinshasa: Editions du BEC, 1971. 214p.

The author has assembled documents, speeches, and position papers by individuals and
organizations dealing with the need to reform education in Zaire for purposes of national
development. These texts are drawn from the Catholic educational establishment and
represent the influence of the Church in national education. They reflect the delicate
balance between the laicity and national mission imposed upon Catholic education by the
state and the desire on the part of these educators to deliver a Christian education.

612 **Problèmes de l'enseignement supérieur et de développement en Afrique Centrale: recueil d'études en l'honneur de Guy Malengreau.** (Problems of higher education and of development in Central Africa: a collection of studies in honour of Guy Malengreau.) Edited by Romain Yakemtchouk. Paris: Librairie Générale de Droit et de Jurisprudence, 1975. 225p.

This work is a Festschrift in honour of Guy Malengreau, a professor at the Université Catholique de Louvain in Belgium and closely associated with its Zairian sister school, the Université Lovanium. The topics are varied, but many of the essays discuss the history, curriculum, and administrative organization of the Université Lovanium and consider its incorporation into the umbrella organization of the Université Nationale du Zaïre (Unaza) as a result of the government's determination to reorganize higher education in Zaire and to incorporate Catholic institutions into the state system. Much can be learned about higher education in Zaire from this work.

613 **Problèmes généraux de l'enseignement universitaire.** (General problems of university education.) Rectorat-Kinshasa: Presses Universitaires du Zaïre, 1979. 3 vols.

Focuses on higher education in Zaire, concentrating on the statutory and administrative structure of the university. Many official documents governing the university in Zaire are included in this work which would be very useful for a scholar examining the theoretical and legal basis of higher education in Zaire, but which is of marginal value to the general user.

614 **La Radio scolaire au Zaïre: (cas de l'émission 'Antenne Scolaire').** (Radio school in Zaire: [the case of the 'School of the Airwaves' broadcast].) Bakwa Muelanzambi. Kinshasa: Université Nationale du Zaïre, Campus de Kinshasa, Faculté des Sciences Economiques, Département de Communication Sociale, 1973. 42p.

Because this short study is a paper presented as a final work for a social communications degree, it may be difficult to locate. The work has the specialized focus of examining the educational radio broadcasting programme aimed at elementary school students. The author makes a distinction between general educational radio, aimed at an adult audience as a supplement to their previous education, and the school radio, aimed at children as the major or sole means of their scolarization. The programme and curriculum of this radio school is examined and the effectiveness of the broadcasts analysed.

615 **The reorganization of higher education in Zaire.** William M. Rideout. Washington, DC: Overseas Liaison Committee, American Council on Education, 1974. 25p. (OLC Paper, no. 5).

Published in 1974, this brief account of Zairian higher education covers the founding of the three universities of Zaire: the Catholic University of Lovanium (1954); the State sponsored Official University of the Congo (1955); and the Protestant sponsored Free University of the Congo (1963). A parallel system of specialized institutes completes the system of Zairian higher education. Until independence, the student body of Zairian universities and institutes, which have all received state subsidies, was predominantly

Education

Belgian. The author discusses the administrative organization of the universities; in the immediate post-independence era, higher education in Zaire expanded at an extraordinary pace of nearly thirty per cent per year. In 1971, the Mobutu régime initiated a reorganization of higher education in Zaire, incorporating all of these previously autonomous institutions into a national university system – Unaza (Université Nationale du Zaïre, or National University of Zaire). The administrative, pedagogical, and financial structure of the new Unaza is extensively analysed.

616 **Revue de Pédagogie Appliquée.** (Review of Applied Pedagogy.)
Université Nationale du Zaïre. Instituts Supérieurs Pédagogiques.
Kinshasa: Presses Universitaires du Zaïre, 1973-79. monthly.

Published from 1973 to about 1979 on a monthly basis, this serial of education and pedagogy in Zaire offers a wide variety of articles aimed at the teaching profession.

617 **Structural problems in education in the Congo (Leopoldville).**
Barbara A. Yates. *Comparative Education Review*, vol. 7, no. 2
(Oct. 1963), p. 152-62. bibliog.

In the early independence period, the Zairian government gave top priority to the expansion of enrolment at all levels. Yates traces this effort and discusses the structural difficulties of this enormous expansion for each of the three levels of education (primary, secondary, higher) and the interrelation of the three levels.

618 **Student attrition in Zaire: the system and the game in the secondary schools of Masomo.**
John D. Studstill.   PhD thesis, Indiana University, Bloomington, Indiana, 1976. 250p. bibliog. (Available from University Microfilms International, Ann Arbor, Michigan, order no. 771939).

This PhD dissertation has a narrow focus on the high rate of failure of secondary school students in Zaire. The author outlines the efforts made by the new Zairian state to educate its young people, expanding greatly the number of people enrolled in secondary schools. Yet despite this effort, in 1969 only eight or nine per cent of the students who entered secondary school managed to graduate six years later. The work is a sociological study on the causes of this student attrition. Despite its narrow focus, it offers a great deal about the difficulties of education in Zaire and both the state system and church schools are discussed.

619 **Survey of education in the Democratic Republic of the Congo.**
William M. Rideout, David N. Wilson, Crawford Young.
Washington, DC: American Council on Education, Overseas Liaison Committee, 1969. 102p. (Report [American Council on Education. Overseas Liaison Committee], H).

The authors provide a dated but comprehensive review of the education system of Zaire, surveying the colonial past and dealing with each level of education in separate sections. They also discuss the social, political, and economic context of education in Zaire.

620   **To honor the sacred trust of civilization: history, politics, and education in Southern Africa.**
Dickson A. Mungazi.   Cambridge, Massachusetts: Schenkman Publishing, 1983, p. 205-40.
In a chapter devoted to Zaire the author first resumes the political history of Zaire from colonial times to the ascendancy of Mobutu Sese Seko. In the second part of the text there is a brief history of education in Zaire, discussing the rôle of the churches and of the state. The coverage of education is rather superficial, but does include interesting observations on the relationship of education and politics throughout the work.

621   **Travailler et réussir: initiation aux méthodes d'étude dans l'enseignement supérieur et universitaire.** (Studying and succeeding: an introduction to the methods of study in higher and university education.)
Bokeme Sha Ne Molobay.   Kinshasa: Service de Pédagogie Universitaire, 1982. 95p. maps.
This is a very specialized work on the pedagogy of Zairian higher education. It is primarily a handbook for students undertaking a higher education in Zaire, advising them on how to organize their time, prepare for classes, take examinations, and negotiate the bureaucratic maze of the university system in Zaire. The work reveals much about the atmosphere of a Zairian university and although not appropriate for the general user, it might be a very useful introduction to Zairian higher education for foreign students or a faculty interested in study or work in this Central African nation.

622   **The triumph and failure of mission vocational education in Zaire 1879-1908.**
Barbara A. Yates.   *Comparative Education Review*, vol. 20, no. 1 (June 1976), p. 193-208. bibliog.
This article consists of a brief history of early education in Zaire. The primary focus is mission education for vocational purposes.

623   **University education and alienation: the dilemma of the 'Université nationale du Zaïre' and national development.**
Rudahindwa Chizungu.   PhD thesis, Stanford University, Stanford, California, 1979. 308p. maps. bibliog. (Available from University Microfilms International, Ann Arbor, Michigan, order no. 8001889).
Students often play a major political rôle in developing countries, and Zaire proves no exception. Zairian students are an élite group, aware of the inadaptation of their education to the development and employment needs of their country, and resentful of the economic rôle that they are called on to play in a neo-colonial economic and political system. They are also conscious of the Mobutu régime's wishes to control their institutions and their destiny contrary to their own wishes. The author's focus is primarily in the sociological description and definition of alienation among Zairian students. He analyses the political and social atmosphere on Zairian university campuses, sums up the crisis and decline of Unaza, the national university system, and discusses the development of higher education in this Central African country.

Education

Zaïre-Afrique.
See item no. 11.

Zaire, what destiny?
See item no. 14.

The emerging physician: a sociological approach to the development of a Congolese medical profession.
See item no. 308.

Science and
Technology

624 **Directory of institutions and individuals active in
     environmentally-sound and appropriate technologies.**
     Oxford: Published for the United Nations Environment Programme by
     Pergamon Press, 1979. 152p. (UNEP Reference Series, vol.1).

This UNEP directory lists ten organizations and five individuals under Zaire (p. 122-24).
Each entry lists name, address, contact person, subject areas covered, and a brief
description of activities.

625 **Recherche scientifique et développement: 1980 répertoire des
     institutions francophones.** (Scientific research and development:
     1980 repertory of Francophonic institutions.)
     Paris: Agence de Coopération Culturelle et Technique, 1980. 2 vols.

In this directory of French-speaking institutions specializing in scientific research,
technical assistance and the development of Third World countries, thirty-five Zairian
institutions, each specifying its activities (such as biology, soil science and food
technology) are included.

626 **La recherche scientifique zaïroise à l'étranger de 1976 à 1979.**
     (Zairian scientific research in foreign countries from 1976 to 1979.)
     Pilipili Kagabo. Brussels: Centre de Recherches Scientifiques
     Zaïroises, 1979. 80p.

This volume documents the first three years of CEREZA's efforts to systematize Zairian
scientific research in foreign countries. It includes brief descriptions of its major projects
as well as detailed financial accounts of the organization.

Literature

627 **The aborted sun: the image of postindependence Africa in recent Zairian fiction.**
Janice Spleth. In: *African literature 1988: new masks.* Washington, DC: Three Continents Press; African Literature Association, 1988, p. 73-78. bibliog.

In focusing on Bolya Baenga's *Cannibale* (q.v.), Thomas Mpoyi-Buata's *La ré-production*, and Pius Ngandu Nkashama's *La mort faite homme* (q.v.), Spleth discusses the theme of despair over the repressive and violent post-independent Zairian political climate.

628 **Anthologie des écrivains congolais.** (Anthology of Congolese authors.)
Kinshasa: SNEC; Ministère de la Culture, 1969. 264p.

This collection of short stories, plays, poems and proverbs contains the works of the winners of the 1969 Concours Littéraire National Léopold Sédar Senghor, including Zaire's most famous female poet Clémentine Nzuji (Clémentine Faïk-Nzuji Madiya) and her brother Dieudonné Kadima-Nzuji (Kadima Nzuji Mukala).

629 **La bataille de Kamanyola, ou, Bataille de la peur et de l'espoir: théâtre.** (The battle of Kamanyola, or, Battle of fear and hope: theatre.)
Mboyem M. K.-Mikanza, preface by Mbemba Yowa. Kinshasa: Les Presses Africaines, 1975. 56p.

Written by leading Zairian playwright Mikanza, also known as Norbert Mikanza, this play is based on actual historical events. In 1964, in Kamanyola, Kivu, the Zairian army battled against rebels until the then General Mobutu Sese Seko arrived and overwhelmed them. The author is also known for his critical works on Zairian theatre.

630 **Between tides.**
V. Y. Mudimbe, translated from the French by Stephen Becker.   New
York: Simon & Schuster, 1991. 160p.
The first of only three Zairian novels to be translated into English, this translation of
Entre les eaux concerns a native Catholic priest who joins the revolution in the former
Congo against the orders of his church superiors. He is tormented by his love for the
Church as well as the feeling that he is betraying his ancestors by being an accomplice to
colonial domination. The novel received the 1975 Grand Prize, International Catholic
Literature, Paris. Mudimbe is also well-known for his works on African intellectual life
and philosophy and other important works include: *Before the birth of the moon* (Le bel
immonde) (New York: Simon & Schuster, 1989); *Shaba deux* (Shaba II) (Paris: Présence
Africaine, 1989); *L'odeur du père: essai sur les limites de la science et de la vie en
Afrique noire* (The smell of the father: essay on the limits of science and life in Black
Africa) (Paris: Présence Africaine, 1982).

631 **Bibliographie littéraire de la République du Zaïre, 1931-1972.**
(Literary bibliography of the Republic of Zaire, 1931-1972.)
Kadima Nzuji Mukala.   Lubumbashi: Université Nationale du Zaïre,
Campus de Lubumbashi, 1973. 60p. (Publications du Centre d'Etude
des Littératures Romanes d'Inspiration Africaine).
This literary bibliography on Zaire, together with Alphonse Mbuyamba Kankolongo's
Guide de la littérature zaïroise de langue française, 1974-1992 (q.v.), constitutes a
national literary bibliography. The publication is organized into sections on anthologies,
forty individual poets and novelists (including a list of their notable works), literary
criticism of Zairian authors by non-Zairians, and Zairian literary criticism on foreign
literatures.

632 **Cannibale.** (Cannibal.)
Bolya Baenga.   Lausanne, Switzerland: P.-M. Favre, 1986. 191p.
(Collection Littératures).
This political allegory which takes place in an imaginary African country is the story of
two violent and corrupt men from rival clans who will stop at nothing to gain control of
international aid destined for the victims of an epidemic. As the novel opens two
children are rescued from a prison camp; they also seek vengeance for crimes against
their family. The novel is notable for its almost delirious and hallucinagetic style. It is
significant that the author chooses to live in the diaspora.

633 **Dictionnaire des oeuvres littéraires négro-africaines de langue
française: des origines à 1978.** (Dictionary of Negro-African literary
works in the French language: from its origins to 1978.)
Edited by Ambroise Kom.   Sherbrooke, Quebec: Editions Naaman;
Paris: ACCT, 1983. 671p. bibliog.
Unlike many anthologies or critical works on African literature, this useful dictionary
contains a wide selection of entries on Zairian authors. No less than forty Zairian authors
are included, such as Zamenga Batukezanga (five entries), V. Y. Mudimbe (five entries),
and Elebe Lisembe or Philippe Elebe (nine entries). Six of the dictionary's contributors
are from Zaire. The entry for each work includes the literary genre and an analysis, as
well as its place in the production of the author. Many lesser-known authors are included.

Literature

634 **Esanzo, chants pour mon pays: poèmes** = Esanzo, songs for my
country: poems.
Antoine-Roger Bolamba, preface by Léopold Sédar Senghor,
translated from the French by Jan Pallister.   Sherbrooke, Quebec:
Editions Naaman, 1977. 73p. (Collection en Traduction, no. 1).

First published in 1955, this collection of poems is the first English translation of a
complete poetic work by a Zairian author. The fourteen poems use the metaphor of
music to describe life in Mongo villages and two of the poems appear in Mongo as well
as in English and French. Also known as Bolamba Lokolé, the author also wrote
L'échelle de l'araignée (The spider's ladder) (The Author, [1939]), a story for which he
won the 1939 Prix de Littérature Orale Indigène, and was Editor-in-chief of the
influential journal *La Voix du Congolais* (The Voice of the Congolese) from 1945-59.

635 **Giambatista Viko, ou, le viol du discours africain: récit.**
(Giambatista Viko, or, the rape of African discourse: narrative.)
Mbwil a Mpaang Ngal.   Lubumbashi, Zaire: Editions Alpha-Omega,
1975. 113p. (Collection 'Création et Recherches').

Also published in Paris by Hatier in 1984, this is the story of an African intellectual who
struggles between an African discourse based on African tradition and his western
training and discourse. Other important works by Ngal are *L'errance* (The wandering), a
novel (Yaoundé: CLE, 1981); *Tendances actuelles de la littérature africaine
d'expression française* (Current tendencies of Francophonic African literature), literary
criticism (Kinshasa: Mont Noir, 1972); and *Aimé Césaire: un homme à la recherche
d'une patrie* (Aimé Césaire: a man in search of a country), literary criticism (Dakar:
NEA, 1975). The author is also known as Georges Ngal.

636 **Guide de la littérature zaïroise de langue française, 1974-1992.**
(Guide to Zairian literature in French, 1974-1992.)
Alphonse Mbuyamba Kankolongo, preface by Bertin Makolo
Muswaswa.   Limete-Kinshasa: Editions Universitaires Africaines,
1993. 113p.

The author picks up where Kadima Nzuji Mukala left off with his *Bibliographie
littéraire de la République du Zaïre, 1931-1972* (q.v.). Sections include: bibliographies;
literary anthologies; literary criticism; bio-bibliographies (of sixty-one authors); and
literary prizes won by Zairians from around the world (1948-68).

637 **Heart of darkness: search for the unconscious.**
Gary Adelman.   Boston: Twayne, 1987. 116p. maps. bibliog.
(Twayne's Masterwork Studies, no. 5).

This full-length, well-rounded critical study is but one of the many critical works which
have been written on Joseph Conrad's famous novel, *Heart of darkness*. It includes
chapters on the novel's critical reception, the situating of the text, a reading of the text,
and a discussion of the levels of meaning in the text. Adelman's excellent bibliography
highlights the critical commentaries which are discussed in some detail in his study.

638 **Heart of darkness: an authoritative text, backgrounds and sources, criticism.**
Joseph Conrad, edited by Robert Kimbrough.   New York: Norton, 1988. 3rd ed. 420p. map. bibliog. (Norton Critical Editions).

In this edition of Conrad's novella about the Congo, in addition to the text which dates from the turn of the century, a wide variety of background and source material, a section on Conrad in the Congo, and extensive critical material are included.

639 **Lettres d'Amérique.** (Letters from America.)
Zamenga Batukezanga.   Kinshasa: Zabat, 1982. 175p.

Using the epistolary form, Zamenga writes about his 1981 travel experiences in the United States. He thinks of himself as an explorer, in the same way that Portuguese explorer Diogo Cão probably felt when he came to Zaire in the 15th century. Some of Zamenga's numerous other works include: *Les hauts et les bas* (The highs and the lows) (Kinshasa, Saint Paul Afrique, 1971), *Mon mari en grève* (My husband on strike) (Kinshasa: Zabat, 1986), and *Guérir le malade et la maladie* (To cure the sick person and the illness) (Kinshasa: Kikesa, 1981).

640 **Littérature cyclique et roman zaïrois: tradition, mythe et art romanesque au Zaïre.** (Cyclical literature and the Zairian novel: tradition, myth and art of the novel in Zaire.)
Ikupasa O'Mos.   Kinshasa: Centre de Recherches Pédagogiques, 1988. 19p. bibliog.

The author takes issue with the idea that the novel is essentially a Western product and that it did not exist in traditional Africa. All legendary heros were first conceived in oral literature before they were given new life in written form. Numerous Zairian legendary heros are briefly discussed in this work.

641 **La littérature zaïroise.** (Zairian literature.)
Notre Librairie, no. 44 (Oct.-Nov. 1978), 63 (Jan.-March 1982), 144p., 127p.

This journal devoted two entire issues to a panorama of Zairian literature, from poetry, theatre, and the novel to literary criticism, book reviews, and the history of Zairian publishing houses. The second volume was also reissued in 1989.

642 **La littérature zaïroise de langue française, 1945-1965.** (Zairian literature in the French language, 1945-1965.)
Kadima-Nzuji Mukala.   Paris: ACCT; Editions Karthala, 1984. 342p. bibliog.

A major analysis of the formation of a Francophonic Zairian literature, this covers the period of 1945 to 1965, from the birth of the press in *La Voix du Congolais* (The Voice of the Congolese) to the rise of reading occasioned by the opening of public libraries and the foundation of the university in Zaire. Because of the aesthetic qualities as well as the sociological significance of their writings, poet Antoine-Roger Bolamba, storyteller Paul Lomami-Tshibamba, and novelists Dieudonné Mutombo and Timothée Malembe are discussed at length.

643 **La mort faite homme: roman.** (Death makes man: novel.)
Pius Ngandu Nkashama.   Paris: L'Harmattan, 1986. 257p.

The narrator of this novel is a prisoner of conscience, arrested during a demonstration when he was a medical student. As he thinks about his dream of being a doctor, he loses hope, and sinks into despair. After being pardoned, because he cannot forget how he was exploited by the government, he finally becomes mad.

644 **Le mystère de l'enfant disparu.** (The mystery of the missing child.)
Timothée Malembe.   Leopoldville: Bibliothèque de l'Etoile, 1962. 86p. (Collection L'Afrique Raconte, no. 1).

The kidnapped child Kalamay, who is held captive in an enemy village, subsequently escapes, then meets the first white men who are just arriving in the region of the Bangoli, before he finally returns to his family. This work was reprinted in Nendeln by Kraus Reprint in 1970. The author is also known as Malembe Wankani ko Ng'emwu.

645 **Ngando (le crocodile).** (Ngando [the crocodile].)
Lomami-Tshibamba, Paul.   Brussels: Editions G. A. Deny, 1948. 117p.

In this long tale, the supernatural mingles with a realistic recounting of daily life in Leopoldville (Kinshasa) during the period of 1945 to 1948. Ngando is one of the great early works of Zairian literature and the 1948 winner of the Foire Coloniale de Bruxelles. It was reprinted with Timothée Malembe's *Le mystère de l'enfant disparu* (Nendeln: Kraus Reprint, 1970).

646 **Papier blanc, encre noire: cent ans de culture francophone en Afrique centrale: Zaïre, Rwanda et Burundi.** (White paper, black ink: one hundred years of Francophonic culture in central Africa: Zaire, Rwanda and Burundi.)
Cellule 'Fin de Siècle', edited under the direction of Marc Quaghebeur by Emile Van Balberghe, with the collaboration of Nadine Fettweis, Annick Vilain.   Brussels: Editions Labor, 1992. 2 vols. (Archives du Futur).

Although the subtitle indicates that this large work of 690 pages is about Francophonic culture, it is primarily a literary criticism. The thirty-three articles largely concern Zaire, and several cover lesser-studied topics such as comic strips, the first writings of Zairian university élites, Francophonic literature and Protestantism in the Congo.

647 **Papier blanc, encre noire: cent ans de littérature francophone en Afrique centrale: Zaïre, Rwanda et Burundi.** (White paper, black ink: one hundred years of Francophonic literature in central Africa: Zaire, Rwanda and Burundi.)
Cellule 'Fin de Siècle', established under the direction of Marc Quaghebeur by Annick Vilain, with Nadine Fettweis, Antoine Tshitungu Kongolo, Emile van Balberghe. Brussels: Editions Labor, 1992. 73p.

This slim volume supplements the two-volume set with the same title (q.v.). A chronological look at Zairian literature is attained with one and two sentence quotes from writers, followed by bio-bibliographical information. Its strength lies in its coverage of pre-independent colonial writers living in the Belgian Congo.

648 **Pour mieux comprendre la littérature au Zaïre.** (To better understand Zairian literature.)
Kabongo Bujitu. Kinshasa: La Grue Couronnée, 1975. 152p. bibliog.

In this publication are brought together the author's lectures, interviews, radio and television programmes, and other research on Zairian and African literature.

649 **Promesses: anthologie provisoire d'une jeune littérature zaïroise.** (Promises: provisional anthology of a young Zairian literature.)
Centre Africain de Littérature, preface by Olivier Dubuis. Kinshasa: Les Presses Africaines, 1975. 142p.

This is an anthology of fifty-three poems and stories by eighteen Zairian writers, most of them quite young and perhaps still finding their own style. The authors write using the new literary movement of concretism (a rejection of colonial culture in favour of oral tradition coupled with a desire to witness contemporary Zairian life without false illusions, that is to say, concretely). Two of the writers, Zamenga Batukezanga and Tito Yisuku Gafudzi, have become well known today.

650 **La ré-production.** (The re-production.)
Thomas Mpoyi-Buatu. Paris: L'Harmattan, 1986. 243p. (Collection Encres Noirs).

In this political denunciation of modern Zaire, the novel's main character is in jail, fantasizing about sexual encounters, looking towards a new autonomous society. This is one of several important recent novels written by Zairians living in the diaspora.

651 **The rift.**
V. Y. Mudimbe, translated from the French by Marjolijn de Jager. Minneapolis, Minnesota: University of Minnesota Press, 1993. 126p. (Emergent Literatures).

The second of only three Zairian novels to be translated into English, this translation of *L'écart* is a fictional diary of an historian working on his thesis describes the last seven anguished days of his life. Although he is clearly not schizophrenic, he is unable to believe in anything or anyone, and his soul is separated from life.

652 **Les tortures de Eyenga: roman.** (The tortures of Eyenga: a novel.)
Kompany wa Kompany. Kinshasa: UEZA, 1984. 183p.

This is a novel about a tormented man resisting the evolution of customs, particularly the change from polygamy to monogamy, brought about by the rise of Christianity in Zaire.

653 **Traite au Zaïre.** (Slavery [of women] in Zaire.)
Antoine Junior Nzau. Paris: L'Harmattan, 1984. 252p. (Polars Noirs).

This popular detective novel is another recent example of social criticism, particularly of prostitutes and other offenders. The corruption of the Zairian military security force depicted in the novel is based on actual events. Nzau lives in the diaspora.

654 **V. Y. Mudimbe, ou, Le discours, l'écart et l'écriture.** (V. Y. Mudimbe, or, Discourse, the rift and writing.)
Bernard Mouralis. Paris: Présence Africaine, 1988. 143p. bibliog. (Critique Littéraire).

This is a major critical work on one of Zaire's most famous intellectuals, in which Mudimbe's poetry, essays and novels are studied. The bibliography (p. 133-41) includes works by and about Mudimbe as well as on Francophonic African literature in general.

655 **Victoire de l'amour.** (Victory of love.)
Dieudonné Mutombo. Leopoldville: Bibliothèque de l'Etoile, 1953. 128p.

The two people in this love story must overcome various obstacles such as being from different ethnic backgrounds (Luba and Kongo). The work was also reprinted with Timothée Malembe's *Le mystère de l'enfant disparu* (Nendeln: Kraus Reprint, 1970) and the author is also known as Mutombo da Fungu.

656 **Zamenga Batukezanga: vie et oeuvre.** (Zamenga Batukezanga: life and works.)
Prosper Ngoma-Binda. Limete, Kinshasa: Editions Saint Paul Afrique, 1990. 80p. bibliog.

An excellent biographical and critical study of Zamenga, one of Zaire's most prolific and controversial writers, this first takes a look at the life of Zamenga, and then covers each aspect of his writings, including essays, travel accounts, short stories, and poetry as well as novels which reflect Zairian popular life. The author concludes that it is difficult to classify Zamenga's works by literary genre, since they are often both literature and sociology.

657 **Zamenga of Zaire: 'novelist, historian, sociologist, philosopher and moralist'.**
Wyatt MacGaffey. *Research in African Literatures*, vol. 13, no. 2 (summer 1982), p. 208-15.

For the English-language reader, this is an excellent brief analysis of Zamenga Batukezanga's works and his impact on Zairian society.

L'éléphant qui marche sur des oeufs.
See item no. 741.

Congo/Zaire.
See item no. 790.

The Arts

General

658   **The arts of Africa: an annotated bibliography.**
Compiled by Janet L. Stanley.   Atlanta, Georgia: African Studies
Association Press, 1989- . 3 vols. (to date).

This is the most comprehensive bibliography for recent books, chapters of books, and periodical articles on African art, compiled by the Branch Chief of the National Museum of African Art in Washington, DC. Chapters are geographically arranged with coverage beginning in 1986 where Daniel Biebuyck's *The arts of Central Africa* (q.v.) leaves off. Each volume also includes a basic list of books recommended for academic libraries developing their collections on African art. This outstanding bibliography contains four indexes, including a detailed subject index, which makes finding the citations on Zaire more convenient.

659   **The arts of Central Africa: an annotated bibliography.**
Daniel P. Biebuyck.   Boston, Massachusetts: G. K. Hall, 1987. 300p.
(Reference Publications in Art History).

Biebuyck's comprehensive bibliography on Zairian visual arts, culture, ethnology, and early travelogues is the best bibliographical source on early to pre-independent Zairian art. Brief but useful annotations are not evaluative, and are arranged by geographical regions within Zaire. The bibliography covers books and periodical articles in all languages and in addition to the usual indexes, there is also an index of ethnic groups. The book won the African Studies Association's prestigious Conover-Porter award for excellence in Africana reference works.

660 **Sura Dji: visages et racines du Zaïre.** (Sura Dji: faces and roots of Zaire.)
Paris: Musée des Arts Décoratifs, 1982. 165p. maps. bibliog.

The aim of this 1982 French exhibition catalogue is to expose the French public to the richness of Zairian civilization. It contains essays on the full range of Zairian arts and intellectual life (archaeology, ancient and contemporary visual arts, music and literature) as well as reflections of the western view of central Africa. Some 183 objects are illustrated, primarily in black-and-white.

661 **Zaïre: peuples/art/culture.** (Zaire: people/art/culture.)
Joseph-Aurelien Cornet. Anvers, Belgium: Fonds Mercator, 1989. 405p. 17 maps. bibliog.

In this authoritative and beautifully illustrated book Zaire is described in its totality, including its geography, administration, and ethnology as well as artistic life. Important historical events, oral history, archaeology, natural resources and European exploration of each region are also covered. One helpful feature is that the characteristics of each ethnic group's artistic style are delineated and contrasted with that of neighbouring groups.

Visual arts

662 **African reflections: art from Northeastern Zaire.**
Enid Schildkrout, Curtis A. Keim, with contributions by Didier Demolin, John Mack, Thomas Ross Miller, Jan Vansina.   Seattle, Washington: University of Washington Press; London; New York: American Museum of Natural History, 1990. 271p. 3 maps. bibliog.

The focus of this book is on the art of the Mangbetu and Zande people. Most of the objects illustrated are from the American Museum of Natural History and were collected during its Congo Expedition between 1909-15. Liberal use is also made of the Museum's archival photographs which illustrate these cultures as they were during the early 20th century. In Chapter twelve, the authors discuss the influence of colonial contacts in the first quarter of the 20th century, as anthropomorphic objects developed and then disappeared from the Zairian artistic repertoire. Chapter ten consists of a discussion of the music, dance and musical instruments of Northeastern Zaire.

663 **Anthologie des sculpteurs et peintres zaïrois contemporains.**
(Anthology of contemporary Zairian sculptors and painters.)
Bamba Ndombasi Kufimba, Musangi Ntemo.   Paris: Nathan, Agence de Coopération Culturelle et Technique, 1987. 109p. bibliog.

Eight contemporary Zairian sculptors and nineteen painters are included in this anthology which provides a biographical sketch, a portrait, a summary of where the artist's works have been exhibited, a brief discussion of each artist's style, as well as illustrations of two or three recent sculptures or paintings. In addition, the authors devote a brief chapter to the various contemporary Zairian schools such as the New Generation, the Ecole de Lubumbashi, and the producers of tourist art called here 'de très mauvais goût' (in very bad taste).

664 **Anthropomorphe Gefässkeramiken aus Zaïre: Ausstellung 13. Oktober-14. November, 1987.** (Anthropomorphic terracotta vessels of Zaire: exhibition October 13-November 14, 1987.) Text by Leo Polfliet, edited and translated from the German by Jens Jahn. Munich: Galerie Fred Jahn Studio, 1987. 50p.

Eighteen anthropomorphic Zairian terracotta pots and jugs as well as one funerary stele, all from fourteen ethnic groups, are illustrated in this thin exhibition catalogue. Little information is given about when or where they were collected, although the author states that the earliest pieces probably date from the 17th century, and several were collected before the first quarter of the 20th century. Although archaeological excavations to date reveal that Zairian anthropomorphic vessels only occur after contact with Europeans, further research is still needed. The text is in both German and English.

665 **L'architecture tropicale: théorie et mise en pratique en Afrique tropicale humide.** (Tropical architecture: theory and application in tropical humid Africa.) Paul Dequeker, Kanene Mudimubadu. Kinshasa: Centre de Recherches Pédagogiques, 1992. 295p. maps. bibliog. (U, 40).

This excellent recent architectural manual not only encompasses the theoretical foundation of architecture in wet climates, but also discusses Zairian architecture in particular. The photographs and plans of hundreds of buildings in Zaire illustrate the variety and practicality of modern Zairian architecture.

666 **Art and healing of the Bakongo commented by themselves: minkisi from the Laman collection.** Wyatt MacGaffey. Stockholm: Folkens Museum-Ethnografiska; distributed by Indiana University Press, Bloomington, Indiana, 1991. 184p. map. bibliog. (Monograph Series, no. 16).

This unique monograph on Kongo *minkisi* (ritual fetishes, often accompanied by medicines in bags) brought to Sweden between 1910 and 1920 by ethnographer Karl Edvard Laman, is remarkable in that it documents forty-five *minkisi* and provides the original Kongo text collected by Laman as well as an English translation. Although Laman himself had published on this subject in *The Kongo* (Uppsala: [n.p.], 1953), his work was difficult to use because of a lack of indexes. MacGaffey, who is a translator and editor of Kikongo texts, has compiled new indexes of about 370 *minkisi* which include the name of the Kongo author, location from which the object came, and the catalogue number assigned by Laman. The publication is divided into four functional categories: divination; healing; wealth and warfare; and attack. It is illustrated with line drawings and occasional detailed photographs.

667   **Art bakongo: les centres de style.** (Bakongo art: style centres.)
Raoul Lehuard.   Arnouville-les-Gonesse, France: Arts d'Afrique
Noire, 1989. 2 vols. maps. bibliog. (Arts d'Afrique Noire, supplement
to tome 55).

Lehuard uses anthropomorphic wooden sculptures to illustrate his morphological
classification of Kongo art (Lower Congo) into style centres: Dondo-Kamba, Bwende,
Zombo-Sosso-Nkanu, Vili, Lari, Woyo-Kakongo, Bembe, Kougni, Mayanga,
Yombe-Sundi West, Sundi East, Solongo, and Kongo-Ndibu. Kongo art is found in
Zaire, Congo-Brazzaville, Angola and Gabon. A very useful glossary of
magical-religious forces contains the translations of Kongo terms and offers variant
spellings.

668   **Art from Zaire: 100 masterworks from the National Collection =**
L'art du Zaïre: 100 chefs-d'oeuvre de la Collection nationale.
Joseph Cornet, text, translation from the French and introduction by
Irwin Hersey, foreword by Mobutu Sese Seko Kuku Ngbendu Wa Za
Banga.   New York: African American Institute, 1975. 132p. map.
bibliog.

This exhibition catalogue is noteworthy because it commemorates the first exhibition of
works from the Institute of the National Museums of Zaire in the United States. In his
foreword, President Mobutu makes a plea to museums and collectors to return Zairian art
'plundered' during the colonial era: 'If we had not been deprived of some treasures, we
could have shown to the world, especially the American people, a more representative
sampling of our vast artistic heritage' (p. 10). This very topic, concerning who has the
right to own cultural treasures from Africa (and other parts of the world), was hotly
debated by art historians attending the 1992 African Studies Association meeting in
Seattle, Washington. Despite the lack of certain important objects such as Kongo nail
fetishes and Songye masks, this volume, arranged by ethnic group, pictures and
describes to scholars a representation of the most prized artworks located in Zaire.

669   **Art history in Africa: an introduction to method.**
Jan Vansina.   London; New York: Longman, 1984. 233p. maps.
bibliog.

A methodological study of African art history by the noted ethnologist and historian
Vansina, this is an excellent overview for both the general reader and scholar. Although
the text covers the entire continent, the Congo basin is his area of expertise, and Zaire is
represented throughout, including many of the illustrations.

670   **Art of Africa: treasures from the Congo.**
Joseph Cornet, translated from the French by Barbara Thompson.
New York: Phaidon, 1971. 365p. map. bibliog.

In this monumental work by the foremost authority on Zairian art, Father Joseph Cornet,
Director General of the Institute of the National Museums of Zaire, the reader is
reminded that an African work of art must be understood not in purely aesthetic terms,
but in the context of its religious function in the society from which it emanated. The
book is organized by four main geographical regions and thirty-three ethnic groups. The
180 plates of art objects primarily include statues, fetishes, and masks, but also other
objects such as pendants, adzes, pots, pipes, divining instruments, thrones, drums,

whistles, stools and staffs. These objects are made primarily out of wood, nails and ivory, but also of clay, feathers, stone, bronze, fibres and iron.

671 **Art of Central Africa: masterpieces from the Berlin Museum für Völkerkunde.**
Hans-Joaquim Koloss. New York: Metropolitan Museum of Art; distributed by Harry Abrams, 1990. 87p. map. bibliog.

The sixty-one objects illustrated here are primarily Zairian, although some originate from neighbouring Congo and Angola. They represent the best of the Berlin Ethnographic Museum's remaining Central African collection, half of which was destroyed or missing as a result of the Second World War. Nine prominent art historians have catalogued the exhibition, which ranges from *minkisi* (power figures or ritual fetishes) and masks to whistles, crucifixes, hammock pegs, cups, and pipes. The major ethnic groups represented include the Kongo, Yombe, Suku, Kuba, Luba, Songye, and Hemba.

672 **Art of the Yaka and Suku.**
Arthur P. Bourgeois, text in English and French. Meudon, France: Alain & Françoise Chaffin, 1984. 271p. maps. bibliog.

This book primarily contains black-and-white illustrations of nearly 250 objects of Yakalega and Suku sculpture from collections the world over. The text begins with the historical context, then explores the political and social life, and finally devotes the bulk of the discussion to the material culture and daily life of the two southwest Zairian groups including a discussion of five styles of masks and various statuettes, differentiated largely by their treatment of the eyes.

673 **Art pictural zaïrois.** (Art of painting in Zaire.)
Edited by Bogumil Jewsiewicki. Sillery, Quebec: Septentrion, 1992. 282p. bibliog. (Nouveaux Cahiers du CELAT, no. 3).

Popular urban painting of contemporary Zaire is broadly discussed in this recent monograph. Aspects such as the rural exodus, urban population structure, and contemporary popular sculpture have influenced this art and are therefore included among the eighteen essays (three in English, fifteen in French). Tshibumba Kanda-Matulu, painter of the history of society, receives special attention in several essays. Some fifty black-and-white and twelve colour reproductions of paintings are included.

674 **The arts of Zaire.**
Daniel P. Biebuyck. Berkeley, California; Los Angeles; London: University of California Press, 1985-86. 2 vols. bibliog.

In the first volume, Biebuyck analyses the art of thirty-three ethnic groups from southwestern Zaire, while the second volume covers twenty-one ethnic groups related to the Lega of Eastern Zaire. The author critically summarizes historical research in Zairian ethnographical studies and the classification of art, and states that there are gaps in scientific ethnographical studies because documentation is dispersed, uneven, or even lacking for many cultures. In volume one, the ethnography of each ethnic group is discussed, major art forms are identified along with their cultural context and use in rituals. Volume two is organized by chapters on the *bwami* association (a hierarchical association operating within various autonomous communities), Lega art, anthropomorphic and zoomorphic figurines, masks, other sculptures and *bwami* traditions. Biebuyck has written extensively on Zairian art and ethnology, including other works on the Lega such as: *La sculpture des Lega* (Sculpture of the Lega) (New York: Galerie Leloup, 1994), an exhibition catalogue which includes an English translation; and *Lega culture: art, initiation, and moral philosophy among a central African people* (Berkeley, California: University of California Press, 1973).

675 **Au royaume du signe: appliqués sur toile des Kuba, Zaïre.** (In the kingdom of the sign: appliques on cloth of the Kuba, Zaire.)
Fondation Dapper. Paris: A. Biro; Fondation Dapper, 1988. 96p. map. bibliog.

The *ntshak*, or female loin-cloth, are raffia cloths covered with symbols which are worn by women of the Kuba court. The abstract and geometric appliqué work is not uniformly distributed throughout the piece of cloth. The seven authors note that the Kuba designs are not unfamiliar to Westerners who have studied the works of Paul Klee and other European artists from the period 1920 to 1940.

676 **Contribution à l'étude historique de l'art plastique zaïrois moderne: fin XVe siècle-1975.** (Contribution to the historical study of modern Zairian plastic arts: end of the 15th century-1975.)
Badi-Banga Ne-Mwine. Kinshasa: Editions Malayika, 1977. 138p. bibliog. (Collection Propos sur l'Art).

Although this book claims to discuss only the 'plastic' arts, it actually touches on the full range of Zairian visual arts, while focusing equally on sculpture and painting. The first section is an historical review of Zairian art, including Portuguese, Asian, and Arabic influences as well as some sixty pages on colonial influences. The second section covers in some detail the era of Mobutu (1967 onwards) from the formation of art schools, protection of art and artists, and the rehabilitation of art and artists into Zairian society.

677 **Eglises tropicales.** (Tropical churches.)
Paul Dequeker. Kinshasa: Editions CEP, 1984. 157p.

Little text accompanies this book of black-and-white illustrations of Catholic churches designed by Belgian-born priest and architect Dequeker, and built nearly exclusively in Zaire. The architectural plan as well as interior and exterior photographs illustrate each building.

678 **Emil Torday and the art of the Congo, 1900-1909.**
John Mack. London: British Museum Publications, 1990. 96p. map. bibliog.

Hungarian ethnographer Emil Torday lived in the southern part of Zaire from 1900 to 1909. His contribution today is that of field anthropologist, not field collector of art/ethnographic objects. Illustrations include a few of the objects Torday collected, field photographs from his archives, and paintings by Norman Hardy, the painter on expedition with him.

679 **Face of the spirits: masks from the Zaire Basin.**
Edited by Frank Herreman, Constantijn Petridis.   Antwerp: Martial &
Snoeck, 1993. 261p. maps. bibliog.

Translated from French and Dutch, this richly illustrated scholarly exhibition catalogue
contains full-page colour representations of 113 masks from the major Zairian ethnic
groups, as well as chapters by fifteen renowned authorities on African art. The masks of
each ethnic group are defined in their socio-cultural as well as artistic contexts, and their
functions and symbolism are addressed. In order to differentiate often similar-looking
masks, Marc Leo Felix, in his chapter on Eastern Zairian animal masks, provides an
unusual set of maps useful to the novice and scholar alike. Maps of anthropomorphic,
simian, leopard, horned, bird and composite masks are each broken down into forty-eight
ethnic groups and their frequency of occurrence. In addition, a single detached oversize
colour map illustrating representative masks also accompanies this notable monograph.

680 **Fired brilliance: ceramic vessels from Zaire.**
Patricia Darish.   Kansas City, Missouri: University of
Missouri-Kansas City Gallery of Art, 1990. (unpaged) 2 maps. bibliog.

This exhibition catalogue of fifty-four terracotta Zairian vessels represents four broad
geographical regions: Lower Zaire; western Kasai; Shaba; and northeastern Zaire. A
brief introduction includes discussions of tradition and technique in the process of
manufacturing pottery, as well as form and function of the vessels.

681 **Late beads in the African trade.**
Elizabeth Harris, photography by Richard Todd.   Lancaster,
Pennsylvania: The Center; G. B. Fenstermaker, 1984. 16p. map.
bibliog.

This little book illustrates in colour and describes each of the 140 beads found in a
warehouse of a Belgian company doing business in the Belgian Congo. The beads
probably date from the 1950s and were likely European made.

682 **Maniema: an essay on the distribution of the symbols and myths
as depicted in the masks of greater Maniema.**
Marc L. Felix.   Munich: Fred Jahn, 1989. 313p. maps. bibliog.

Felix uses masks from various Zairian ethnic groups in Maniema (eastern Zaire, west of
the Great Lakes region) to hypothesize on their symbolism and typology (types of
objects produced). Seventy-nine black-and-white illustrations show masks from
twenty-five ethnic groups in Maniema. An analysis of migration patterns in Maniema
helps the reader to understand the influences of other cultures and ethnic groups on
Maniema art. The text is in English and German.

683 **Mon idée de l'architecture.** (My idea of architecture.)
Sante Ortolani.   Kinshasa: La Grue Couronnée, 1980. 158p.
(Collection Mosaïque).

Ortolani, an Italian who was both a university professor and architect in Zaire in the
1970s, wrote this book to explain his philosophy of architecture. Included in this
publication is the entire text of his *Manifeste de l'architecture zaïroise authentique*
(Manifesto of authentic Zairian architecture), first published in 1975. The second half of

the book is an essay by Lonoh Malangi Bokelenge entitled, 'L'architecture: réflet d'un humanisme' (Architecture: the reflection of a humanism), in which he discusses architecture from the Black African point of view. Illustrations of nine of Ortolani's buildings in Zaire are included.

684 **100 peoples of Zaire and their sculpture: the handbook.**
Marc Leo Felix. Brussels: Zaire Basin Art History Research Foundation, 1987. 246p. maps. bibliog.

Written for collectors, scholars, and students, this essential handbook devotes two pages to each ethnic group: one page of background characteristics (sociopolitical organization, economy, history, religion, sculpture, art style, brief bibliography) as well as one page of line drawings of sculptures exemplifying the group. A glossary and index of alternative names of ethnic groups are also included.

685 **Shoowa design: African textiles from the kingdom of Kuba.**
Georges Meurant, translated from the French by Sebastian Wormell.
London: Thames & Hudson, 1986. 205p. maps. bibliog.

The Shoowa, the least studied of the Kuba peoples, create geometrical rectilinear designs on cut-pile embroidery (or velvets). The designs are analysed in terms of Shoowa mythology, and are amply illustrated with embroidery, body scarification, wood engravings, as well as some basketwork, barkcloth and pottery examples. A glossary and index of the names of design motifs are included.

686 **Songye masks and figure sculpture.**
Dunja Hersak. London: Ethnographica, 1986. 189p. 3 maps. bibliog.

In this excellent study of Songye masks and figures, Hersak describes Songye society and the rôle of witchcraft within it, details the making and symbolism of the masks, and discusses the primary visual characteristics of *minkisi* figures used in benign magical operations. The author also classifies *bifwebe* striated masks used to malign magic in witchcraft, placing them in their social context. Nearly 130 objects are illustrated, primarily in black-and-white. Also included is a useful glossary of Songye terms, with explanations of singular versus plural forms of words.

687 **Statuary from the pre-Bemba hunters: issues in the interpretation of ancestral figurines ascribed to the Basikasingo-Bembe-Boyo.**
Daniel P. Biebuyck. Tervuren, Belgium: Royal Museum of Central Africa, 1981. 163p. maps. bibliog.

This catalogue includes fifty-nine black-and-white plates of pre-Bemba ancestral figurines in the Royal Museum of Central Africa. Lineages of the Basikasingo (eastern Zaire) are shown to be complex and analysed in depth in the text. Biebuyck's problems of identification include an analysis of seven Basilugezi-Basikasingo figurines and sixteen figurines ascribed to the Bembe when they arrived by 1913 at the Museum.

688 **Style, classification and ethnicity: design categories on Bakuba raffia cloth.**
Dorothy K. Washburn. Philadelphia: American Philosophical Society, 1990. 157p. map. bibliog. (Transactions of the American Philosophical Society, vol. 80, pt. 3).

In this study of Kuba raffia cloth, the author uses a psycho-anthropological approach to analyse how people categorize the patterns on the cloth. Kuba patterns classified by the Kuba people themselves do not always follow the traditional Western design elements of motif and layout.

689 **A survey of Zairian art: the Bronson collection.**
Joseph Cornet. Raleigh, North Carolina: North Carolina Museum of Art, 1978. 379p. 13 maps. bibliog.

Collectors Lee, Dona, and Robert Bronson formed a collection of Zairian art that related to their careers in fashion, interior design and decoration. This publication uses the collection and covers representative artistic styles, including 'lesser-known tribal styles'. Cornet here emphasizes artistic and stylistic appreciation and briefly discusses the cultural context of each of the 207 objects. The survey updates Cornet's *Art of Africa* (q.v.): 'new sculptures have been found, new styles discovered, stylistic relationships among neighboring tribes clarified, and tribal areas redefined and renamed through political evolution. . . .' (p. 16).

690 **Zaire 1938/39: photographic documents on the arts of the Yaka, Pende, Tshokwe and Kuba** = Fotodokumente zur Kunst bei den Yaka, Pende, Tshokwe und Kuba.
Hans Himmelheber. Zurich: Museum Rietberg, 1993. De-luxe ed. 164p. maps.

These field photographs, taken in 1938 and 1939, are accompanied by brief English and German text on the Yaka, Suku, Tshokwe, Biomo and Kuba of southwestern Zaire. The photos capture the dress, material culture, customs, and traditions of that era.

Music and dance

691 **African children's songs for American elementary schools.**
Kazadi wa Mukuna. East Lansing, Michigan: Michigan State University, African Studies Center and Music Department, 1979. 40p. (Resources for Teaching and Research in African Studies, no. 2).

The ten children's songs here are from the Luba, in the Kasai and Shaba regions of Zaire. The music is printed with Luba words, but the phonetic pronunciation and rhythmic structure are also given and some of the songs are translated into English. The author explains how to make four rhythm instruments: bottle cap instruments, rattles, rhythm sticks, and clappers.

692 **African music and oral data.**
Ruth M. Stone, Frank J. Gillis.   Bloomington, Indiana; London:
Indiana University Press, 1976. 412p. (African Field Recordings
Survey / Archives of Traditional Music, Indiana University).

This catalogue summarizes collections of phono-recordings of African music and oral
data collected throughout the world. It lists both commercial and non-commercial
collections. There are indexes to countries (Zaire lists 42 citations), culture groups and
subjects.

693 **African music: a bibliographical guide to the traditional, popular,
art, and liturgical musics of Sub-Saharan Africa.**
John Gray.   New York; Westport, Connecticut; London: Greenwood
Press, 1991. 499p. (African Special Bibliographic Series, no. 14).

Although this recent bibliography on African music is not annotated, its comprehensiveness is noteworthy. The author gathered his sources from printed materials as
well as five CD-ROM databases and his own database. Zaire is covered in the sections
on traditional music as well as popular music, together containing nearly 300 citations.
The ethnic group and subject indexes are helpful.

694 **African music in perspective.**
Alan P. Merriam.   New York; London: Garland, 1982. 506p. bibliog.
(Critical Studies on Black Life and Culture, vol. 6).

This republication of the author's essays and articles includes eight chapters on the
ethnomusicology of Zaire, including work about the Bashi, Basongye (Songye), and Bala
peoples.

695 **African music on LP: an annotated discography.**
Alan P. Merriam.   Evanston, Illinois: Northwestern University Press,
1970. 200p.

This reference tool by noted ethnomusicologist Merriam lists commercially-made LPs on
African music and songs, dating from the beginning of recorded music to 1965. It
includes no less than eighteen indexes such as language of song texts and 'tribal
groupings' (for example, ethnic groups). To find the several dozen entries on Zaire, go to
Index IX, Places of Recording, and look under Congo (Democratic Republic of). Each
band on the record is indexed.

696 **African music: a pan-African annotated bibliography.**
Carol Lems-Dworkin.   London: H. Zell, 1991. 382p.

This bibliography on African music from 1960 to the present contains fifty-six detailed
annotated entries on Zaire. It is intended as an update on four earlier bibliographies
published between 1936 and 1965 (J. P. Gaskin, A. P. Merriam, D. Thieme, and
D. Varley).

697 **African pop: goodtime kings.**
Billy Bergman. Poole, Dorset: Blandford Press, 1985. 143p. maps. bibliog. (Planet Rock Series, no. 3).
Zairian popular music is covered in the chapter entitled '*Soukous*' (having a good time) (p. 44-55). The historical growth of *soukous* is given, and Zairian pop singers Franco, Rochereau (Tabu Ley), and M'bilia Bel are highlighted. It includes a list of American and British stores in which African music may be purchased.

698 **Bobongo: la grande fête des Ekonda (Zaïre).** (Bobongo: the great festival of the Ekonda [Zaire].)
Daniel Vangroenweghe. Berlin: Reimer, 1988. 332p. maps. bibliog. (Mainzer Afrika-Studien, Bd. 9).
The thorough ethnological introduction to the Ekonda is followed by an analysis of their funeral and mourning customs. The text concludes with the Ekonda dialect and French texts of two *bebongos* (polyphonic songs) and two *bayaya* (dances and songs).

699 **Bodies of resonance: musical instruments of Zaire =**
Resonanz-Körper: Musikinstrumente aus Zaïre.
Leo Polfliet. Munich: Fred & Jens Jahn, 1985. 71p. maps. bibliog.
Zairian music is classified into five linguistic groups: Bantu; Central Sudanic (northern Zaire); Nilotic (northeast Zaire); Nilotic-Hamitic (lakes area of Zaire); and Pygmies. Although there is no single Zairian musical style, polyrhythm is the common denominator. Forty plates of black-and-white instruments illustrate this volume which treats the objects primarily from an artistic perspective. The text is written in English and German.

700 **Chansons de danse mongo: Rép. du Zaïre.** (Songs of Mongo dance: Republic of Zaire.)
G. Hulstaert. Bandundu, Zaire: Ceeba, 1982. 127p. bibliog. (Ceeba Publications. Série II, vol. 78).
Father Hulstaert transcribed the song texts of Mongo dances along with the French translations. Some commentary and explanations of the dances are included in this volume.

701 **Chants mongo: Rép. du Zaïre.** (Mongo songs: Republic of Zaire.)
G. Hulstaert. Bandundu, Zaire: Ceeba, 1982. 175p. bibliog. (Ceeba Publications. Série II, vol. 76).
This publication contains Mongo song texts and French translations collected by the author, although the recordings that he made are now housed in Tervuren, Belgium. The songs are classified into: paddling; drinking; fighting; hunting; complaining; specialists in singing; and songs of folktales.

702 **Cinquante ans de musique du Congo-Zaïre (1920-1970): de Paul Kamba à Tabu-Ley.** (Fifty years of music from the Congo and Zaire [1920-1970]: from Paul Kamba to Tabu-Ley.)
Sylvain Bemba. Paris: Présence Africaine, 1984. 188p. bibliog.

Bemba's history of Zairian and Congolese music is arranged chronologically from its origins, and its Western influences, to chapters on each of the decades from the 1920s up to the 1970s. The major musicians and orchestras are covered and a chronology of important historical and musical events (1807-1978) in the world/Africa, the Congo, and Zaire is included.

703 **La condition de la femme à travers la musique zaïroise moderne de 1964 à 1984.** (The condition of women as seen through modern Zairian music from 1964 to 1984.)
Nkangonda Ikome, Amisi Manara Bakari. *Afrikanistische Arbeitspapiere*, vol. 20 (1989), p. 5-47.

Songs are examined which highlight the following themes: the degraded image of women; the weight of tradition; the factor of polygamy; the infidelity of men; and the dependence of women on men.

704 **Congo-Zaire.**
Ronnie Graham. In: *The Da Capo guide to contemporary African music.* New York: Da Capo, 1988, p. 184-214. map. bibliog.

Chapter eighteen covers both Congolese and Zairian music, here characterized as 'the most potent musical form in the entire continent' (p. 187). It is largely devoted to a description of forty-four Zairian and Congolese popular singers and bands, including brief biographical sketches and discographies. Only one page, however, is devoted to traditional Zairian music. This text was also published in London in 1988 under the title: *Stern's guide to contemporary African music.*

705 **Les cordophones du Congo belge et du Ruanda-Urundi.** (The cordophones of the Belgian Congo and Ruanda-Urundi.)
Jean Sébastien Laurenty. Tervuren, Belgium: Musée Royal du Congo Belge, 1940. 2 vols. maps. bibliog. (Annales du Musée Royal du Congo Belge. Nouvelle Série in-4o, Sciences de l'Homme, vol. 2).

This volume on musical instruments is one of several published by the museum, and covers stringed instruments from Zaire, Rwanda and Burundi. Volume two contains thirty-seven plates and five maps.

706 **Enquête sur la vie musicale au Congo belge, 1934-1935: questionnaire Knosp.** (Study of musical life in the Belgian Congo, 1934-1935: Knosp questionnaire.)
Gaston Knosp. Tervuren, Belgium: Musée Royal de l'Afrique Centrale, 1968. 3 vols. maps. (Archives d'Ethnographie, no. 11-13).

In 1934-35, Knosp sent out a survey on musical instruments and vocal music to some administrators in the Belgian Congo. The respondents, however, did not usually have specialized musical training and the questions suffered from a lack of established ethnomusicological terminology since the field was then in its infancy. Nevertheless, although the survey does have some faults, it contains information that is still useful today.

707 **Essai de commentaire de la musique congolaise moderne.**
(Commentary on modern Congolese music.)
Michel Lonoh. [N.p.]: [n.p.], [1967-71]. 95p. bibliog.

This is the first comprehensive monograph on the music of Zaire. It is divided into four parts: the historical background of traditional Zairian music; the sociological analysis of modern Zairian music (for example, treatment of themes such as love, death, propaganda, and politics); the impact of the Zairian independence revolution on music; and sketches of prominent contemporary Zairian musicians and orchestras. The author is also known as Lonoh Malangi Bokelenge.

708 **Modern Zairean music: yesterday, today and tomorrow.**
Lonoh Malangi Bokelenge. In: *The Arts and civilization of Black and African peoples. Volume 1, Black civilization.* Lagos: Centre for Black and African Arts and Civilization, 1986, p. 132-51.

The author puts Zairian music into a historical perspective. The origin of modern Zairian music, considered ethnologically and linguistically, lies in the musics of the Bantu, Sudanese, Nilotic and Hamitic peoples. External contributions are discussed as well. For the future, new aesthetics must guide Zairian musical art.

709 **Musical instruments of the Belgian Congo.**
Blair M. Benner. BA thesis, Boston University, 1948. 147p. maps. bibliog.

Despite its age and sparse ethnographic background, this is a useful English language source on Zairian musical instruments. The author examined the musical instruments in the Peabody Museum of Harvard University in preparation for this description of a variety of Zairian idiophones, membranophones, chordophones, and aerophones.

710 **Musique d'animation politique & culturelle: festival de Kinshasa du Zaïre 14 octobre 1979.** (Political and cultural music for mass entertainment rallies: festival of Kinshasa, Zaire, October 14 1979)
Kanza Matondo ne Mansangaza. Kinshasa: [n.p.], 1979. 31p.

In this brief monograph the author describes *musique d'animation* (music for mass entertainment rallies) which combines features of modern ballet, traditional dancing, and popular political rallies. These shows, performed throughout Zaire, promote the Popular Revolution Movement. The author, a supporter of the policy of a return to authenticity, finds much to criticize in contemporary urban Zairian music: for example, ancestral costumes are not uniformly worn when music is performed, and electronic amplification is not appropriate.

711 **La musique et son rôle dans la vie sociale et rituelle luba.** (Music and its rôle in Luba social and ritual life.)
Jos Gansemans. Tervuren, Belgium: Musée Royal de l'Afrique Centrale, 1978. p. 47-121. maps. bibliog. (Annales. Série in-8, Sciences Humaines, no. 95).

Gansemans briefly describes Luba society before discussing Luba musical instruments. The primary focus moves on to music accompanying Luba rites and ceremonies such as those used in rites of passage, nuptials, and those used with healers and hunters. Song texts are recorded in Luba and in French.

712 **Musique traditionnelle de l'Afrique noire: discographie. Zaïre.** (Traditional music of Black Africa: discography. Zaïre.)
Chantal Nourrit, William Pruitt. Paris: Radio-France Internationale, Centre de Documentation Africaine, 1982. 257p. maps.

Volume fourteen of this comprehensive set of discographies of African music covers Zaire in 967 entries, with each band of the recording separately numbered. It includes ninety-two commercially-made LPs and two audio cassettes. Although the dates of issue are often not given, coverage appears to span from the 1950s to 1981 and the reader is freqently referred to Alan P. Merriam's *African music on LP* (q.v.). Each LP is classified into the following categories: traditional (popular music with traditional instruments); traditional/learned music (music of professionals); modernized traditional contemporary music in traditional style; and variety. An introductory essay by Benoît Quersin on Zairian traditional music is included.

713 **Musique zaïroise moderne: extrait d'une conférence illustrée donnée en 1969 au Campus Universitaire de Kinshasa.** (Modern Zairian music: extract from an illustrated lecture given in 1969 at the University Campus of Kinshasa.)
Kanza Matondo ne Mansangaza. Kinshasa: Publications du CNMA, 1972. 84p. bibliog.

This text discusses pre-colonial Zairian music's qualities of notation, tonality, theme and harmony, as well as colonial music such as the polka and quadrille. However, it mainly concentrates on the current musical scene, covering topics including the rôles of the song, new orchestration, the composer, the singer, and the accompanist. In the final chapter, the author exhorts the reader not to permit the stagnation of contemporary Zairian music.

714 **Le ndunga: un masque, une danse, une institution sociale au Ngoyo.** (The ndunga: a mask, a dance, a social institution to the Ngoyo.)
Zdenka Volavka. *Arts d'Afrique Noire*, no. 17 (spring 1976), p. 28-43.

In the western part of Zaire and the Cabinda territory, in the former Ngoyo kingdom, the *ndunga* (sacred dance) is still practised. The performer wears the *ndunga* mask and a huge costume of dry banana leaves, and is accompanied by a long and short drum. An English summary accompanies the French text treating this topic.

715   **New Grove dictionary of music.**
Alan P. Merriam.   Washington, DC: Grove's Dictionaries of Music,
1980. 20 vols. map. bibliog.

The entry under Zaire (p. 621-26) provides an excellent historical overview and a brief
bibliography of Zairian music.

716   **The origin of Zairean modern music: a socio-economic aspect.**
Kazadi wa Mukuna.   *African Urban Studies*, no. 6 (winter 1979-80),
p. 31-39. bibliog.

In 1899 when the Chemin de Fer du Congo was created, and in 1906 when the Union
Minière du Haut Katanga (Gécamines) was created, detribalized centres were formed,
impacting the various tribal groups and foreigners employed on the railroad and in the
mines. Zairian modern music was thus born there and in other urban centres (but not
Kinshasa) in the late 1930's.

717   **Shaba diary: a trip to rediscover the 'Katanga' guitar styles and
songs of the 1950s and '60s.**
John Low.   Vienna: Fohrenau, 1982. 123p. bibliog. (Acta
Ethnologica et Linguistica, nr. 54) (Series Musicologica, no. 4)
(Series Africana, no. 16).

Low recounts his eight-month trip through Shaba (formerly Katanga) and neighbouring
countries in 1979. The author travelled to meet guitarists Jean Bosco Mwenda, Losta
Abelo, and Edouard Masengo, in order to study their finger-styles when playing the
guitar and also to learn and record the songs he encountered along the way. An appendix
on the origin of non-tribal Katangan guitar styles and a discography are included.

718   **Sounding forms: African musical instruments.**
Edited by Marie-Thérèse Brincard.   New York: American Federation
of Arts, 1989. 205p. map. bibliog.

Approximately half of the 178 musical instruments illustrated here are identified as
Zairian, and originating from numerous ethnic groups. Of particular relevance are two
introductory essays: 'Body and voice: Kongo figurative musical instruments', by Robert
Farris Thompson and 'Anthropomorphism, zoomorphism, and abstraction in the musical
instruments of Central Africa', by Jean-Sébastien Laurenty.

719   **Sweet mother: modern African music.**
Wolfgang Bender.   Chicago; London: University of Chicago Press,
1991. 235p. bibliog. (Chicago Studies in Ethnomusicology).

In Chapter two (p. 42-73) entitled 'Francophone connections', the author discusses
music from both Congo-Brazzaville and Zaire, called at least seven different names, but
here known by the term 'African jazz'. The musical scene is covered beginning in the
1950s, and includes discussions of record labels, some of the major musicians, a
description of the Katanga guitar style, and a brief mention of the influence of politics on
Zairian music.

720 **La systématique des aerophones de l'Afrique centrale.** (The
systematics of aerophones of central Africa.)
Jean-Sébastien Laurenty.   Tervuren, Belgium: Musée Royal de
l'Afrique Centrale, 1974. 2 vols. bibliog. (Annales. Nouvelle Série
in-4o, Sciences Humaines, no. 7).
Slit drums are the subject of this volume on Zairian musical instruments. Volume one
contains 479 pages of text and volume two contains 124 plates.

721 **Les tambours du Congo belge et du Ruanda-Urundi.** (Drums of the
Belgian Congo and Ruanda-Urundi.)
Olga Boone.   Tervuren, Belgium: Musée du Congo Belge, 1951.
120p. maps. bibliog. (Annales du Musee du Congo Belge. Nouvelle
Série in-4o, Ethnographie, vol. 1).
This volume on musical instruments covers drums from Zaire, Rwanda and Burundi. It
contains forty plates and five maps.

722 **Les xylophones du Congo belge.** (The xylophones of the Belgian
Congo.)
Olga Boone.   Tervuren, Belgium: Musée du Congo Belge, 1936.
p. 69-144. maps. bibliog. (Annales du Musée du Congo Belge.
Ethnographie, Série III, Notes Analytiques sur les Collections du
Musée du Congo Belge, tome III, fasc. 2).
Zairian xylophones are the subject of this volume which, despite its age, is still an
excellent source of information. It contains five maps.

Theatre and film

723 **Le cinéma dans les pays des grands lacs: Zaïre, Rwanda, Burundi.**
(Cinema in the countries of the great lakes: Zaire, Rwanda, Burundi.)
Rik Otten, with the collaboration of Victor Bachy.   Paris:
OCIC/L'Harmatttan, 1984. 122p. map. bibliog. (Cinémedia).
Separate sections cover the cinemagraphic history of Zaire, Rwanda, and Burundi and
the brief chapter on the Belgian Congo is followed by several chapters on Zaire.
Noteworthy topics include film distribution, the censoring of films in Zaire as well as a
catalogue of fifty-one Zairian filmmakers and their filmographies up until 1982.

724 **La critique coloniale et la naissance du théâtre au Zaïre.** (Colonial criticism and the birth of theatre in Zaire.)
Lye Mu-Daba Yoka. *L'Afrique Littéraire et Artistique*, no. 5 (1975), p. 83-91.

The author presents errors made by colonial ethnologists and missionaries such as G. Hulstaert, A. De Rop, and O. De Bouveignes on the subject of Zairian theatre. The author then analyses the birth of Zairian theatre, cornered between colonial Aristotelian conceptions and reminiscences of African oral tradition.

725 **Dictionnaire du cinéma africain.** (Dictionary of African cinema.)
Association des Trois Mondes. Paris: Karthala, 1991- . vol. 1.

This current catalogue of African films contains brief biographical information and filmographies of fifty-six Zairian films by fifty-one Zairian filmmakers. Occasionally, the subject of the film is briefly described. Surprisingly, the catalogue contains only a few more recent films but the same filmmakers as listed in Rik Otten's *Le cinéma dans les pays des grands lacs* (q.v.).

726 **Le Groupe Mufwankolo.** (The Group Mufwankolo.)
Recorded and edited by Walter Schicho in collaboration with Mbayabo Ndala. Vienna: Institut für Afrikanistik, 1981. 333p. bibliog. (Beiträge zur Afrikanistik, Bd. 14) (Veröffentlichungen der Institute für Afrikanistik und Agyptologie der Universität Wien, Nr. 20).

Each of the twelve people in the theatrical Group Mufwankolo is interviewed and asked when and why he or she joined the group and about the characters he or she portrays on radio and television. That text, as well as the four plays that follow, all appear in Lubumbashi Swahili and in French translation. The plays which portray the middle class and workers who lived in Lubumbashi in the 1970s, are also a linguistic documentation of Lubumbashi Swahili.

727 **Histoire du cinéma colonial au Zaïre, au Rwanda et au Burundi.**
(History of the colonial cinema in Zaire, Rwanda and Burundi.)
Francis Ramirez, Christian Rolot. Tervuren, Belgium: Musée Royal de l'Afrique Centrale, 1985. 527p. bibliog. (Annales. Série in-8o. Sciences Historiques, no. 7).

Belgian Congo is the primary focus of this analysis of the history of the cinema of the Belgian Congo and Ruanda-Urundi. It includes chapters on the cinematic view of traditional African life as well as colonial life from both the white colonizer and Black African perspectives. The second part of the book is an analysis of the cinema of missionaries and a filmography is included.

728 **Musical play in Zaire: a contemporary interpretation of African oral literature.**
D. M. Pwono. In: *African literature 1988: new masks.* Washington, DC: Three Continents Press; African Literature Association, 1988, p. 79-86. bibliog.

The musical plays of the *Liandja* epic and *Ngembo*, produced by the National Dance Company of Zaire, serve as examples of new Zairian theatre. The themes are relevant to Africans, the plays are performed primarily in Lingala (the language spoken in Kinshasa), and the resulting experience is a combination of political ideology and traditional music, dance, costume and oral literature.

729 **Les spectacles d'animation politique en République du Zaïre: analyse des méchanismes de reprise, d'actualisation et de politisation des formes culturelles africaines dans les créations spectaculaires modernes.** (The spectacles of political mass rallies in the Republic of Zaire: analysis of the mechanisms of renewal, realization and the politicizing of African cultural forms in the modern creation of the spectacle.)
Kapalanga Gazungii Sang'Amin. Louvain-la-Neuve, Belgium: Editions des Cahiers Théâtre Louvain, 1989. 262p. bibliog. (Cahiers Théâtre Louvain, nos. 63-65) (Arts du Spectacle).

This is the most thorough analysis of the Zairian phenomenon, the *'spectacle d'animation'*, a theatrical event combining elements of theatre, dance, and music along with political slogans.

730 **Sub-Saharan African films and filmmakers: an annotated bibliography** = Films et cinéastes africaines de la région subsaharienne: une bibliographie commentée.
Nancy Schmidt. London: H. Zell, 1988. 401p.

This well-researched bibliography on African films and filmmakers contains twenty-four citations (six books and eighteen periodical articles) relevant to Zaire. It is updated annually in Schmidt's articles entitled, 'Recent films by Sub-Saharan African filmmakers,' which appear in the *African Literature Association Bulletin.* A supplement covering the years 1987-92 is expected to be published in 1994 by Hans Zell.

731 **Théâtre populaire de marionnettes en Afrique sud-saharienne.**
(Popular theatre of marionnettes in Sub-Saharan Africa.)
Olenka Darkowska-Nidzgorska. Bandundu: CEEBA, 1980. 259p. bibliog. (Publications CEEBA. Série II, vol. 60).

The marionnettes and puppets described here are not usually children's toys, but living creatures which are capable of producing drama or theatre. The chapter on Angola, Congo and Zaire (p. 195-235) describes the cultural setting, the use and method of manipulation of a variety of marionnettes such as giant mortuary puppets, marionnettes that are musical instruments, divinatory marionnettes and mask marionnettes. The Chokwe, Sanga, Luba, Luntu, Ngbaka, Sonde, and Abarambo are each briefly discussed in relation to their use of marionnettes.

732 **Le théâtre zaïrois: dossier du premier festival.** (Zairian theatre: documents from the first festival.)
Kinshasa: Editions Lokole, 1977. 138p.

This record of the 1977 festival includes the speeches, minutes of the debates, a summary and photographs from each of the fourteen 'spectacles' or plays performed at the festival, and several essays on Zairian theatre. The four themes of the festival are: Zairian theatre and language; Zairian theatre and criticism; Zairian theatre and its problems; and Zairian theatre from dilettantism to technicality.

Ethnographische Notizen aus den Jahren 1905 und 1906.
See item no. 187.

Power and performance: ethnographic explorations through proverbial wisdom and theater in Shaba, Zaire.
See item no. 201.

La bataille de Kamanyola, ou, Bataille de la peur et de l'espoir: théâtre.
See item no. 629.

Folklore and Customs

733 **Africa adorned.**
Angela Fisher. New York: Harry Abrams, 1984. Reprinted 1991.
304p. bibliog.
This 'coffee table' book includes a brief text on the history of Zairian personal adornment, as well as some colour photographs of Zairian coiffures, neck torques, bracelets, pendants, clothing, hats, and hairpins.

734 **African dress.**
Vol. 1 compiled by Joanne Bubolz Eicher; vol. 2 compiled by Ila M.
Pokornowski, Joanne Bubolz Eicher, Moira F. Harris, Otto Charles
Thieme. East Lansing, Michigan: Michigan State University, African
Studies Center, 1970-85. 2 vols.
Because there are few books written on Zairian dress, this annotated bibliography is especially welcome. The authors have cast a wide net to locate information within publications on topics such as African dress, body ornamentation, jewellery, and hairdressing. The annotations provide specific information on the relevant parts of the book or periodical article. There are eighty-nine citations on Zaire in the two volumes.

735 **Chants de cultes du Zaïre: chants et possession dans les cultes du**
Butembo et des Mikendi chez les Bahemba et les Baluba: essai
d'étude ethnolinguistique. (Chants of cults in Zaire: chants and
possession in Butembo and Mikendi cults of the Bahemba and Baluba:
ethnolinguistic approach.)
Ntole Kazadi. Louvain, Belgium: Peeters; Paris: SELAF, 1990.
271p. 3 maps. bibliog. (Langues et Cultures Africaines, no. 8)
(SELAF, no. 117).
The purpose of this comparison of Hemba and Luba spiritual possession is to confirm the essential rôle of chants in the phenomenon of possession. Using an ethnolinguistic

approach, the author analyses twenty Butembo and eighteen Mikendi chants. An English summary is included.

736 **Coiffures du Zaïre.** (Hairstyles of Zaire.)
   Tayeye Mayanga.   Bandundu, Zaire: CEEBA, 1979. 304p. bibliog.
   (Publications CEEBA. Série II, Mémoires et Monographies, vol. 53).

The primary purpose of this book is twofold; it aims to describe the origins of hairstyles and to illustrate various male and female hairstyles from Zaire. Seventeen examples are also included of ancient hairstyles taken from Ivan de Pierpont's *Un broussard heroïque* (A heroic man of the bush) (Charleroi, Belgium: Dupuis, 1937).

737 **Congo fireside tales.**
   Phyllis Savory, illustrated by Joshua Tolford.   New York: Hastings House, 1962. 88p. map.

As the art of storytelling is enjoying a rebirth in some parts of the world today, storytellers are always interested in locating interesting ethnic tales. This collection of fourteen Zairian tales is noteworthy because the author includes a variety of tales, including one about cannibalism. In her introduction, Savory states 'American and European readers would do well to remember the Fee, Fi, Fo, Fum element in many of our own beloved tales before being critical' (p.8).

738 **Contes du Zaïre: contes des montagnes, de la savane et de la forêt au pays du fleuve Zaïre.** (Tales from Zaire: tales from the mountains, from the savanna, and from the forest in the region of the Zaire River.) Compiled and translated by N'Sanda Wamenka, adapted by Alain Tashdjian.   Paris: Conseil International de la Langue Française, 1975. 114p. (Fleuve et Flamme).

Animals are the protagonists in this collection of fifty-four representative tales, translated into French. The stories originate from different regions of Zaire, and are written in relatively simple French.

739 **La cuisine de Bandundu (Rép. du Zaïre).** (The cookery of Bandundu, [Republic of Zaire].)
   Sona Gisangi.   Bandundu: CEEBA, 1980. 245p. (Publications CEEBA. Série II, vol. 63).

This is a comprehensive cookbook from the region of Bandundu, Zaire. The chapters include recipes on vegetables, fruits, starches, mushrooms, eggs, caterpillers, shrimps, insects, fish, tortoise, fowl and birds, rodents, hoofed animals, monkey, crocodile, tripe, liver, animal feet, and a few breads, cakes, and sweets.

740 **Dictionnaire des rites.** (Dictionary of rites.)
   Edited by Hermann Hochegger.   Bandundu, Zaire: CEEBA, 1984-92. 20 vols. (Publications CEEBA. Série 1, vols. 8-28).

Based on the observation of traditional religious phenomena, this massive dictionary of Zairian rites contains an entry for each concept (for instance, *sorcier* (witch), abstinence, *tombe* [tomb]) as well as a proverb translated into French. Its symbolic language is then explained. Various ethnic groups in the region of Bandundu are represented in the work, primarily including the Yansi: one of several Bantu-speaking peoples living in the Bandundu region, and also comprising the majority of the authors of this work. The index at the end of each volume will assist the reader in finding related entries. A complement to this twenty-volume set is Hochegger's *Le langage des gestes rituels* (The language of ritual signs) (Bandundu, Zaire: CEEBA, 1981-83), which is a three-volume dictionary on non-verbal communication in ritual language. Hochegger is the director of CEEBA, which has published over 100 volumes in the series *Publications CEEBA*, focusing primarily on folklore, but also covering other topics such as ethnology, language, and religion.

741 **L'éléphant qui marche sur des oeufs.** (The elephant who walks on eggs.)
T. Badibanga, preface by G. D. Perier, G. Dwlonge, illustrations by Djilatendo.   Brussels: L'Eglantine, 1931. 90p.

This collection of Luba fables and tales is generally regarded as the first work by a Black Congolese author. Although some scholars doubt that Badibanga ever existed, current research indicates that he did indeed exist.

742 **Forms of folklore in Africa: narrative, poetic, gnomic, dramatic.**
Edited by Bernth Lindfors.   Austin: University of Texas Press, 1977. 281p. bibliog.

Two articles are of particular interest for the study of Zaire. Wyatt MacGaffey's 'The black loincloth and the son of Nzambi Mpungu' (p. 144-51) is an analysis of a Kongo folktale. Denise Paulme's 'The impossible imitation in African trickster tales' (p. 64-103) describes the trickster in many African cultures, of which the Mongo, Zande, Luba, Lulua, and Buma are from Zaire. The articles were previously published in the periodical *Research in African Literatures*.

743 **Les insectes comme aliments de l'homme.** (Insects as food for man.)
Tango Muyay.   Bandundu, Zaire: CEEBA, 1981. 177p. map. bibliog.
(Publications CEEBA. Série 2, vol. 69).

Insects are a rich source of protein, and are readily available for eating year-round in Zaire. Each type of insect eaten by the Yansi is described and illustrated and any customs associated with gathering, cleaning, or cooking them are also discussed. The texts of traditional songs and lullabies which contain examples of insects as food are then provided. Detailed cooking instructions follow.

744 **Kasala: chant heroïque luba.** (Kasala: Luba heroic chant.)
Clémentine Faïk-Nzuji Madiya.   Lubumbashi, Zaire: Presses Universitaires du Zaïre, Université Nationale, Campus de Lubumbashi, 1974. 250p.

The *Kasala* is a traditional Luba heroic chant, in danger of being abandoned in favour of programmed ceremonies. Faïk-Nzuji, Zaire's pre-eminent poet and expert on oral literature, transcribes the Luba oral text and supplies a French translation, an introduction to the reading of the *Kasala* genre and a literary and cultural analysis. Her work complements Patrice Mufuta's *Kasala* texts and social analysis called, *Le chant Kasala des Luba* (Paris: Julliard, 1970).

745 **Lega dress as cultural artifact.**
Daniel P. Biebuyck. *African Arts*, vol. 15, no. 3 (May 1982),
p. 59-65.

African sculptural art would have more meaningful classifications if scholars studied the material culture, that is, the costumes, body ornamentation, and hats, for example in their ethnohistorical and cultural contexts. The Lega of eastern Zaire here serve to exemplify this approach.

746 **Littérature orale africaine: quelques mythes et contes du Zaïre.**
(African oral literature: some myths and tales from Zaire.)
Maria Haler. Lubumbashi: Editions Saint-Paul Afrique, 1980. 40p.
map. (Recherches Africaines).

This slim volume on Zairian oral literature is an analysis of stories, myths, and proverbs translated from various Zairian languages.

747 **Mwindo, a Nyanga epic hero and Mubila, a Lega epic hero.**
Daniel P. Biebuyck. *Cahiers de Littérature Orale*, vol. 32 (1992),
p. 39-62. bibliog.

Two eastern Zairian epic heroes, one from the Nyanga and the other from the Lega, are compared and their similarities and differences are analysed in their cultural contexts.

748 **Mythes et contes populaires des riverains du Kasaï.** (Riparian
myths and popular tales of Kasai.)
Leo Frobenius, translated from the German by Claude Murat.
Wiesbaden, Germany: F. Steiner, 1983. 326p. (Studien zur
Kulturkunde, 70 Bd).

Dating from 1928, the original German edition of this work was written by Frobenius who is remembered today for his pioneering ethnological studies. This impressive collection of tales and myths from south-central Zaire is translated into French, and divided into chapters on magic and the mystical, myth, man, and animal fables. For each entry, the ethnic group and location of where it was recorded is followed by the French translation of the myth or tale. There is unfortunately no index of ethnic groups, which would have been useful in a monograph of this length and importance.

749 **Myths & legends of the Congo.**
Jan Knappert. Nairobi: Heinemann, 1971. 218p. (African Writers
Series, no. 83).

One of the few English-language books on myths and legends of Zaire, this collection of stories represents ten ethnic groups: the Alur, the Kongo, the Nkundo, the Woyo, the Makere, the Ngbandi, the Azande, the Mayombe, the Bwaka, and the Luba.

750 **N'ouvre pas à l'ogre: Zaïre.** (Don't open the door to the ogre: Zaire.)
Compiled and translated by Kazadi Ntole, Ifwanga wa Pindi. Paris:
Conseil International de la Langue Française, 1982. 142p. map.
(Fleuve et Flamme).

These Zairian tales, translated into French, consist of seventeen Luba and twenty Kongo tales, all about human beings.

751 **Récits épiques des Lega du Zaïre.** (Epic stories of the Lega of Zaire.)
N'Sanda Wamenka. Paris: Agence de Coopération Culturelle et
Technique, 1992. 2 vols. map. bibliog. (Musée Royal de l'Afrique
Centrale. Annales. Sciences Humaines, vols. 135-36).

The Lega epic tales of *Kiguma Kya Kansindi* (Kiguma son of Kansindi), *Museme w'Idali* (Museme son of Idali) and *Wabugila-Ntondi, Mwana wa Musimba* (Wabugila-Ntondi, son of Musimba) are recorded here in Lega and French. The author's introduction provides the historical and socio-cultural background on the Lega.

752 **Recueil de littérature orale kongo.** (Collection of Kongo oral
literature.)
Nsuka zi Kabwiku. Kinshasa: PNUD/UNESCO/IMNZ, 1986. 122p.
maps.

This collection of Kongo oral literature includes the original Kongo text and a French translation of fourteen different myths and tales.

753 **Storytelling among the Chokwe of Zaire: narrating skill and
listener responses.**
Rachel Irene Fretz. PhD thesis: University of California, Los
Angeles, 1987 438p. bibliog. (Available from University Microfilm
International, Ann Arbor, Michigan, order no. 8719989).

Fretz provides an analysis of indigenous evaluation and responses to narrating skills by listeners among the Chokwe storytellers of Shaba.

754 **Tabwa tegumentary inscription.**
Allen F. Roberts. In: *Marks of civilization.* Edited by Arnold
Rubin. Los Angeles: Museum of Cultural History, University of
California, Los Angeles, 1988, p. 41-56. bibliog.

This essay examines the social significance of scarification of the Tabwa of southeastern Zaire, and their reasons for abandoning the practice. The illustrations of Tabwa material culture and art mimic the photographic portraits of the Tabwa from the turn of the century.

755 **We test those whom we marry: an analysis of thirty-six Nyanga tales.**
Daniel P. Biebuyck, Brunhilde Biebuyck.   Budapest: Lorand Eotvos University, Department of Regional Geography, African Research Program, 1987. 115p. bibliog. (Traditional Cultures in Modern Africa, no. 1).

In this analysis of Nyanga folktales with a focus on suitor contests and an unfit bride or bridegroom, the authors delineate the plot outline, stylistic analysis and sociological conclusion drawn by the Nyanga narrator. The English translations for all the tales from this eastern region of Zaire are also included.

756 **Word and world: Luba thought and literature.**
Jacques A. Th. Theuws.   St. Augustin, West Germany: Anthropos-Institut, 1983. 198p. bibliog. (Studia Instituti Anthropos, vol. 32).

The whole range of Luba folklore is included in this collection: proverbs; invocations; incantations; funeral songs; praise songs; allocutions; myths; tales; fables and stories. The Luba text and English translations are preceded by introductory chapters on the Luba and their language.

Sport and Leisure Activities

757 **Les Cahiers du Congo.** (Reports from the Congo.)
Ivoz-Ramet, Belgium: Groupement des Collectionneurs du Congo,
filiale du Phila Club Flemalle, 1988- . 30 vols. to date. bi-monthly.

This bi-monthly periodical on philately of the Belgian Congo only began publication in 1988. Each slender volume contains many illustrations of stamps, postmarks, and photocopies of envelopes, some in colour.

758 **L'enfant africain et ses jeux dans le cadre de la vie traditionnelle au Katanga.** (The African child and games in traditional life in Katanga.)
Thomas H. Centner. Elisabethville, Zaire: CEPSI, 1963. 412p. map.
bibliog. (Collection Mémoires CEPSI, no. 17).

An extensive study of the rôle of games and toys in traditional culture in the Zairian province of Shaba.

759 **Evolution du sport au Congo.** (Evolution of sport in the Congo.)
Pius Théophile Muka. Kinshasa: Editions Okapi, 1970. 109p.

Follows the origin and evolution of Zairian sport during the colonial era and after independence. This work contains much information about personalities and organizations involved in the promotion of physical education and sport in Zaire.

760 **Jeux congolais.** (Congolese games.)
S. Comhaire-Sylvain. *Zaire*, vol. 6, no. 4 (April 1952), p. 351-62.

The author discusses three indigenous Zairian games – *nzango*, *minoko*, and *mangola* – and describes how they are played.

761 **Les jeux de Mankala au Zaïre, au Rwanda et au Burundi.**
(Mankala games in Zaire, Rwanda and Burundi.)
Philip Townshend.   Brussels: Centre d'Etudes et de Documentation
Africaines, 1977. 76p. maps. bibliog. (Cahiers du CEDAF, no. 3).

Numerous versions of *mankala*, a popular game of strategy in Zaire, are described and analysed in detail. To play, hollows in the ground are made in various patterns, according to the version being played, and seeds or stones are placed in the hollows. The seeds or stones are moved around the holes to capture the opponent's pieces.

762 **Les makuta dans le passé.** (The makuta in the past.)
François Bontinck.   *Zaïre-Afrique*, vol. 27, no. 216 (June-July 1987),
p. 357-79. bibliog.

This is a rather interesting history of the *makuta*, the currency used before King Leopold's Belgian franc was minted in the late 19th century. When the Portuguese first came into contact with the Kongo in the 15th century, shells were the local currency but by the 16th century squares of Kongo cloth had become the method of exchange. In the 17th century, Angolan coins called *macutas* were used in the Congo. The article includes a few black-and-white illustrations of the cloth squares and Angolan *macutas*.

763 **Numismatique du Congo, 1485-1924: instruments d'échange,
valeurs monétaires, méreaux, médailles.** (Numismatics in the
Congo, 1485-1924: instruments of exchange, monetary values, tokens,
medals.)
Alfred Mahieu.   Brussels: Imprimerie Médicale et Scientifique, 1925.
2nd ed. 150p. maps. bibliog.

Mahieu's is the most comprehensive book written on the numismatics of colonial Zaire, Rwanda, and Burundi. Topics covered include metal coins, shells, fabric, and tokens struck for payment of taxes as well as other objects fashioned from metal.

764 **Philatélie congolaise.** (Congolese philately.)
Théodore Heyse.   London: [n.p.], 1944. 16p. bibliog. (Cahiers Belges
et Congolais, no. 1).

This slender volume on the philately of the Belgian Congo also contains twelve black-and-white illustrations of postage-stamps as well as a brief bibliography. A more complete colonial bibliography on this topic is contained in the author's *Bibliographie du Congo belge et du Ruanda-Urundi (1939-1951), documentation generale: folklore-philatelie-sports-tourisme* (q.v.).

765 **Scott 1994 standard postage stamp catalogue.**
Sidney, Ohio: Scott Publishing, 1993. 150th ed. 5 vols.

This annual reference tool contains 234 black-and-white illustrations of stamps from four separate listings: Belgian Congo, Congo Democratic Republic, Katanga, and Zaire. Because of its comprehensiveness and the inclusion of descriptions of stamps that are not illustrated, this catalogue is essential for any philatelist, whether expert or novice.

766 **Sport in Zaire.**
Bangela Lema. In: *Sport in Asia and Africa: a comparative handbook.* Edited by Eric A. Wagner. New York: Greenwood Press, 1989, p. 229-47.

This chapter begins with an historical overview of sport in Zaire and continues with a presentation on the organization of Zairian sport. The author then provides details on the levels of participation in sports within Zaire and on the international scene, concluding with an assessment of Zairian sport at present and how it could develop in the future. This is an excellent source of information on the current state of sport in Zaire.

767 **Le sport scolaire et universitaire en R.D.C.** (School and university sport in the Congo Democratic Republic.)
Pius Théophile Muka. Kinshasa: Okapi, 1971. 40p. (Collection C'est Quoi?, no. 2).

Discusses the organization of sports in Zairian schools and universities.

768 **Sports, loisirs en R.D.C. et dans le monde.** (Sport and recreation in the C. D. R. and the world.)
Eugène Luboya. Kinshasa: Okapi, 1971. 150p. bibliog.

A general discussion of a wide variety of popular sports and leisure activities in Zaire and the world.

769 **Standard catalog of world coins.**
Chester L. Krause, Clifford Mishler, edited by Colin R. Bruce II.
Iola, Wisconsin: Krause Publications, 1994. 22nd ed. 2,216p.

The coins of the Belgian Congo, Congo Democratic Republic, Katanga, and Zaire are illustrated in black-and-white in this annual catalogue. A similar recent source for Zairian coins is *Collecting world coins* (Iola, Wisconsin: Krause Publications, 1992. 4th ed.).

Libraries, Archives, Museums and Research

770 **The African studies companion: a resource guide & directory.**
Hans M. Zell. London; Munich; New York: H. Zell, 1989. 165p.
bibliog. (Hans Zell Resource Guides, no. 1).
This compact guide is packed with a variety of sources of information which will be useful to anyone studying Africa or Zaire, or those who are interested in Africana publishing. The first section is an annotated bibliography of major general and current reference sources, followed by current bibliographies and continuing sources, and a selective listing of important African studies periodicals and magazines. It names publishers with African studies lists and dealers and distributors of African studies materials. In addition, the guide features awards and prizes in African studies and organizations; African studies associations and societies; foundations; donor agencies; and network organizations which support African studies research or which are active in Africa.

771 **African studies information resources directory.**
Compiled and edited by Jean E. Meeh Gosebrink. Oxford: H. Zell, 1986. 572p. bibliog.
The 1988 winner of the African Studies Association's Conover-Porter award is this directory of resources of American libraries, archives, and missions containing Africana collections. Ample material on Zaire, much of it unique, may be located through the index.

772 **Catalogue des archives: historiques, linguistiques, imprimés en langues africaines, cartographiques.** (Catalogue of archives: historical, linguistic, printed in African languages, cartographic.) Honoré Vinck. Borgerhout, Belgium: Aequatoria, 1993. 129p. bibliog. (Bibliothèque Aequatoria Bamanya).
This catalogue of the archives of the periodical *Aequatoria* was produced when these valuable historical archives were microfilmed in 1992-93. The subjects covered are: dialectology and Mongo literature; history of schools; problems of colonization; history of the Equator; church and school books in African languages; the history of the missions; geographical maps; and the flora and fauna of the central Congo basin.

773 **Des photos faites en Afrique centrale: un inventaire des archives et de leurs dépôts en Belgique.** (Photographs taken in central Africa: an inventory of archives and of their collections in Belgium.)
Guido Convents. In: *Photographs as sources for African history.*
London: SOAS, 1988, p. 115-23.

Photographs are difficult to inventory for two reasons: they have a fragile nature (many of these were taken on glass plates); and a large number are untraceable. This preliminary inventory of the major public and private Belgian archives of pre-1960 photographs is therefore a welcome addition to the study of Zaire. The public institutions covered are: Le Musée Royal de l'Afrique Centrale; Ministère des Affaires Etrangères; Ministère de la Défense; Musée Royal de l'Armée; Provincie Antwerpen Museum voor Fotografie; Instituut voor Tropische Geneeskunde; Instituut voor Volkskunde Stad Antwerpen; and the Palais Royal Bruxelles. The private institutions include: Katholiek Documentatie en Onderzoekscentrum; L'Agence Belga; Union Royale Belge pour les Pays d'Outre-Mer et l'Europe Unie; and the Union Colonial Belge. Certain journals, corporations and universities are also included.

774 **Development of libraries in Zaire: inventory and review of the literature 1888- .**
J. Wasonga Mutaboba. *African Research and Documentation*, no. 52 (1990), p. 10-19, no. 53 (1990), p. 7-18.

This two-part article contains the most recent comprehensive information on Zairian libraries available in English. An excellent bibliography (most of the material is in French) appears at the end of the second part.

775 **Directory of museums in Africa** = Répertoire des musées en Afrique.
Edited by Suzanne Peters, Jean-Pierre Poulet, Alexandra Bochi, Elisabeth Jani. Paris: ICOM; London; New York: Kegan Paul, 1990. 211p.

Twenty-one Zairian museums are listed in this directory (p. 171-75), for which not much more information is given, other than their location and status (national, provincial, or private). The subject index is also inadequate. Five of these museums are also covered among the nine listed under Zaire in *Museums of the world* (Munich: Saur, 1992, 4th ed.).

776 **Guide to federal archives relating to Africa.**
Researched and compiled by Aloha P. South. Waltham, Massachusetts: Crossroads Press, 1977. 556p. bibliog. (The Archival and Bibliographic Series).

This catalogue of material housed in the National Archives in Washington, DC includes both textual and non-textual materials covering the US Congress and other government agencies and committees. Separate indexes of subject, places, and ethnic groups are excellent and permit easy access to information on Zaire.

777 **Guide to non-federal archives and manuscripts in the United States relating to Africa.**
Researched and compiled by Aloha P. South.   London; New York: H. Zell, 1989. 2 vols. bibliog.
This catalogue of American archives and manuscripts is a companion to the author's *Guide to federal archives relating to Africa* (q.v.). It is arranged by state.

778 **International guide to African studies research** = Etudes africaines, guide international de recherches.
Compiled by Philip Baker.   London: H. Zell, 1987. 2nd ed., fully revised and expanded. 264p.
This directory of research on Africa includes entries for thirty research institutions in Zaire, including longer entries on the Centre de Linguistique Théorique et Appliquée, the Centre d'Etudes des Religions Africaines, the Institut des Musées Nationaux, and the Université de Lubumbashi.

779 **Inventaire des archives relatives au développement extérieur de la Belgique sous le règne de Léopold II.** (Inventory of the archives relative to the external development of Belgium under the reign of Leopold II.)
Emile Vandewoude.   Brussels: Archives Générales du Royaume, 1965. 293p. (Archives des Palais Royaux, no. 1).
The first part, which concerns the Belgian archives of the Congo (up to page 175) contains 242 entries. It includes correspondence and press clippings as well as the archives of the Comité d'Etudes du Haut-Congo, the Association Internationale du Congo, the Conférence de Berlin, and the Etat Indépendent du Congo et Colonie du Congo Belge.

780 **Inventorying moveable cultural property: National Museum Institute of Zaire.**
Shaje Tshiluila.   *Museum (Paris)*, vol. 39, no. 153 (1987), p. 50-51.
This brief description of the inventorying of the collections in the NMIZ, established in 1970, also summarizes efforts to return items from Belgium. The author explains how the NMIZ documents objects in other African, European or American museums and private collections, with a view towards their eventual return to Zaire.

781 **The Lubumbashi Museum: a museum in Zaire that is quite different.**
Guy de Plaen.   *Museum (Paris)*, vol. 41, no. 162 (1989), p. 124-27.
The curator of the Lubumbashi Museum writes about the establishment of the museum, describes the collections (prehistory, protohistory, ethnography and art of Shaba and Zaire) and its activities such as training, conservation, research, and inspection missions regulating the sale of antiques. The museum is working on these topics: Yaka masks and statuary; northern Shaba and Maniema insignia of power; and ancient iron and copper-working in Shaba. The last page explores the concept of authenticity, and demonstrates how techniques such as x-ray photography can prove that an artifact is bogus.

782 **Recherches africanistes au Zaïre: actes du Colloque du cinquantenaire d'Aequatoria, du 11 au 13 octobre 1987.** (Africana research in Zaire: acts of the colloquium on the fiftieth anniversary of Aequatoria, from 11 to 13 October 1987.)
Colloque du Cinquantenaire d'Aequatoria (1987). Bamanya, Mbandaka, Zaire: Centre Aequatoria, 1989. 275p. bibliog. (Etudes Aequatoria, no. 6 [7]).

This colloquium on fifty years of the periodical *Aequatoria* includes fifteen essays on specific archives (Zairian National Archives, Archives of the town of Mbandaka) and libraries (Centre Aequatoria), as well as other topics on the current and future state of research in Zairian art, history, linguistics, literature, and ethnology. Although the papers are in French, they are each preceded by a brief English summary.

783 **The SCOLMA directory of libraries and special collections on Africa in the United Kingdom and in Europe.**
Tom French. London; New York: H. Zell, 1993. 5th ed., revised and expanded. 355p.

Significant Africana collections are mentioned in this directory of libraries, including entries on Zaire for thirteen institutions in five European countries (the United Kingdom, Belgium, Germany, Italy, and the Netherlands). Many other institutions are not specifically indexed under Zaire, but mention is made of significant holdings (for example, the Musée Royal de l'Afrique Centrale, Tervuren).

784 **Zaire, libraries in the Republic of.**
Mamosi Nsilulu Lelo. In: *Encyclopedia of library and information science.* New York: Dekker, 1982, vol. 33, p. 486-507.

This is an excellent overview of libraries in Zaire, covering the period up to 1980.

Répertoire des recherches agronomiques en cours, au sein de la Communauté économique des pays des grands lacs (C.E.P.G.L.): Burundi, Rwanda, Zaïre.
See item no. 526.

The African book world & press: a directory = Répertoire du livre de la presse en Afrique.
See item no. 786.

A publication survey trip to Equatorial and East Africa, France and Belgium.
See item no. 792.

A publication survey trip to West Africa, Equatorial Africa, Tunisia, France and Belgium.
See item no. 793.

Books and Publishing

785 **The African Book Publishing Record.**
Edited by Hans Zell.   Munich: H. Zell & K. G. Saur, 1974-
quarterly.

Bibliographical information is provided in this journal along with reviews of significant new and forthcoming books from the African continent and its offshore islands. Publications from Zaire are regularly covered.

786 **The African book world & press: a directory** = Répertoire du livre de la presse en Afrique.
Edited by Hans Zell.   London; Munich: H. Zell, 1989. 4th ed. 306p.

This source attempts to provide current and accurate information on libraries, publishers and the retail book trade, major periodicals and newspapers, government and commercial printers, research institutions with publishing programmes, and book industry and literary associations throughout Africa, including Zaire. A series of appendices provides details about book fairs and book promotional events, book clubs, African news agencies, and book prizes and literary awards. Includes subject indices to special libraries and periodicals.

787 **African books in print** = Livres africains disponibles.
Edited by Hans Zell.   London: H. Zell, 1993. 4th ed. 2 vols.

Lists more than 23,000 titles published through to the end of 1991 from 745 publishers in 45 countries. In addition to commercial trade books, publications of libraries, university departments, research institutes, and professional and scholarly societies are also included. Since Zaire, like many other African countries, seldom publishes a regular national bibliography, this work, and its previous three editions, is indispensible in providing an impression of the extent of publishing in Zaire and the continent. The first volume includes author and title lists; the second, the subject list.

788   The book in francophone Africa: a critical perspective.
Gunter Simon.   *African Book Publishing Record*, vol. 10, no. 4
(1984), p. 209-15.
An in-depth analysis of the state of the book and the book industries in francophone
African countries, including Zaire.

789   The book trade of the world. Vol. IV: Africa.
Edited by Sigfred Taubert, Peter Weidhaas.   Munich; New York:
K. G. Saur, 1984. 391p. maps. bibliog.
Provides information on the structure of the book trade in Zaire as well as every other
African country, including its history, important publishers, the state of Zairian
publishing, and literary prizes.

790   Congo/Zaire.
Kadima-Nzuji Mukala.   In: *European-language writing in
Sub-Saharan Africa*.   Edited by Albert S. Gerard.   Budapest:
Academiai Kiado, 1986, p. 541-57. (Histoire Comparée des
Littératures de Langues Européennes, vol. 6).
This is a part of a section in chapter seven, which deals with francophone countries,
called *The emergence of local publishing*. Although the emphasis is somewhat heavier
on the evolution of Zairian creative writing and literature after the Second World War,
the development and growth of a local publishing industry during that time, and the links
between the two, are also discussed.

791   Le financement de la culture et de l'industrie du livre au Zaïre.
(The financing of the book industry and culture in Zaire.)
Lukomo Bivuatu Nsundi.   Kinshasa: Société d'Etudes et d'Edition,
1979- . (Collection 'Economie & Finance').
The first volume, *Les problèmes de l'édition au Zaïre* (The problems of publishing in
Zaire), is an economic analysis of specific problems that prevent the existence of a
flourishing publications industry in Zaire. An intended second volume, *Essai sur
l'authenticité monétaire et la croissance économique* (Essay on monetary authenticity
and economic growth), has apparently not been published.

792   A publication survey trip to Equatorial and East Africa, France
and Belgium.
Julian W. Witherell.   Washington, DC: Library of Congress, General
Reference and Bibliography Division, Reference Department, 1965.
48p.
This report documents the publishing activities of government agencies, research
organizations, universities, libraries, archives and museums of select African countries,
including Zaire, plus France and Belgium, at the time of publication.

793 **A publication survey trip to West Africa, Equatorial Africa,**
     Tunisia, France and Belgium.
     Samir M. Zoghby.   Washington, DC: Library of Congress, General
     Reference and Bibliography Division, Reference Department, 1968.
     53p.

This title is a complement to Julian Witherell's report (q.v.) of his trip to Equatorial and
East Africa, France and Belgium in 1964-65. Like the previous report, this documents
the major publishing activity in Zaire at the time, and includes changes that occurred
since Witherell's work was issued.

794 **Publishing and book development in Africa: a bibliography** =
     L'édition et le développement du livre en Afrique : une bibliographie.
     Compiled by Hans Zell.   Paris: UNESCO, 1984. 143p. bibliog.
     (Studies on Books and Reading, no. 15).

With almost 700 entries, this work covers material published on all aspects of publishing
and the book trade in Africa, with the exception of South Africa. Entries specific to Zaire
are few, but general works listed here on African publishing as a whole do contain
information on Zaire. An overview of publishing in Zaire is included in the introductory
material.

La recherche scientifique zaïroise à l'étranger de 1976 à 1979.
See item no. 626.

The African studies companion: a resource guide & directory.
See item no. 770.

Mass Media

795 **Broadcasting in Africa: a study of Belgian, British and French colonial policies.**
Geoffrey Z. Kucera. PhD thesis, Michigan State University, East Lansing, Michigan, 1968. 395p. bibliog. (Available from University Microfilms International, Ann Arbor, Michigan, order no. 6811069).

This PhD dissertation discusses the colonial media/communications policies and the history of broadcasting under Belgian, British, and French rule. The highly paternalistic Belgian régime in Zaire excluded the local African population from any participation in decisions affecting the colony and the policies on communications are here examined in the context of the general political and economic policies of the colonial régime. The author follows the development and introduction of new media (telegraphy, telephony, and later radio) in the African colonies and the character of the institutions that supported the new mass media.

796 **La cible manquée: une étude de la pratique des média dans une ville africaine, Lubumbashi.** (Missed target: a study of the practices of the media in an African city, Lubumbashi.)
Mukamba Longesha. Louvain-la-Neuve, Belgium: Cabay, 1983. 214p. bibliog.

The author discusses new concepts of communication in Africa, using the example of Lubumbashi, a major mining/industrial centre and the capital of Shaba Province, Zaire. The history of film, radio, and television in Lubumbashi is examined in the context of mass media communication and the author studies the economic and social aspects of access to the media.

797 **Communication policies in Zaire: a study.**
Botombele Ekanga Bokonga. Paris: Unesco, 1980. 59p.

This is a short but comprehensive review of the media in Zaire from colonial times to the present (1980). It covers the press, radio, television, and cinema, with an emphasis on the national communications policy. The author, writing for a Unesco series, appears to be a spokesman for the Zairian government and presents a rather antiseptic, uncritical view of the media situation in Zaire. Several official documents are included; among them are: the Zairian decree on the freedom of the press and a manifesto of the national press organization.

798   **L'origine, l'évolution et le fonctionnement de la radiodiffusion au Zaïre de 1937 à 1960.** (The origin, evolution and the functioning of radio broadcasting in Zaire from 1937 to 1960.)
      Greta Pauwels-Boon.   Tervuren, Belgium: Musée Royal de l'Afrique Centrale, 1979. 341p. bibliog. (Annales. Série in-8o. Sciences Historiques, no. 5).
Awarded a prize by Belgian Radio and Television, this doctoral thesis covers the history of radio broadcasting in Zaire from its beginning in 1937 to independence in 1960. The first half of the work examines the official government radio service in Zaire and the second half looks at the private radio stations and their individual history. This well-documented study is limited to a single media – radio broadcasting – and to the colonial period.

799   **Philosophie et communication sociale en Afrique: IIIe Séminaire Scientifique National de Philosophie du 29 novembre au 03 décembre 1987.** (Philosophy and social communication in Africa: IIIrd National Scientific Seminar of Philosophy from 29 November to 03 December 1987.)
      Kinshasa: Facultés Catholiques de Kinshasa, 1989. 198p. bibliog. (Recherches Philosophiques Africaines).
These conference proceedings on communication in Africa include several papers on mass media in Africa, applying most particularly to Zaire.

800   **The press in Africa: communications past and present.**
      Rosalynde Ainslie.   London: Gollancz, 1966. 256p. bibliog.
Also including general chapters on radio and television broadcasting, this publication is a general work on the press in Africa. The study devotes a short chapter (p. 120-29) to the press in Zaire, in which the history of the major newspapers of the colonial and the immediate post-colonial period is traced. Previously dominated by the Belgians, the Zairian press by the mid-1960s was thoroughly 'Africanized'. The author briefly characterizes the newspaper establishment and its political connections, stating that, as in earlier Belgian times, the press in the 1960s in Zaire was strongly aligned around leading political personalities.

801   **La presse quotidienne au Congo belge.** (The daily press in the Belgian Congo.)
      Jean Marie van Bol.   Brussels: Pensée Catholique; Paris: Office Général du Livre, 1959. 112p. bibliog. (Etudes Sociales. Série 3, nos. 23-4).
This short but detailed, well-documented work covers the history of the daily press in Zaire during the colonial period. The work states that the colonial press was written and

published by and for Belgians living in Zaire, and the author looks into the awkward question of freedom of the press in a tightly controlled, paternalistic, white-dominated colony. The Zairian colonial press managed to extend its distribution and reporting to the entire country.

802 **Radio-trottoir: une alternative de communication en Afrique contemporaine.** (Sidewalk-radio: an alternative communication in contemporary Africa.)
Duasenge Ndundu Ekambo. Louvain-la-Neuve, Belgium: Cabay, 1985. 238p. bibliog. (Questions de Communication, no. 13).

Radio-trottoir is not about an electronic media but rather the spontaneous oral communication of the people of Kinshasa, Zaire, circulating rumour and information and supplying the media needs that are not met by the official government-controlled mass media. This 'sidewalk radio' has become the major means of fulfilling the public's need for lively, free, untrammelled information in modern urban Zaire. The work studies this means of popular mass communication, which circumvents the formal media, controlled by an authoritarian régime.

La Radio scolaire au Zaïre: (cas de l'émission 'Antenne Scolaire')
See item no. 614.

Encyclopaedias and Dictionaries

803 **Le dictionnaire colonial (encyclopédie): explication de plus de 7.000 noms et expressions se rapportant aux diverses activités coloniales, depuis l'époque heroïque jusqu'aux temps présents.** (Colonial dictionary [encyclopaedia]: explanation of more than 7,000 names and expressions relating to various colonial activities, from the heroic era to the present.)
Maurice Louis Bevel.   Brussels: Imprimerie E. Guyot, 1950-51.
2 vols. 1 map. bibliog.

As the only dictionary on the Belgian Congo, this handy reference tool has entries ranging from geographical, personal, corporate and botanical names to useful entries on specific industries, administrative terms, and colonial concepts, as they apply to the Belgian Congo.

804 **Encyclopédie du Congo belge.** (Encyclopaedia of the Belgian Congo.)
Brussels: Bieleveld, 1950-53. 3 vols. maps.

This is the only encyclopaedia ever written about Zaire although since it was written in colonial times, it naturally has its prejudices and weaknesses. However, certain chapters are still particularly useful, such as those on botany, agriculture, fauna, the diseases of domestic animals and crops, and geology and minerals. Rwanda and Burundi are also included in the encyclopaedia.

Historical dictionary of Zaire.
See item no. 102.

Biographie coloniale belge = Belgische koloniale biografie.
See item no. 124.

Dictionnaire des oeuvres littéraires négro-africaines de langue française: des origines à 1978.
See item no. 633.

Dictionnaire des rites.
See item no. 740.

Bibliographies

General

805 **Africa Bibliography.**
Compiled by Christopher H. Allen, with assistance from A. M. Berrett,
in association with the International African Institute. Edinburgh:
Edinburgh University Press, 1984- . annual.

Before 1991 this bibliography was compiled by Hector Blackhurst and published by
Manchester University Press. It appears as a separate number of *Africa*, contains books,
chapters from books by single authors, essays in edited volumes, and periodical articles
about the entire African continent and associated islands, all published in the previous
year. Principally, subject areas covered are the social sciences, environmental sciences,
and the humanities and arts; a selection of items from the medical, physical, and
biological sciences is also included and government publications and literary works are
excluded. Arrangement is by region and country, with a preliminary section for the entire
continent; within each section entries are arranged by subject. This is a good source for
material in English.

806 **Africa south of the Sahara: index to periodical literature, 1900-[ ].**
Boston: G. K. Hall; Washington, DC: Library of Congress, 1971-85.
4 vols. 3 supplements.

The aim of this work is to provide citations to the contents of journals not covered in
standard guides to periodical literature. The main work, published by Hall in 1971,
covers 1900-70; the first supplement, covering 1971-72, was published in 1973 and
indexes 960 serials; the second supplement, covering 1973-76, was issued in 1982. The
last supplement, the first to be published by the Library of Congress, appeared in 1985
and covers 1977. Cards are not reproduced, as in all other parts of this title; instead, it
has a newly adopted six-part subject division (anthropology, languages and the arts;
education, health, social conditions; geography, history and religion; economic
development; politics and government; and international relations). The *Cumulative*

bibliography of African studies (q.v.) and its successors, together with this work, which has been suspended, are essential for preliminary access to the extensive periodical literature on Zaire.

807 **American and Canadian doctoral dissertations and master's theses on Africa, 1974-1987.**
Compiled by Joseph J. Lauer, Gregory V. Larkin, Alfred Kagan.
Atlanta, Georgia: Crossroads Press for the African Studies Association, 1989. 377p.

Arranged primarily by country, then broad discipline, this publication lists theses focused on the entire continent of Africa, plus islands of the Indian and Atlantic oceans typically counted as African territories or countries. It continues *American & Canadian doctoral dissertations & master's theses on Africa, 1886-1976* (Waltham, Massachusetts: African Studies Association, 1976), compiled by Michael Sims and Alfred Kagan.

808 **Bibliographie de l'Afrique Sud-Saharienne: Sciences Humaines et Sociales.** (Bibliography of Sub-Saharan Africa: Humanities and Social Sciences.)
Tervuren, Belgium: Musée Royal de l'Afrique Centrale, 1978- .
annual.

The title of this bibliography is somewhat misleading as it lists journals and collective works which primarily deal with Central Africa, especially the ex-Belgian possessions. It is well-indexed and includes many materials about Zaire. This is also the best source of current periodical literature relating to the area it covers although one drawback is that it is arranged in the difficult-to-use fiche format and is not as current as other bibliographical works.

809 **Bibliographies for African Studies 1970-1986.**
Yvette Scheven. London; New York: H. Zell, 1988.

This title won the Conover-Porter Award, presented by the African Studies Association for the best Africana reference tool, in 1990. It is a well-organized, regularly updated bibliography of bibliographies in the social sciences and humanities, in which annotated entries are divided between topical sections for subject bibliographies and country for geographical ones. Titles included appear as books, articles, or parts of edited volumes, and are restricted almost entirely to sub-Saharan Africa. This work is intended primarily for those working in English and French, although bibliographies published in other major European languages and Afrikaans are included. This latest edition is supplemented by a forthcoming edition (London; New York: H. Zell, 1994) that covers the years 1987-93. Few other bibliographies of African bibliographies have been published. See also Theodore Besterman's *A world bibliography of African bibliographies,* revised by J. D. Pearson (Totowa, New Jersey: Rowman & Littlefield, 1975); books only are included and the period up until the end of 1973 is covered. The earliest work of substance is the outdated *A bibliography of African bibliographies covering territories south of the Sahara* (Cape Town: South African Public Library, 1961. 4th ed. 79p. [Grey bibliographies, no. 7]), which covers the period through to 1960.

810 **Cumulative bibliography of African studies.**
International African Institute. Boston: G. K. Hall, 1973. 5 vols.

A cumulative index listing all the titles of books and articles published in the bibliographical section of *Africa*, a quarterly journal, from 1929 to 1970, and in the *International African Bibliography* from 1971-72. Entries are in catalogue card format, and are arranged by author or broad topic within countries or geographical areas. References for Zaire appear in vol. 2, p. 511-636. It is continued by the *International African Bibliography* (q.v.).

811 **Current Bibliography on African Affairs.**
Edited by Paula Boesch. Farmingdale, New York: Baywood Publishing, 1962-67. New series, 1968- . quarterly.

A broad, annotated bibliography of African and international sources, including books, periodical articles and documents. Its greatest coverage is on contemporary political and social concerns, as well as materials appearing in non-scholarly journals that tend to escape notice in other serial Africana bibliographies. Frequently containing items on Zaire, this is an excellent source for more works in English.

812 **French-speaking central Africa: a guide to official publications in American libraries.**
Julian W. Witherell. Washington, DC: Library of Congress, 1973. 314p.

This is an excellent bibliography that lists official and quasi-official documents of former Belgian and French possessions, some international and government-sponsored organizations, and selected Belgian and French government publications relating to their former territories. Including works from the colonial era through the immediate post-independence period, it contains 436 specific entries on Zaire, plus some general material with information on Zaire.

813 **Index Africanus.**
J. O. Asamani. Stanford, California: Hoover Institution Press, 1975. 452p. (Hoover Institution Bibliographies, no. 53).

This work lists citations for articles in Western languages found in over 200 Africana serials, 20 Festschriften, and nearly 60 conference proceedings. All were published between 1885 and 1965. Arrangement is primarily by geographical area, then by subject, with the total number of citations approximately 25,000; those for Zaire number just over 1,800.

814 **International African Bibliography: Current Books, Articles and Papers in African Studies.**
London: Mansell for the School of Oriental and African Studies, 1973- . quarterly.

Compiled at the SOAS, this bibliography lists works, current at the time, on Africa in general subject areas of the social sciences. Each issue is arranged thematically under Africa first, then by individual country; the number of references on Zaire varies, but there is usually a minimum of ten. In 1981 Mansell published a five-year cumulation for 1973-78 (of 368 pages and with almost 20,000 references). Previous to 1973 this work existed in various forms back to 1929 and was issued by the International African Institute in its journal *Africa*.

815 **Joint Acquisitions List of Africana.**
Evanston, Illinois: Northwestern University, Melville J. Herskovits Library of African Studies, 1962- . bimonthly.
This is not a true bibliography, but an accessions list; therefore, no journal articles are included. All entries have been published within the past five years, and frequently include titles on Zaire.

816 **Recently Published Articles.**
Washington, DC: American Historical Association, 1976-90.
tri-annual.
Initially published as an informal column in the *American Historical Review*, this valuable serial bibliography has unfortunately ceased publication. Every available issue of the work is divided into almost twenty geographical areas, each prepared by a specialist in that area. Africa is thoroughly covered and articles on Zaire, many of which are in English, are easily located, as the section on Africa is further divided by country. A drawback to this tool is its lack of indexes, but its coverage is broad.

817 **Répertoire des Thèses Africanistes Françaises.** (List of French Africanist Theses.)
Paris: CARDAN, 1977- . annual.
Lists theses on Africa, including ones about Zaire, completed at universities in France.

818 **Sources d'information sur l'Afrique noire francophone et Madagascar: institutions, répertoires, bibliographies.** (Information sources on francophone black Africa and Madagascar: institutions, lists, bibliographies.)
Laurence Porgès.   Paris: Ministère de la Coopération, 1988. 389p.
(Collection Analyse des Sources d'Information).
This guide, which strives to provide all present and former information sources available, is an excellent source of both general and specialized bibliographies on Zaire. Also listed is information on scientific research, and technical institutions, universities, and learned societies.

819 **U.S. Imprints on Sub-Saharan Africa: A Guide to Publications Cataloged at the Library of Congress.**
Washington, DC: Library of Congress, 1986- . annual.
This title lists monographs published or distributed in the United States and catalogued by the Library of Congress during the current and previous two years. An excellent source for contemporary materials on Zaire in English.

820 **United Kingdom Publications and Theses on Africa.**
Standing Conference on Library Materials on Africa.   Cambridge,
England: Heffer, 1963- . irreg.

Arranged by sections on Africa in general, regions, and individual countries, each of
which is subdivided by subject, this title lists books, journal articles, and theses.

821 **The United States and Africa: guide to U.S. official documents and
government-sponsored publications on Africa, 1785-1975.**
Julian W. Witherell.   Washington, DC: Library of Congress, 1978.
949p.

Winner of the Conover-Porter Award in 1980, this is a large, general bibliographical
reference work that contains approximately 400 entries on Zaire, and covers a variety of
topics.

Zaire

822 **Bibliographie du Congo belge et du Ruanda-Urundi.** (Bibliographie
of the Belgian Congo and Ruanda Urundi.)
Théodore Heyse.   Brussels: G. Van Campenhout, 1947-51. 14 vols.
(Cahiers Belges et Congolais, nos. 4-6, 9-12, 16-22).

Heyse compiled a series of separately published bibliographies on the following topics
and groups of topics: land tenure; languages; economic conditions; transportation and
telecommunication; art and motion pictures; education and missions; folklore, sports,
philately, and tourism; journalism; natural history; geology, mining and mineral
resources; and medicine, languages, and ethnology. Most works cited are in French.
Although these bibliographies are dated, the information presented is still valuable from
an historical perspective, especially for certain subjects.

823 **Bibliographie du Katanga. I: 1824-1899. II: 1900-1924. III:
1925-1949.** (Bibliography of Katanga.)
Michel Walraet.   Brussels: Académie Royale des Sciences
d'Outre-Mer, 1954-60. 3 vols.

Each volume of this bibliography is a source of books, journal and periodical articles,
and maps dealing with the Zairian province now known as Shaba, important for its rich
mineral deposits. Despite the fact that this bibliography is geographically limited, it is a
work of substance and valuable as a source of older material.

824 **Bibliographie du Zaïre 1987-1988. Tome 1: Imprimés.**
(Bibliography of Zaire 1987-1988. Volume 1: Imprints.)
Bibliothèque Nationale du Zaïre.   Kinshasa: Bibliothèque Nationale
du Zaïre, 1990. 89p. (Collection Travaux, no. 1).

This is another attempt by the National Library of Zaire to provide coverage of the
national imprint. This first volume includes printed materials; a second and third volume

will contain theses and dissertations and audiovisual materials, respectively. Arrangement is by year and within each year arrangement is by the nine main Dewey classes. Included also is a list of Zairian research institutions and publishing houses, as well as periodicals published in Zaire. It is interesting to note that there is a dominance of religious material among the publications listed.

825 **Bibliographie Nationale.** (National Bibliography.)
Direction des Archives et Bibliothèques. Kinshasa: Direction des
Arts et Cultures, 1977-80. annual.

Lists titles published in Zaire and acquired by the National Library, including government publications; arrangement is by Dewey Decimal Classification. Publication has apparently now ceased, with the last known issue dated June 1980. This continues the same title published by the Congo's Direction des Archives et Bibliothèques, and which was first issued in 1971 when the National Library was begun.

826 **An introductory bibliography for modern Zairian studies.**
Edited by Guy Gran. In: *Zaire, the political economy of
underdevelopment.* New York: Praeger, 1979, p. 319-31.

This bibliography is intended to be used as a guide to works on postcolonial Zaire, especially Zaire of the 1970s. It is not comprehensive; rather, it lists the best, most current, and most representative titles available at the time of publication. Works are divided between published and unpublished, and are mostly examples of North American and European work in the social sciences.

827 **Les périodiques congolais, 1960-1969.** (Congolese periodicals,
1960-1969.)
Edwine Simons, with the collaboration of Danièle Sinechal, Marc
Meurrens. Brussels: CEDAF, 1978. 244p. (Bibliographies
Analytiques sur l'Afrique Centrale, t. 2).

This bibliography contains summaries of 855 articles which appeared in ten Congolese periodicals from 1960 to 1969. Arrangement is alphabetical by title of each periodical; articles are listed in chronological order under the periodical title in which they appeared, and treat a variety of topics.

828 **République du Zaïre, Kivu-Maniema: bibliographie.** (Republic of
Zaire, Kivu-Maniema: bibliography.)
Max Liniger-Goumaz. Geneva: Editions du Temps, 1977. 235p.

A large bibliography which lists periodical articles on Kivu, one of the most remote and densely populated of Zaire's eight regions, and Maniema, one of Kivu's three rural sub-regions. Entries are grouped under the broad areas of physical, biological, and human aspects, with a heavy concentration on the latter.

829 **A study guide for Congo-Kinshasa.**
Edouard Bustin. Boston: Development Program, African Studies
Center, Boston University, 1970. 167p.

Although much of the material is now dated, this represents a well-organized survey of most of the important literature on Zaire up until 1968. Entries are divided into broad subject areas and most of the works listed are in French. A particularly useful feature of this volume is the fact that the author has singled out some of the more important works and provided valuable background and critical information on them, in bibliographical essay style, at the beginning of each chapter.

Préhistoire et protohistoire de la République démocratique du Congo: bibliographie.
See item no. 89.

Guide de l'étudiant en histoire du Zaïre.
See item no. 100.

Historical dictionary of Zaire.
See item no. 102.

African historical demography: a multidisciplinary bibliography.
See item no. 150.

La politique en République du Zaïre: 1955-1er semestre 1981.
See item no. 364.

L'économie de la République du Zaïre, 1960-1er semestre 1980.
See item no. 453.

Bibliographie analytique pour l'agronomie tropicale: Zaïre, Rwanda, Burundi.
See item no. 519.

Bibliography of the soils of the tropics: Vol.1: Tropics in general and Africa.
See item no. 520.

L'éducation en République du Zaïre, 1960-1979.
See item no. 605.

Bibliographie littéraire de la République du Zaïre, 1931-1972.
See item no. 631.

Guide de la littérature zaïroise de langue française, 1974-1992.
See item no. 636.

The arts of Africa: an annotated bibliography.
See item no. 658.

The arts of Central Africa: an annotated bibliography.
See item no. 659.

African music: a bibliographical guide to the traditional, popular, art, and liturgical musics of Sub-Saharan Africa.
See item no. 693.

African music: a pan-African annotated bibliography.
See item no. 696.

The African studies companion: a resource guide & directory.
See item no. 770.

Publishing and book development in Africa: a bibliography = L'édition et
le développement du livre en Afrique : une bibliographie.
See item no. 794.

Indexes

There follow three separate indexes: authors (personal and corporate); titles; and subjects. Title entries are italicized and refer either to the main titles, or to other works cited in the annotations. The numbers refer to bibliographical entry rather than page numbers. Individual index entries are arranged in alphabetical sequence.

Index of Authors

250

Index of Titles

261

Index of Subjects

Kilo-Moto *see* Mining
industry (gold)
Kimbangu, Simon 280
Kimbanguism 243, 256, 262,
268-71, 275, 277,
280-81
Kinshasa 46, 578, 581-84,
589
government 400
statistics 567-68
Kinship 194, 200
Kisangani 585
Kongo Kingdom 105-07,
491
Kongo language 221, 223,
227
French influence 226
Kongo people 156, 176, 191,
200, 202, 299, 318,
666-67, 752
religion 253-54, 278, 281
Kuba people 177, 675,
688

L

Labour 300, 542-52
Labour productivity 465
Labour supply 553
Land tenure 513, 524
Language maps 209, 213
Languages 205-08, 210-12,
214
French 215-16
Kongo 221, 223, 226-27
Lingala 228, 230, 234,
236-38
Luba 222, 224-25, 229,
231, 239-41
Swahili 201, 217-20,
232-35
Laws 294, 391
civil rights 388
electoral 341, 365
private law 393
rights of defendants 387
treaties 383
Lega people 185, 745, 747,
751
Legendary heros 640
Leopold II *see* History
(Leopold II)

Lese people 190, 204
Lexicography 212
Libraries 775, 782-84, 786,
792-93
Limnology 45, 49
Lingala language 228, 230,
234, 236-38
Literature 640-41, 790
analysis 627, 637, 642,
646-48, 654, 656-57
anthologies 628, 649
bibliographies 631, 636,
785
correspondence 639
dictionaries 633
fiction 630, 632, 635,
643-45, 650-53, 655
plays 629
poetry 634
Livestock 523, 533
Loans 488
Local government 11, 399,
403, 405
Kinshasa 403
Lomami-Tshibamba, Paul
642
Luba Empire 106, 108
Luba
language 222, 224-25,
229, 231, 239-41
people 195-96, 201, 711,
735, 741, 744, 756
Lubumbashi 586, 590
Lubumbashi Museum 781
Lumumba, Patrice 139, 335,
348, 352, 356, 368,
420
Lunda Empire 106
Lunda people 128

M

Malembe, Timothée 642
Malnutrition 306, 309
Mammals 64, 76
Man and Biosphere 525
Mangbetu art 662
Maniema 682
Maps 54
Marketing 494
Marriage 180
Masks *see* Art (masks)

Mass media 795, 797, 799
film 796
newspapers 800-01
policy 795, 797
radio 614, 796, 798
television 796
Material culture 187, 745
Mbuti people 183, 189
Medical assistance 320
Medical care 313
Medical education 308
Medical policy 313
Medicinal plants 70
Medicine 305, 308, 315,
318-19, 322
Mercenaries 132, 141
Migration 151, 167
Military intervention 326,
373, 417, 428
Minerals 503-05
Mineworkers 544-47, 552
Mining industry 503-07,
509-10, 512, 521,
545-46, 552
copper 508, 539, 544,
547
diamonds 498-500
gold 501
Missionaries 21, 29
Missions 246-47, 251, 255,
260, 263, 272
Mobutu Sese Seko 142,
145-47, 149, 328-29,
339, 345-46, 351-53,
369-70, 377, 379, 410,
429, 436, 446
Money 480, 490, 762, 769
Mongo people 172, 700-01
Mortality 159
Mouvement Populaire de la
Révolution 344
Mpoyi-Buata, Thomas 627
Mudimbe, V. Y. 654
Museum für Völkerkunde,
Berlin 671
Museums 775, 780-81
Mushrooms 67
Music 691, 693-94, 696-98,
702-04, 707-08,
710-11, 713, 715-17,
719
discographies 692, 695,
712

Musical instruments 699,
705-06, 709, 718,
720-22
Mutombo, Dieudonné 642

N

National Museum Institute
of Zaire 780
Natural history 43, 580
Navigation 48
Neocolonialism 332
Newspapers 786, 800-01
Ngandu people 181
Numismatics 762-63, 769
Nutrition 316, 320
Nyanga people 747, 755

O

Onchocerciasis 317
Oral tradition 195, 692
Organization of African
Unity see Foreign
Relations (OAU)

P

Painting see Art (painters;
painting)
Periodicals 786
Persecution
political 325, 554,
557-58, 561
religious 325, 558
Pharmacology 319
Philately 757, 764-65
Photographs 302, 773
Physical education 759
Pius Ngandu Nkashama 627
Political class 360
Political opposition 338
Political parties 131, 336,
344, 359, 361
Political trends 476
Politics 3, 10-11, 14, 131,
133, 135, 143, 146-49,
325-63, 365-82, 398,
431, 437, 448-49, 554,
556-57, 561

bibliographies 364
Kinshasa 403
Politicization 351
Polygamy 180
Population 3, 150-51,
153-54, 156-59,
161-63, 165, 167-68
density 154
foreign 154
policy 166
refugees 152, 155, 160,
164, 169
statistics 564
Pottery see Art (pottery)
Prehistory 77-79, 82, 84, 86,
90-92, 95-96, 205
bibliographies 89
Primates 56, 75
Prophetism 250, 253, 262,
271, 273, 275, 281
Prostitution 287
Protestantism 246, 248, 251,
255, 260, 263-64, 272,
607
Proverbs 740
Public health 304, 310,
312-13, 315, 320,
324
see also Health
Public opinion
Belgian 337
Publishers and publishing
785-93
bibliographies 794
Puppets 731
Pygmies 172, 198

R

Race relations 117, 292
Radio 614, 796, 798
Radio plays 726
Raffia 675, 688
Reading see Books and
reading
Recipes see Cookbooks
Recreational activities
768
Reforms 371
Refugees 155, 169
Angolan 152, 164
Rwandan 160

Religion 245-49, 251-52,
254-55, 257-58,
260-61, 263-64, 272,
274, 276, 279, 282
popular 243-44, 253, 256,
259, 262, 266-71, 273,
275, 277-78, 280-81
traditional 242, 250, 265
Religion and development
257
Research centres 770-71,
778, 782
Rice 492
Rifts 53
Rites and ceremonies 203,
740
Roman Catholic Church
244-45, 247, 257-58,
261, 266-67, 274, 279,
282
see also Church and state
Rural conditions 468
Rural development 537, 588
Ruwenzori Mountains 43

S

Sanga 80-82, 95
Scarification 754
Scientific research 625-26
Sculpture see Art (sculpture)
Sects 279
Shoowa people 685
Slave trade 110, 120, 491,
495
Slavery 114
Social classes 285, 297, 331,
343, 358, 360, 362,
395
Social conditions 10-11, 14,
145, 284-85, 288-89,
291-92, 294-97,
299-300, 302, 333, 354,
452, 468
aged 293
peasants 283
women 286-87, 290, 298,
301, 549, 703
Social networks 290
Social policy 143, 296, 464
Social status
women 286, 295, 298

Map of Zaire

This map shows the more important towns and other features.

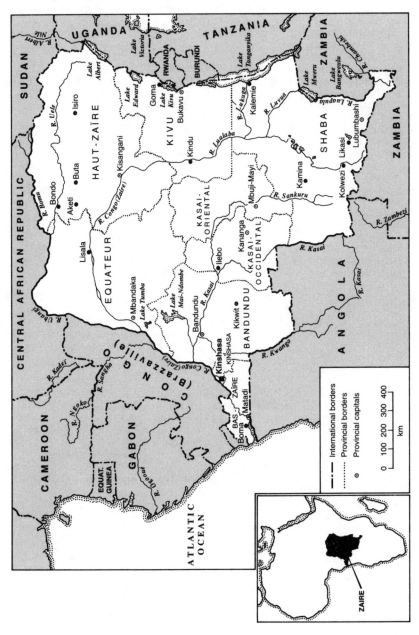

ALSO FROM CLIO PRESS

INTERNATIONAL ORGANIZATIONS SERIES

Each volume in the International Organizations Series is either devoted to one specific organization, or to a number of different organizations operating in a particular region, or engaged in a specific field of activity. The scope of the series is wide-ranging and includes intergovernmental organizations, international non-governmental organizations, and national bodies dealing with international issues. The series is aimed mainly at the English-speaker and each volume provides a selective, annotated, critical bibliography of the organization, or organizations, concerned. The bibliographies cover books, articles, pamphlets, directories, databases and theses and, wherever possible, attention is focused on material about the organizations rather than on the organizations' own publications. Notwithstanding this, the most important official publications, and guides to those publications, will be included. The views expressed in individual volumes, however, are not necessarily those of the publishers.

VOLUMES IN THE SERIES

1 *European Communities*, John Paxton
2 *Arab Regional Organizations*, Frank A. Clements
3 *Comecon: The Rise and Fall of an International Socialist Organization*, Jenny Brine
4 *International Monetary Fund*, Anne C. M. Salsa

5 *The Commonwealth*, Patricia M. Larby and Harry Hannam
6 *The French Secret Services*, Martyn Cornick and Peter Morris
7 *Organization of African Unity*, Gordon Harris
8 *North Atlantic Treaty Organization*, Phil Williams

TITLES IN PREPARATION

British Secret Services, Philip H. J. Davies
Israeli Secret Services, Frank A. Clements
Organization of American States, David Sheinin

United Nations System, Joseph P. Baratta
World Bank, Anne C. M. Salda